My Story

SELWYN HUGHES

My Story

From Welsh mining village to worldwide ministry

CWR

Dedicated to the Partners of
Crusade for World Revival
whose loyalty and support to CWR and myself
have been a continued source of inspiration over the years.

———————————

ACKNOWLEDGEMENTS

My grateful thanks to Eddie Tait and John Peters for overseeing the manuscript and suggesting changes and improvements. My thanks also to Jennifer Oldroyd for her work in the final editing of the manuscript and to the current Creative Services team at CWR whose contribution is deserving of the highest commendation.

I wish to record my deepest appreciation to the trustees and directors of CWR (both past and present), who have over the years supported my ministry, encouraged me and given me the benefit of their friendship and wise counsel. My appreciation also to all staff of CWR (again past and present) whose commitment to the task of making Christ known has been a constant source of encouragement to me.

My apologies to the many people whose lives have interfaced with mine but whose names are not mentioned in this autobiography. It has been impossible to include the names of everyone who has helped or ministered to me along the way but I wish to assure them that they have been much in my thoughts as I have sought to tell my story.

Selwyn Hughes
Life President, CWR

CONTENTS

Acknowledgements   vi

Introduction   1

1. 'The Little Village on the Cheek of the Hill'   3

2. A glimpse of the future   13

3. My search for satisfaction   21

4. The most important decision of my life   31

5. First steps into discipleship   41

6. From coal pit to pulpit   49

7. 'The Revival Boy'   59

8. Preparing for Bible college   69

9. My days at Bible college   79

10. Trekking – and my first church   89

11. A time of spiritual crisis   97

12. My time in Llandeilo   107

13. Taking on two churches   115

14. First days in Yorkshire   123

15. Breakthrough in evangelism   131

16. Storm over Sheffield   141

17. A new field of service   151

18. Broadening my horizons   159

19. An amazing offer   167

20. My time in the wilderness   177

21. 'Think big'   187

22. 'The Midnight Express'   197

23. Penetrating the London drug scene   207

24. A watershed year   217

25. Korean joy – and a parting   227

26. Getting my priorities right   237

27. An unexpected new venture   245

28. 'I can do that'   253

29. Partnership with Trevor   263

30. A significant anniversary   271

31. A new level of personal discovery   281

32. Around the world in 30 days   289

33. A dream is realised   297

34. Refurbishing and healing of a rift   307

35. The loss of my wife   315

36. The opening of Waverley   325

37. Waverley – the first three years   333

38. My battle with cancer   343

39. 70 years, and still going strong   353

40. A year of highs and lows   363

41. My legacy to the next generation   373

Epilogue   381

INTRODUCTION

This autobiography, written at the age of 75, is the most honest and authentic account of my life that I am able to provide. The younger Selwyn, resurrected from the past, has been taking me back over the old roads, and my heart is overflowing with gratitude to a loving heavenly Father, who has filled my life with such happy and blessed memories. Of course, there are some not-so-happy memories also, but in the hands of a God who, according to Romans 8:28, is able to take every setback and turn it into a springboard, everything ultimately works out for good. Circumstances and situations may not have looked good when I was passing through them, but good has always come out of them.

C.S. Lewis said that in relation to what God is doing in our lives we must look and go on looking until we have seen exactly what is there. As I have reviewed the landmarks of my 75 years (so far) on this earth I have sought to do just that – look at exactly what was there. Why did God allow that to happen? What purpose could He have had in what I considered were undue delays? How could a stumbling-block become such a stepping-stone? The more I looked, and the more I realised just how God has orchestrated the stops and starts of my life, the more my heart has been lifted in praise.

How the world has changed since I first entered it! Few people had phones, but you could guarantee a letter arriving in any part of the United Kingdom the next day after posting it. Divorce was something one heard of only occasionally. It was not enough to say a marriage had broken down – you had to prove it

1

through something really serious, like adultery. And had I been writing my autobiography in the middle of the twentieth century instead of the beginning of the twenty-first, I would have had to hammer it out on a typewriter. Now I can sit at my computer and in seconds move whole chunks of material into different positions.

A story that has come to mind often as I have looked back, is one that seems to sum up my life. I have not been able to find the source of the story but it tells of a man who had a dream in which he saw himself standing on the top of a cliff and, because of his fear of heights, felt greatly alarmed.

Suddenly he heard God's voice boom out of the heavens saying, 'Go to the edge!'

'It's dangerous there,' he answered.

'Go to the edge.'

'But I might fall!'

'Go to the edge.'

Eventually he made his way to the edge. Suddenly he felt the hand of God push him from behind ... and he flew!

Time and time again throughout my life I have felt God calling me to do things, and fear has risen up to prevent me from trusting myself to the divine commands. But each time as I have moved to the edge I have found that instead of falling ... I flew.

In telling my story I have come to realise more than ever that life is an incredible, immeasurable gift. Yours, as well as mine. And it is there to be cherished. It should not be casually received but embraced with the deepest gratitude and thanks. How I thank God for the privilege of being part of His purposes in this world and for the special joy of representing His cause here on planet Earth.

My story is no better than yours. It may be different, but it is not better.

Let me take you now to where *my* story began.

CHAPTER 1

'THE LITTLE VILLAGE ON THE CHEEK OF THE HILL'

―――――――――――

I was born on 27 April 1928, in a hamlet consisting of just four unprepossessing cottages on top of a small mountain near the town of Dowlais, in the county of Glamorganshire, South Wales. In those days 27 April was marked in the diaries as 'Forget–me-not Day'. For some reason, which I have been unable to trace, it seems to have been dropped from all diaries somewhere around the beginning of the 1940s.

My parents were living in two rooms with my maternal grandparents at the time, as due to the difficult economic conditions they had no money to rent or purchase a home. My father, John Wyndham Hughes, was an electrician working in the mines, and my mother, Lily (née Marshallsea), had left school at 14 to enter into what was then called 'service'. This was a live-in position serving a well-to-do household with cleaning, cooking and so on. My father was one of six children, my mother one of twelve. They were ordinary people, but people of great character. Coming from large families, my parents placed a lot of value on family ties. I'll tell you a little more about my parents later, but for now I just want to say this about them: they were people with a strong moral make-up.

Just a few weeks after I was born I was taken to a little mission hall in the nearby village of Fochriw, a distance of about three miles, where my parents worshipped, to be dedicated to God.

'Dedication' is a practice not unlike infant baptism except that no water is used. I was named Selwyn, which in Welsh means 'clear voice'. My parents said that they gave me this name because they hoped and prayed that I would use my voice in the service of Jesus Christ.

The pastor of the mission hall, David Thomas, who conducted the service of dedication, also happened to be my uncle – my mother's sister's husband. Some of those present told me years later that as he took me in his arms to pray over me they were surprised when, after finishing his prayer, he paused for a moment and said, 'And Lord I ask that one day you will make this child a preacher of the gospel.'

Over the years, I have often pondered on my uncle's apparent afterthought. Scripture says, 'The prayer of a righteous man is powerful and effective' (James 5:16). Believe me, there was no one more righteous than my uncle. That godly man, I believe, caught something of God's desire for my life as he held me in his arms and prayed a prayer of dedication that was in harmony with the purposes of God.

I have told congregations all over the world the story of my uncle's dedication prayer and I remember on one occasion recounting it in a church in Kuala Lumpur, Malaysia. As I did so, a ten-year-old boy turned to his parents sitting next to him and whispered, 'Was I dedicated to God in the same way as Mr Hughes?' 'Yes,' they said. 'You were.' After a few moments' reflection he said, 'And did you ask God to make me a preacher of the gospel?' 'No, we didn't,' they said and the young boy began to cry. 'But I want to be a preacher when I grow up, too,' he said. 'I wish you had prayed for me the same as that pastor did for Mr Hughes.'

After the service ended the boy's parents brought him to me to pray that God would make him a preacher. I hesitated for a moment because I did not want to pray in a way that might not be in harmony with the Holy Spirit's purposes for his life. But as I laid my hands on his head and began to pray I felt the Spirit's confirmation that he, too, would one day become a preacher. I shall never forget the expression of gratitude and pleasure on that young boy's face as I finished my prayer. Malaysia has some wonderful preachers and there is no doubt in my mind that in God's good time he will take his place alongside these great men and women of God and contribute to the spiritual health and vitality of that nation.

In terms of economy and lifestyle, things in the little hamlet where I spent the first few years of my life were difficult. John Peters, in his biography of me, said this about the economic conditions in Wales during the 1930s:

> At that time coal mining was the principal industry of South Wales. From 1920 onwards the miners – then the most vociferous and powerful men in industry – were enraged by the continually falling wages and in 1926 took part in the General Strike. The beautiful valleys stretching from Cardiff northwards to Brecon were torn apart by frustration and bitterness as well as by the ravages of the industrial revolution.[1]

Although my early years were punctuated by strikes and unemployment that brought in its train inevitable hardships and poverty, my parents never allowed the situation to depress them psychologically or spiritually. Money was scarce. There was enough for basic food supplies but little for anything else. One summer the residents of the hamlet where I lived had to ask the ice-cream man who lived outside the area not to bring his van into the small community to avoid disappointing the children. When a hole appeared in the sole of a shoe, many children had to make do with thick cardboard being put inside it until their parents could afford to pay for a proper repair.

I remember my early years as happy ones and even though at times there was not very much on the table, my father would always say grace before a meal as if we were sitting down to a banquet.

I started school in Fochriw on my fifth birthday and apparently, when my mother left me at the school gates, I cried, because I was not sure whether she would remember to come back and collect me. But I loved it at that infants' school. It meant a two-and-a-half mile walk there and back every day from my home on top of the mountain, but I never remember it being much of a problem, except of course, when it was wet or exceptionally cold. In those days we began school each morning by reciting the Lord's Prayer in Welsh and ended the day in the same way. Although I was never fluent in Welsh, I knew enough to follow a conversation. Sometimes, when my mother and father wanted to discuss something they did not want me to understand, they would do so in Welsh, little knowing that I could get the gist of what they were saying!

There was one school in the village, four churches, a railway station and one pub. The railway station and three of the churches have now vanished. The only religious building remaining is the little mission hall in which I was dedicated. In fact, half of the village has been demolished and the people who lived there have been re-housed in another valley. The ground on which the houses stood has now been re-seeded and I imagine it looks much the way it was two centuries ago, before the village came into being.

In my childhood, of course, there was no television, no mobile phones, personal computers, radar, credit cards, ballpoint pens, washing machines, electric blankets, air conditioners, video recorders, artificial hearts, jet aircraft or yoghurts. I do not believe, however, that my childhood was impoverished by the absence of television. Sometimes I wonder whether the flood of new inventions have actually benefited the human condition. Most of our toys were home-made. Oxo tins would serve as motor-cars and cardboard boxes as garages. We listened incessantly to the wireless. Tommy Handley, *In Town Tonight*, *Workers' Playtime* and, of course, *Toytown*. I would race home from school, change my clothes and do my homework so I could listen to the children's programmes that began at five o'clock. My favourite radio programme was *Dick Barton Special Agent*, which came on just before my bedtime. The news was always read by some plummy-voiced character who, I later learned, wore evening dress. During the reading of the news my father forbade my mother and me to speak; listening to the news in our home was sacrosanct. So was the King's Christmas Day address.

Some of my earliest memories of home life are of listening to my father praying at his bedside for a long list of missionaries. He was missionary secretary for the mission hall, chosen for the position because of his great love for overseas missions. In fact my parents came close to becoming missionaries themselves. A visit to our little church from India of an evangelist by the name of Jonathan Edwards, who spoke of the need for missionaries in his country, resulted in my mother and father deciding to offer themselves as missionaries there. However, wise counselling from the elders of the church made clear to them that they were responding to the emotion of the moment rather than a clear call from God.

When I was six my world was turned upside down. My father and mother decided to uproot from the village and move to Birmingham. It was a decision that was not taken lightly. Birmingham was just over 100 miles away, but to a little boy it seemed like a move to the other side of the world! The reason for the shift was due to the problem of strikes, which meant that sometimes no money would come into the home for weeks. My father went ahead of us to Birmingham in 1934 and after he had obtained work in that city we were soon on our way in a furniture van to settle there.

I never liked the city of Birmingham. I see it through different eyes now, of course. These days it is always a place I delight to visit, but as a child I hated the grimy smoke that seemed to always hang over the city and when I started school it took me several weeks to adjust to the thick Midlands accent. But the other children also couldn't understand my Welsh accent and would mock me by imitating the way I spoke. Within a few months, however, I had lost my Welsh accent and dropped into the 'Birmingham brogue'.

Although we lived for three years in Birmingham, my memories of life there are very few. It's interesting how the subconscious mind helps us forget those things we don't want to remember. There is, however, one memory of my time in the city that I recall with pleasure.

After our arrival in the city and looking around several churches, my parents decided to join a Baptist congregation. Within weeks the church discovered that my father was an acceptable preacher. Often on a Sunday they would arrange for him to preach in other Baptist churches in the city – churches that were too small to support a full-time minister. On those occasions my father would take me with him.

There was one church, I remember, in which two old ladies would sit in the front and as soon as my father started to preach they would both drop off to sleep. This always bothered my father and I remember him saying as we approached the church one Sunday evening, 'If those two old ladies go to sleep tonight when I preach they are going to get a big surprise!'

I sat in the front alongside them and when my father began to preach I wondered what surprise he had planned. Sure enough, within five minutes of my father ascending the pulpit to preach, the two old ladies were fast asleep.

My father was a great storyteller. He began to tell a story about a little girl called Mary who was trapped in her bedroom when her house caught fire. In subdued tones he told how the girl ran to the window, opened it and shouted for help. 'The word she shouted was this,' he said as he cupped his hands over his mouth and with the loudest voice shouted, 'FIRE!' The two old ladies jumped up in their seats as if they had been stung, and everyone laughed at their confusion. I suppose it was rather mean and I never found out whether it cured them of sleeping through a sermon, but I can tell you that in my childhood mind I was very proud of my father that night!

In my own preaching I often find myself repeating many of the stories my father told. They have lain in the fallow fields of my memory and often come to my aid whenever I search for a sermon illustration.

Although I had had lots of friends in Wales it was not the same in Birmingham. So I spent a great deal of time on my own. But being an introvert I did not find that much of a hardship. I developed a love of reading and I could read so well that often my mother and father would 'show me off', so to speak, and make me read a passage from a book whenever we had visitors to our home.

I would read dozens of comic books in a week and always looked forward to going down to the Bull Ring in Birmingham and the old 'Rag Market' where you could buy a dozen old comics such as the *Hotspur*, the *Dandy*, the *Tiger*, and so on, for just one penny. When I would tell my mother a few days later that I had read all the comics I had brought the previous Saturday, she thought I was one of the quickest readers she had ever known. Little did she know that I was reading them after lights out with a flashlight under the blanket!

Three years after our move to Birmingham, my parents decided to return to Wales. My father, who worked in the Metropolitan Vickers factory in Saltley, installing the wiring of railway carriages destined for overseas, developed a serious illness. At first the cause of it was difficult to diagnose. The symptoms were acute pains in his chest and stomach. It was later discovered that, at the same time as my father worked on wiring the carriages, others were painting them and the build-up of lead fumes from the paint affected his stomach and lungs. Due to this my father and mother decided to return home to Wales, especially as the economic situation there had improved. I can't begin to tell you how excited I was when I got the news that we were going home.

On our return to Wales, just before the outbreak of the Second World War in 1939, we lived with my grandparents in the hamlet where I was born for a few months, until my mother and father found a house to rent in Fochriw, immediately opposite my paternal grandparents. 'Fochriw' is a Welsh word meaning 'cheek of the hill'.

It was wonderful to be back in the area again, not just to return to my old school but also to live in a larger community than I had been used to in the hamlet on top of the mountain. It meant I could meet up with my friends in the evenings and visit other members of the family, my aunts and uncles, most of whom lived in the village.

I have very vivid memories of two things that happened during those early months of settling back into the village. One is the communal lamp post at the top of the street where several of us used to assemble after dark, talking and playing under the soft circumference of light until one by one our parents called us to come home to bed. The second is going down to the railway track at the bottom of my street with a few friends and, when no one was about, putting pennies on the polished rails, waiting until a train had run over them and then, at an appropriate moment, returning to find them as thin as oak leaves.

In the first few months after our return to Wales, I met up with the same problem I had encountered when we moved to Birmingham. I had developed a strong Birmingham accent, and the mocking I got when I started school in Birmingham because of my different accent was now in reverse. Within a few months, however, I soon picked up the Welsh accent again and became one of the boys.

The village of Fochriw at that time had a population of less than 2000 people, most of the men being miners. It was a friendly and tightly-knit community. I have always been grateful that most of my childhood was spent in a village. I am sure that it gave me a sense of belonging that I think is difficult to experience in a town or city.

What happened to me in that little village on the cheek of the hill formed and shaped a good deal of the way I now think and feel concerning many of life's issues. Above everything else, it was there that I decided to become a follower of Jesus Christ – a decision that affected my life not just for time but for all eternity.

Notes

1. *Selwyn: Every Day with Jesus* by John Peters (CWR 1990).

CHAPTER 2

A GLIMPSE OF THE FUTURE

It is often said that of all our memories none are more poignant than those of our childhood. We may leave home but the memories never leave us. I once heard the famous broadcaster and writer, Malcolm Muggeridge, talk about the power and importance of memory. He said that no matter how fast we drive on the road of life, or how far away, we can never escape our past. It is always there behind us in our rear-view mirror. What surprises me is that the older I get, things appear larger in the rear-view mirror of my memories. Often they are no more than a glance away. And sometimes they appear so large I have to turn the car round and go back, so to speak.

Although none of my family now live in the little village where I was brought up, whenever I am in South Wales for a preaching appointment or to visit my mother and sister who live in the next valley (my father died in 1986), I always drive through the village, park my car on top of the hill overlooking it, and reflect on some of the things that took place there in the days of my childhood.

What is it about the place, I often ask myself, that pulls me back so insistently? Is it to discover something I may have forgotten? What may I have inadvertently left behind? Is it simply nostalgia or a desire to escape from the pressures of the present and find comfort in the quiet and comparatively carefree days of the past? Or is it perhaps to savour those things I gulped down too quickly?

Much consideration of this matter has brought me to the conclusion that one of the major reasons why I love to return to 'the little village on the cheek of the hill' is because it was there in my childhood *that I had a glimpse of the future*. Writer Graham Greene says in *The Power and the Glory*: 'There is always a moment in childhood when the door opens and lets the future in.'[1] I can't begin to tell you the impact that quote made on me when I first came across it many years ago. I began to realise that some of the things that had happened to me in the first twelve years or so of my life were windows that looked out on to my future, even though I did not realise it at the time.

There are several very special experiences that took place in those first twelve years of my life which loom large in my rear-view mirror. The first is of the hours I spent as a child under my maternal grandparents' kitchen table. Let me explain. On occasions my grandparents would invite a few family members and friends into their home just for the pleasure of spending an evening drinking tea and chatting together. It was always a great social occasion when they met up like this. Grandmother would light the oil lamp that was suspended over the large kitchen table and, whilst the adults would gather round it, one of my favourite cousins and I would huddle under it to play with our toy cars and listen to the fascinating conversation. What is it about little boys and their liking for huddling under tables, I wonder?

That table must have been fifteen feet long and five feet wide. Fourteen or fifteen people could easily sit around it. It was made of pine and my grandmother scrubbed its surface every day. On these social evenings the table would be covered with such things as Welsh cakes, buttered scones, jam, bread, cheese, and, of course, a large tea pot from which appeared to flow a never-ending supply of tea.

Almost invariably the conversation on those occasions would turn to the events of the great spiritual awakening, which took place in Wales between the years 1904 and 1905 and was known as the Welsh Revival. I did not realise it at the time, but by listening in to those conversations a longing was being awakened in me that was to play an important part in my life. I became fascinated with the stories of the Welsh Revival and the more I heard the more I wanted to hear.

During the Welsh Revival a great movement of the Holy Spirit swept through the Principality in such tremendous spiritual power that within six months around 100,000 men and women had flooded into the churches, either to become Christians for the first time or to have their spiritual lives revived. Such was the power of the Holy Spirit at work that, in some mining communities, prayer meetings would be held on the surface before the miners descended in the cages to the heart of the mine.

Stories were told of miners down in the bowels of the earth crying out to God under intense conviction of sin to save them. Many times they would come up to the surface at the end of their shifts with white streaks on their blackened faces showing where the tears of repentance had flowed down their cheeks.

I heard stories, too, of how sometimes little children in school would bow their heads on the desks in front of them and begin to cry. When the school teacher would ask what was wrong they would say, 'Please, I want to be saved, Miss!'

In the public houses people would drink beer, but instead of singing bawdy public house songs would join together in singing hymns. Crime figures plummeted. In one place, the magistrates were given white gloves in recognition of the fact there were no criminal cases to conduct.

People would pay off old debts – a factor which, more than any other, in some cases, convinced sceptics that God was at work. I found it thrilling to hear stories of how drunkards would come to scoff and stay to pray, of stories about strong men who would weep like children as the Spirit met with them.

Often these social occasions would end in a prayer meeting and I would hear my mother and father and other family members, most of whom were Christians, cry out in deep anguish of soul, 'O God, do it again … do it again.' Something happened in my soul during those experiences. A door was opening into my future and I never realised it. Revival came to be the theme that has dominated my life. And nowadays, when people ask me how I got turned on to the subject of revival, I tell them that it all began under my grandmother's table!

A second experience that gave me a glimpse of the future happened when I was about 11 years old. It began when the headmaster, Danny Jones, came into my classroom to hand out marked papers of the essays we children had written. As he stopped at my desk he turned to the class and said, 'For a boy of his age, Hughes has written the best essay I think I have ever read.' The feeling of pride and pleasure that swept through me at that moment is as real to me today as it was when I first experienced it. In his office later that day he said to me, 'You know, Selwyn, when I said that for a boy of your age you had written the best essay I have read, I really meant it. I think when you grow up you might become a writer.'

Yet another experience that gave me a hint of what was to come took place when I was about 12, after I had joined the local youth dramatic society. I was very much drawn towards the idea of acting and public speaking and so when an opportunity occurred to join the local acting group I jumped at the chance.

The very first production in which I took part was held in the local village hall. It was a drama about a group of commercial travellers stranded in an old reputedly ghost-ridden hotel on top of a Welsh mountain, and during their enforced stay there weird things began to happen. The opening scene was set in the bar of the hotel and before the curtains opened it was explained to the audience that the commercial travellers were somewhat scared by all that was happening. Some very amateur sound effects were provided – howling wind, ghostly screams and so on – and as the curtain opened I spoke the very first lines of the play: 'Well, I'm going to have another whisky if anyone will join me.'

Everyone in the audience realised, of course, that these opening lines of mine were a nervous defence against the scary situation in which as commercial travellers we found ourselves, so there was an appropriate titter from them. My mother and father were in the audience, sitting near the front just a few feet from the stage. The fact that my father had come to see me take part in this play made me particularly happy, as normally he would never go to such events. This was because he regarded them as being 'worldly' and tantamount, as he put it, to 'sitting in the seat of the scornful'. My mother, however, persuaded him to attend, making the point that if he didn't then I would be very disappointed.

But as I uttered the opening lines I saw out of the corner of my eye my father get up from his seat and leave the hall. I didn't think much about it at the time, but as the play went on I realised what had happened. My father was a strict teetotaller and would have nothing to do with alcohol in any shape or form. His father was heavily dependent on drink and sometimes on a Saturday night would be brought home in a wheelbarrow, blind drunk. As a result of being brought up in this kind of household my father set his face firmly against everything alcoholic. The fact that his own son was repeating lines that had to do with drink was too much for him, so he got up and left.

I was deeply disappointed with my father's action. He never

mentioned the matter to me when I got home that evening; the confirmation that he had left because of my opening lines came from my mother. I left the dramatic society forthwith. That was my first and only attempt at acting. I wasn't sure whether I wanted to stand up and speak before a group of people again.

It has always been a matter of interest to me that, after vowing in that little hall never to stand up before an audience again, most of my life has been spent just doing that. God has worked through the disappointments to bring me to what He planned for my life – to write and speak for Him.

One other thing that looms large in my rear-view mirror, and gave me another intimation of what I would be doing in the future, was my love affair with words. If anyone asked me what I liked about school when I was a child I would give the same answer as many children do to that question – *holidays*! If they persisted and asked what else I liked, I would say the free milk. But the truth was I loved it most when our teacher, Miss Maria Jones, read to us.

Every day, Miss Jones would spend the last 15 minutes of school time reading us a story. This was always the highlight of the school day. Everyone loved that last quarter of an hour, and not just because it was getting close to 'home time', as we used to call it, but somehow when she read a story it was as if she was weaving a magic carpet that transported us from the dusty, grimy mining village in which we lived to another world.

Sometimes she would punish the class for being unruly by not reading a story. It was an effective deterrent, because we all learned very quickly how important it was to pay attention and the prospect of ending the day without a story, through a temporary lapse in our behaviour, would soon bring us to order.

Miss Jones took us in English and maths. She was tall and slender, and had wonderfully rich, lilting voice, which she used to great effect when reading to us. The stories I loved best were the folk stories of Welsh heroes like Owen Glyndwr and others.

I disliked the rote work of maths intensely. The sound of the whole class reciting, 'One and one make two, two and two make four, four and four make eight, eight and eight make sixteen,' I found utterly boring. I was never very interested in figures and although I became fairly competent with them, my real love was for words. And I have Miss Jones to thank for developing that love and starting me off on a romance with language.

Although she was Welsh-speaking, her command and understanding of the English language was deeply impressive. She instilled in me a love of the language by introducing me not only to the great writers of the past, like Shakespeare, Milton and others, but also to contemporaries who were just breaking into print.

Miss Jones made English lessons come alive for me. She would brighten up what could be a boring session, such as examining the parts of speech or punctuation, by little asides that still live in my memory to this very day. 'Think of a colon,' she used to say, 'like the two headlights of car that show that what comes next in a sentence is an amplification of that which precedes it.' Without exaggeration I can say that from that day to this often when I use a colon I think of Miss Jones.

Other statements she made that are imprinted in my memory are these: 'One idea per sentence. Pick the right words for what you want to say. You don't put on climbing boots to go dancing!' 'Remember, one topic per paragraph and paragraphs must fit together like the couplings of railway carriages.' 'When you think a passage is particularly fine, think again, because it probably isn't.' And there are so many more.

I think I also owe my love of picturesque language to Miss Jones. In my mind I can hear her saying as she put copies of a piece of prose before us: 'Just look at this piece of prose; it is as flowing and fluid as a river. Listen to it as it ripples over and around the rocks of punctuation.' Another phrase she used to use was, 'As you read this, float downstream on the soothing rhythm of the author's words.'

There was no doubt that Miss Jones was the favourite teacher of most of the pupils. Many of us used to wait for her after school just to walk home with her and carry her briefcase or the homework she had to mark. One day she said to me, 'You really like words, don't you?' 'Yes, Miss,' I said, 'but there are so many of them that I find it difficult to remember them all.' She offered to give me a few minutes after school one day a week to help me build up a good vocabulary. I loved those times, which sometimes expanded into half an hour. On one such extended occasion she gave me a list of ten new words to look up in the dictionary. During the next one she got me to use them in a sentence to check that not only did I know the meaning of the word, but also how to use it in the proper way. She also warned me about something in the Welsh nature that is never satisfied with using one word when two will do!

Another thing she would do in these extracurricular sessions was to give me a well-written piece of prose and encourage me to 'just soak your mind in it'. 'Sometimes,' she said, 'artists and painters who work indoors will keep by them a variety of precious stones and, to avoid their awareness and sensitivity to colour being affected by the drabness around them, they will wash their eyes, so to speak, in these colours. You need to do something similar with your mind by soaking your mind in exceptionally well-written prose.' Although I didn't realise it at the time, Miss Jones was being used by God, I believe, to prepare me for the work that He had for me to do in the future.

1. *The Power and the Glory* by Graham Greene (Penguin Books 2003).

CHAPTER 3

MY SEARCH FOR SATISFACTION

It is a fact I believe to be incontrovertible that there is a moment in all our lives when we begin to realise that the things of earth and time cannot satisfy us. Christian psychologists refer to it as an 'existential moment', a time when we begin to realise that deep down within, our souls crave for something that this world cannot give us. For me that 'existential moment' came when I was bordering on 13 years old.

Immediately before it, a couple of things had happened which brought a good deal of pleasure into my life. Firstly, my mother had given birth to a little girl. After being the only child for 12 years the thrill of having a sister, Pamela, to dote upon made me exceedingly happy. Secondly, I had won a scholarship to the technical college in Bargoed, a town about five miles away. A scholarship, to the boys and girls of the village, meant more than just higher education; it meant a five-mile ride on the early morning train and a special rail pass one could also use at weekends.

A few weeks after these two events, in the summer of 1941, I was lying alone on the mountainside just outside my home looking up at a cloudless sky when the thought entered my mind that although there were some good feelings in life there were some pretty unpleasant ones, too. The Second World War had begun two years earlier, on 3 September 1939, and although we were not feeling too much of its effects, apart from carrying gas masks to school, blacked-out streets at night, and food rationing, there was still a great deal of fear around. I wondered why it was that with so many Christians in the village praying for the war to stop God was not answering their prayers.

A number of strange and unnerving thoughts ran through my mind that day. As I looked up at the sky I pondered what kept it from suddenly falling in on itself. I saw no reason why it shouldn't. The thought was quite terrifying. Then my mind turned to the question of God. Is there really a God in the way that my mother and father described Him and believed in Him? Some of my friends said they didn't believe in God. They claimed that the idea that there was a God in heaven watching everything we do was something thought up by adults to get children to behave when their parents were not around. Were they right, I wondered to myself?

But my deepest concern, as I remember it, was why there were not only so many joys in life (like earning a scholarship and having a new baby sister), but also so many disappointments. I wrestled with the thought that so often the people you trust don't always come up to your expectations. I was still deeply puzzled and very much hurt by my father's exit from the play in which I had been involved. Resentment still rankled within me as I thought about that. Although I had not met up with Freudian psychology at that time, there is a lot of truth in Freud's idea that the 'the mind will return again and again to that which caused it pain'. A few years later I learned the importance of forgiving my father for walking out of the play and now, though the memory of it is still clear, there is no accompanying resentment. It was, nevertheless, a defining moment, for it led me to the awareness that there were longings in my heart that even those closest to me could not fully satisfy.

There is a Bible verse that says, 'Foolishness is bound in the heart of a child; but the rod of correction shall drive it far from him' (Proverbs 22:15 KJV). In my case, although there had been a good deal of loving discipline, it had not succeeded in driving out all my innate foolishness. There was still a good deal of rebelliousness and strong determination within me to make my life work without having to accept the beliefs of my parents that God and God alone could give me the satisfaction my heart craved.

Although it is only as I look back that I can realise fully what was happening to me, I am convinced that those musings on the mountainside brought home to me that if I were to find satisfaction then it would be down to me and me alone. So began a three-year period when I threw myself with rebellious abandon into the task of finding ways to create what nowadays we call a 'buzz for the soul'.

I noticed that the ones who were most admired in my circle of friends were the most daring. So I set out to become the most daring of them all! I had already learned to swear, so in order to gain attention I began to do it more and more. When I was with my friends my conversation would be peppered with the most indecent words and phrases I could think of. When I look back now as a servant of Jesus Christ, a shudder goes through me when I consider the extent to which I used to blaspheme His name. Though my friends were obviously impressed with my ability to string swear words and profanities together in a way that far exceeded their own, there were times when even they would say, 'Shut up Selwyn, you are going much too far. If someone hears you we will get into serious trouble.'

Unknown to my parents, I was already smoking and as I had a clear bent to organise things I figured out how our group – mostly 13-year-olds, all of whom also smoked – could get our cigarettes free of charge. One of the shops in the village was owned by a family who lived in the basement. As one entered the shop a bell would ring and it would take about half a minute before someone would make it up the stairs into the shop. I developed a plan that when the shop was empty two of us would enter it. One of us would help ourselves to a packet of cigarettes that was within reach, and then leave, while the other waited to make a genuine purchase of something simple, such as an ice cream or perhaps a packet of sweets. It was always one packet of cigarettes so that it would not become obvious to the shopkeeper. This meant we could follow the same plan again and again. I loved it when the group would say, 'That was a wonderful idea Selwyn. What other ideas have you got for us?' Those words were like a drink to my thirsty soul.

Then, of course, there were girls. My hormones were as active as any other healthy young male and I went out with girls, kissed them, and often fantasised what it would be like to have sex. In those days, sexual experimentation amongst young people was not practised to the extent it is now, and though I often used to boast to my friends about my sexual conquests (which were fictitious) my conscience (which I attribute to parental training), would not allow me to go too far. Of course, there were always girls who made it clear that they would not resist a direct sexual approach, but whenever I was tempted it was as if a warning bell rang in my conscience. My sexual restraint, I believe, was not due to willpower, but the effects of good and godly upbringing.

In September 1941 I began my first term at Bargoed Technical College. There I found a new group of friends and although the restraints of travelling and homework caused me to settle down during the week, there were always the weekends. The rail pass meant that on Saturdays it was possible to travel to Bargoed without cost, meet up with my friends, see a film in the afternoon and in the evening visit a dance hall. Usually the dance finished about 10pm and the last train to Fochriw left at 10.45pm. The hour between the end of the dance and getting on the train was always occupied with buying fish and chips, then trying to entice a girl into some dark corner for a few kisses.

Saturday nights meant I had permission to stay out until 11.30, but when I got home I would always find my mother and father waiting up for me. And always with deeply concerned expressions on their faces. When they asked what I had done or where I had been, it was nothing to lie to them and I would often say it had been a pretty boring evening while, of course, that was far from the case.

The worst thing about Saturday nights was the fact that the next day was Sunday. Oh, how I hated Sundays! What little colour there was in those coal-stained valleys seemed to be completely bleached out when Sundays came. The day began with the sound of the church bells calling people out on to streets as silent as the grave, broken only by the slamming of doors, the barking of a dog or the sound of newspaper boys pushing papers through the letter boxes.

No children were allowed to play in the streets on Sundays. Even those parents who were not churchgoers respected Sunday as a day of rest. What made matters worse was that it always rained on Sundays. Or so it seemed. Near my home was an ammunition dump, which had been there since the beginning of the war. It was always guarded by soldiers and I can remember watching them on several Sundays, standing there in the pouring rain, and thinking to myself, 'Which is worse: having to stand there in the pouring rain or having to go to church on a Sunday?' I decided it would be more fun to stand in the rain.

Sunday meant church three times a day. It seemed that no sooner was I out of one service then it was time for the next. Sunday morning was the family worship service, the afternoon meant Sunday school, and Sunday nights was the evangelistic service. The Sunday evening service was the worst to sit through, as that was the time when direct appeals were made from the pulpit to commit one's life to Jesus Christ.

The pastor, my uncle David, would preach every two Sundays of the month and on the other two Sundays visiting speakers would take the pulpit. I liked it best when my uncle preached because he would be fairly short. I don't remember much about his preaching except that he never told a humorous story or even a joke. He was good, but so serious. He was what I supposed a saint should be like. In those days I felt the very opposite to a saint; more like a deep-dyed sinner.

Often my uncle would plead with me after a service to surrender my life to Jesus Christ, but I would always resist. Sometimes he would pat me on the head and say, 'I believe you are going to be a preacher one day.' That used to irritate me greatly, as the last thing I wanted to be was a preacher. A film star perhaps, but not a preacher. My uncle's wife, Rose, my mother's sister, was someone I loved deeply. She was chatty, down-to-earth and what I liked about her most was that when my uncle would extend his sermon longer than usual she would surreptitiously raise her arm slightly and point to her wristwatch – an action guaranteed to bring his sermon to a quick conclusion.

I must confess, however, there were times when I would think to myself that I needed to change. I would promise myself not to swear, smoke or steal, and try to be better, for my parents' sake, but I kept breaking those good resolutions. When I was with my friends I would once again be the daring boy.

On the Sundays when visiting speakers took the pulpit of our little church it was usually hell-fire and brimstone preaching. There was one man in particular who preached regularly to our congregation and who would point to us group of boys sitting in the back seat and say, 'Young men, if you do not get saved you will land up in hell!' In those days women wore hats to go to church and it was often a comfort whenever this preacher came to be able to duck behind a lady with a wide-brimmed hat and avoid his gaze. We boys would sit there at the back and play noughts and crosses. We couldn't wait to get out and walk the streets in the nearby town of Rhymney for what was called 'Monkeys' Parade', where the boys and girls would walk up and down just to size each other up and attempt to set up a date.

There was the time when I was so disobedient in Sunday school that I was banned from the class for over a month. It happened like this. After the whole Sunday school had spent some time together, singing children's choruses, we would then break up and go into different classes according to our age. Everyone would sit in a circle and the teacher would take us through the lesson for the day. On one occasion I happened to sit next to the teacher and while she was talking I moved my chair slightly behind her and kept dropping screwed up pieces of paper into her wide brimmed hat. My mischievous mind had planned this beforehand when I had taken an old songbook that was lying around, ripped out a number of pages and screwed them up into little balls. Later, when the teacher left the church there was a slight wind which whipped up the pieces of paper and people laughed uproariously as they watched her walk down the street unaware that dozens of bits of paper were flying from her hat. When someone pointed out what was happening she knew right away who was the culprit and stormed into my parents' house, accusing me of making her a laughing-stock and saying she was never going to have me in her Sunday school class again.

For a month I sat on my own at the back of the church during the Sunday school. After that, one of the church elders, a man by the name of Dewi Morgan, took me into his class and treated me with great love and respect. I was deeply touched by his interest in me and have never forgotten it.

My years from 13 to 16 were ones that brought great sadness to my parents. They would smell cigarette smoke on my clothes and worry that I showed no interest in spiritual things. One summer evening I lit a cigarette in my bedroom and blew the smoke out of the window, little realising that the smoke was curling back indoors. My father came into the bedroom and caught me at it. He was very annoyed and although he was careful not to overdo the discipline he did sting my legs with a strap which usually hung in the kitchen beneath a motto that said, 'I need Thee every hour.'

When I was with my friends the more daring I became the more daring I wanted to be. This led to one rebellious act after another. Several times I appeared in court at Pontlottyn, for what I considered were minor reasons but the police thought differently. This of course caused my parents a great deal of distress. They would say to me: 'Why do you do these things? Why don't you give your heart to Jesus and He will help you overcome these things?'

Although I did apply myself to my studies at technical college, I was always on the lookout for the next daring thing to do. There was one occasion in particular when, through a friend who worked in the Principal's office, I secured the examination papers ahead of an exam we were due to take. Nothing was too daring – I was so desperate to be accepted, admired and get this buzz when my friends looked at me in admiration. It was the psychotherapist Sigmund Freud who said that the purpose of living is to minimise pain and maximise pleasure. Most certainly that sums up the general condition of my life at that time.

After two years at college an opportunity opened up for me to join an apprenticeship scheme in the engineering shop at a steelworks in Dowlais, a five-mile train journey from my village. My parents and a family adviser felt that it was too good an opportunity for me to miss. Arrangements were made for me to leave college, become an apprentice and continue my engineering studies on a one-day-a-week leave of absence scheme.

From the moment I walked into the engineering shop I loved it. The whirl of the machinery, the heavy smell of burning steel, the quick movements of the machines, the bustle and busyness, made it a place of great fascination for me. I soon made friends among the other apprentices and joined in their worldly talk and lifestyle, and within a few months I was running the football pool on behalf of the young apprentices. Every week we all paid our contribution and whoever won after the weekend results would receive the money. On one occasion no one came to claim the winnings and I suggested to a friend that he should claim to have the winning ticket and we divided the money between us. If the others had known they would have lynched us!

My goal in life in those early teens was to satisfy the deep thirst that existed in my heart through the pleasures that the world offered. How could I ever find something that would truly satisfy the ache in my soul? It would not be long before I came across the answer.

CHAPTER 4

THE MOST IMPORTANT DECISION OF MY LIFE

I have no hesitation in saying that the greatest and most momentous decision I have ever made in my life was the decision to become a follower of Jesus Christ. Prior to my conversion I had always felt, to some degree at least, that there was a longing within my heart to know God in the way my parents seemed to know him, but I was afraid to pursue it in case I might be disappointed. Many times God had tapped at the window-pane of my soul. Like times just before bedtime when I would kneel to pray – something I had been taught as a child – and the feeling would come over me that I needed to take spiritual realities more seriously. Even in my most rebellious times, I would never slip under the blankets without saying a prayer. It was a simple and short prayer recited very quickly:

If I should die before I wake
I pray the Lord my soul to take. Amen.

Sometimes I would think to myself, 'What would happen if I died? Would my parents' faith be enough to save me?' I think, however, that the kind of person I was prior to my conversion needed more than tapping on the window-pane of my soul – the glass needed breaking! I needed God to confront me, wake me up, wrestle me to the ground, so to speak, pin me there and bring home to me as strongly as possible my need to open up my life to Jesus Christ.

Just before my sixteenth birthday, God began to move in my life in a very powerful way. It began one weeknight early in 1944, when I was making my way to the local dance hall. It was about 8pm and the route to the hall was past the local mission hall where they were holding their weekly prayer meeting. As I walked through the blacked-out streets I heard a familiar voice and was instantly stopped in my tracks. It was the voice of my father, who was obviously taking part in the prayer meeting. I stopped and listened as he prayed for me, pleading with God for my salvation.

I had heard my father pray many times at home and in church, but never with such passion as this. His voice took on a tone and power that penetrated deep into my heart. I was rooted to the spot. What should I do? Something inside me wanted to rush into the prayer meeting in response to this and say that I wanted to be saved. Or should I wait to see if this feeling would pass off? I waited – and it passed. I went to the dance that night but there seemed to be something odd about the whole place. The lights appeared less bright than usual; there was something missing in the music; the whole atmosphere of the place seemed as if it had been changed. God was calling me and I was beginning to see things from a new perspective.

The weeks that followed were difficult. The more I threw myself into the pleasures of the flesh, the less satisfying they were to my soul. I turned from one to the other – smoking, gambling, rugby, football – but for some reason they seemed not to thrill me as much as they once did.

For weeks I fought against the strivings of the Holy Spirit. I would lay awake at night and wonder what was happening to me. Things came to a head on a stormy Sunday night in February

1944. I went to church with my parents, but with so much rain pouring down, no one expected the guest preacher to turn up. The speaker booked for that occasion was a man who lived about six miles away and in order to get to us meant a tortuous bicycle ride over the mountain. As the service began I was, quite frankly, a little disappointed to see him walk in. It meant the service would be longer than usual, with my uncle not being the preacher. Now it meant we would be in church for two hours at least.

The back seat was always reserved for the young people. Seated next to me was a close childhood friend, Ronald Lewis. Ronald was a son of one of the elders of the church and though we were close he was not part of the gang I usually went around with. He was not a Christian, but there was no evidence of the rebellion in him that characterised my own life.

There was something that night about the whole service that was different. I found myself being strangely drawn to what the preacher was saying. There was nothing dynamic about him. He was an ordinary person, not much to look at. I had heard him a few times before, but now his words seemed to have some powerful conviction that reached deep into my soul. His face was irradiated with a strange light. His words seemed to be barbed, reaching deep into my soul. I especially remember these words: 'This is the night when God wants to draw you to Himself. Come to Jesus, who will save you from your sin, live in you and give you the power to be able to serve Him.' I had heard these or similar words many times from that pulpit, but that night they seemed to take hold of me with a power I had never known before.

'What is happening to me?' I thought to myself. The tears were coming into my eyes. I didn't cry often – especially in church. I felt the strong defences I had built against the Spirit were breaking down. My heart was crumbling. The preacher asked if there were any there who would walk to the front and commit themselves to Jesus Christ.

I was the first to move. The church was quite small and it took perhaps ten seconds to move from the back of the church to the front, but that night it seemed like a mile long. It was the most wonderful walk of my life. As I moved toward the front my pastor, who had been sitting on the platform with the preacher, quickly came down to greet me. The same arms that had held me and prayed the prayer of dedication so many years ago were thrown around me to embrace me.

I was conscious that others had come to the front also. My friend Ronald Lewis was there and so was his sister Mary, together with several other young men who had been sitting with me in the back seat. Altogether there were about ten of us who were converted that night. My uncle sat with me and read me these words from the Bible: 'Call to me, and I will answer you, and show you great and mighty things, which you do not know' (Jer. 33:3).

I sobbed out my heart as I knelt at the front seat of the church that evening and asked God to forgive my sins. I received the assurance that Christ was mine, that my sins were forgiven and I was saved. There was no doing the usual Sunday night thing afterwards – walking over the mountain to Rhymney and chatting up the girls. I went home, where my parents rejoiced with me and told me how glad they were for the step I had taken. That night I fell asleep wondering where it would all take me. I knew there were things I must break with – lying, cheating, stealing and so on. What would happen now? How was I going to tell my workmates and friends? I knew what they thought about Christians.

That morning, as I made my way to the railway station at about 6:30 to take the train to Dowlais, my mind was made up.

The cigarettes would have to go. Nothing was said in our church about the evils of tobacco, yet I knew for me it was wrong. There were other habits I knew would have to go also – swearing, for example. I do not say this proudly but I have never used a swear word from the day of my conversion to this.

The train took about 20 minutes to puff its way up the steep incline to the steel town of Dowlais. In those minutes I made the discovery that when someone gives their life to Jesus Christ, He not only changes them but resides in them. 'To them gave He power to become the sons of God,' says the apostle John in the first chapter of his Gospel. The boys took out their cigarettes as usual, but I didn't. 'You're not smoking?' 'No,' I said. 'Last night I gave my life to Jesus Christ and I don't think that is what I should now do.' There was an awkward silence. One of the young men tried to argue about religion but I sat and prayed that God would help me not to fail Him in any way. I proceeded to tell my friends just what had happened the night before, and as I gave my first stammering testimony to Jesus Christ I felt His presence and power wonderfully supporting me.

I needn't have worried about telling the men and boys in the engineering shop about my conversion. When I arrived some of the boys who had been on the train with me had gone ahead to tell everyone that I had become a Christian. When I opened the door of the engineering shop I found the place buzzing with excitement. One of the older men patted me on the back and said, 'Good morning, preacher. Are we going to have a sermon today?' It was all good-natured fun and I felt no animosity in what he said. Another man said, 'I'll give you a month.' Yet another commented, 'I'll give you a week!' I think I finally convinced them I had become a Christian when I said I would no longer be running the football pool. The baiting and teasing continued throughout the day, but though it was difficult for me to handle

I did not feel their comments were malicious.

As the days passed and they saw I was serious, their respect for me grew, until eventually all came to accept the fact that I had become a Christian and I intended to run my life differently. The teasing stopped and there were times when some of the men would ask me to include them in my prayers as they struggled with various difficulties in their lives. In those early days of my conversion I remember ending all my prayer times with this phrase: 'Lord, you have made a world of difference to me; grant that I might make some difference to the world.'

My first weeks as a Christian were ones of joyous discoveries. Anyone who has not experienced the dramatic change of life and mind and the spiritual release that Christ brings to the repentant sinner can never understand the welling up of wonderful gratitude that is in the heart. The greatest news of all is that the blood of Jesus Christ, God's son, cleanses from all sin. I had heard good news. I walked the streets in fellowship with my unseen Friend. I knew now that Jesus Christ was alive, not because others had told me, but because He lived within my heart. The Bible, it seemed, was set to music. Carried on the crest of a boundless enthusiasm, I would burst spontaneously into song. I thirsted to know more of the word of God and read my Bible at every opportunity. I was ready for every new discovery, every new challenge that would beckon to me on the Christian highway.

My appetite for spiritual things was so intense that the more I had of God and His Word the more I wanted. I was in church every night of the week. When there was nothing on in my own church I went to one in a nearby town or village. There was always something special on at weekends somewhere – a convention, a youth rally, a special speaker – so I was never at a loss to find food for the ever-increasing appetite of my soul.

A few weeks after my conversion I was baptised by total immersion, along with the others who had been converted on the same night as myself. The baptismal pool was outside the church building, which meant the public could see what was going on. The baptism was on a bitterly cold March day, but crowds sat on the mountainside opposite the church watching. Never shall I forget the thrill, before entering the baptismal pool, of telling everyone what Jesus Christ had done for me.

After baptism in water I was told about another baptism – the baptism of the Spirit. This was most puzzling to me as I thought I had already received the Holy Spirit at my conversion. My pastor explained that although that was so there was another operation of the Spirit for the impartation of power that I needed to seek God for.

Despite my puzzlement, I acted on my pastor's advice and attended a special service being held the following weekend 20 miles away in the town of Brynmawr for those wanting to be baptised in the Spirit. There, he told me, a young evangelist by the name of Handel Price would be speaking on this subject and praying for those who had not yet received this experience. On the Saturday evening I made my way to the small but crowded church. There were the usual preliminaries – chorus singing, reading of the Scriptures and so on – and then the speaker got up and announced his theme: 'Did you receive the Holy Spirit when you believed?' (Acts 19:2).

My heart began to throb within me as I listened to his powerful exposition of the text and its context. Since my conversion I had testified to different people that I had become a follower of Jesus Christ, but whenever I did so it was always with a little fear – fear that I might be ridiculed or rejected. I wanted to have done with this fear and enjoy the same kind of boldness that characterised the early disciples.

Halfway through his message, Handel Price said that later he would be praying for those who wanted to be baptised in the Spirit. I longed for him to finish his sermon, but he seemed to keep on and on and on. I could hold back no longer. The thirst in my soul was so great that I could not live a minute longer without the promised empowerment of the Holy Spirit. Throwing caution to the wind, I stood up and cried out, 'Please pray for me now! I want to be filled with the Spirit. I can't wait any longer!'

The preacher did not seem to be upset by me interrupting his sermon and said, 'Right, stay where you are, lift your hands to God and begin to praise the Lord.' I did as I was told and as I raised my hands and began to praise the Lord I felt a wave of supernatural power sweep into my soul. The English words I was using to praise Him merged into words that were unintelligible to me. My strongest memory of that moment was not just the feeling of spiritual exhilaration, but the sense that my personality was being endued with a new sense of boldness. I felt at that moment I could have stood in front of a whole stadium of rugby fans and preached to them about their need to put their faith in Christ!

Handel Price didn't finish his sermon. The service turned into one great prayer meeting where dozens of others received their 'personal Pentecost' – a phrase used in those days to describe the experience of being baptised in the Spirit. I left the church that night with a spiritual boldness I had not known before and one that has never left me from that day to this.

The following morning, being a Sunday, I stepped out on to the street where I lived to head for church, when I realised that I had never told my neighbours about my Christian faith. The street on which I lived was called Martin Street, and consisted of about 40 terraced houses (20 on each side), built on a hill. My home, number 17, was at the top of the hill. As I stood there, considering how I could best tell my neighbours about my conversion, I found myself shouting the words of John 3:16: 'For God so loved the world that he gave his only begotten Son, that whosoever believeth in him should not perish, but have everlasting life' (KJV).

Several people appeared in their doorways, some in their pyjamas, wondering what all the shouting was about. Immediately I saw them I began to tell them the most wonderful thing that could ever happen to them would be to give their lives to Jesus Christ. This, I said, was certainly the most wonderful thing that had happened to me. They all seemed to be somewhat bemused by my action, but listened attentively as I spoke for about five minutes on the importance of putting one's faith in Christ. In a sense, that was my first sermon. I can't claim any converts from it, but years later, after I had moved away from the village, people who lived on that street would say to my mother, 'How is Selwyn these days? We still remember how he woke up the village that Sunday morning preaching to us about his conversion.'

CHAPTER 5

FIRST STEPS INTO DISCIPLESHIP

A few months after I became a Christian I became more and more interested in how I could become involved in some type of Christian service. The prayer I referred to earlier was always on my mind: 'Lord, you have made a difference to my world, how can I make a difference to yours?' One day I approached the Sunday school superintendent of our church, Dewi Morgan, and offered myself as a teacher. He accepted my offer immediately, but couldn't resist reminding me, with a wide grin on his face, that just over two years previously one of the Sunday school teachers had refused to have me in her class because of the prank I had played on her.

How strange life is. Two years after being expelled from a Sunday School class I was now volunteering to teach one! The teacher I had embarrassed was, of course, as delighted as anyone in the church that I had put my faith in Christ and made it clear that she had forgiven me. She was the first to shake my hand and welcome me on to the Sunday school staff. Years later I heard that she proudly used to tell the story of my conversion to many of her friends and used it as an illustration of how deep a change Christ is able to make in a person's life.

I also became involved in the musical side of our church's ministry. When I was a boy in Birmingham I had taken some piano lessons and although I was not that proficient, I was able to play well enough to accompany the singing of choruses in our youth meetings. I had also taught myself to play the piano accordion. This came into good use several months after my conversion when another young man, Norman Thomas, became a Christian. Norman was an accomplished accordionist and we joined forces and played together in the Sunday services. We became very close friends and were often invited to provide the music for the many open-air services, which in those days were a regular feature of the evangelical churches in the area.

In the summer of 1944 Norman and I had been to a Saturday evening evangelistic crusade in the village of Pontlottyn and on the way home we met up with two Christian girls who had also been at the meeting. They were from a village beyond ours called Bedlinog, and as we talked we decided to escort them back to their homes. Before we said our goodbyes we had made arrangements to meet with them again. This led eventually to courtship, although in Norman's case it lasted only a few months. Mine went on for just under a year. My girlfriend, blonde and strikingly good-looking, had been a Christian for several years and was also an excellent singer and pianist. Many an evening was spent in her home with around a dozen or so other young people, singing choruses and discussing spiritual issues. Going out together helped my Christian growth in a most wonderful way and I shall always be grateful for the spiritual influence she had on my life. We eventually decided that, romantically speaking, our relationship was going nowhere and we parted company the best of friends.

One of the things I struggled with during that courtship was the whole issue of sexual thoughts. It wasn't there strongly at first, but it arose one night about three months after our relationship began. One summer evening we were lying together on the mountain side when my girlfriend said, 'I think we ought to go now before we do something drastic.' There was something in her words that seemed to awaken the slumbering giant of sex within me and I battled with it afterwards for several weeks. I fought hard against lustful and licentious thoughts until one night, worn down by the conflict that was going on inside me, I shut myself in a room and prayed, 'Lord, inside me is a team of wild horses that are out of control. If you can't control them, no one can. And if they can't be controlled then I would rather die.'

God understood my desperate state and met with me that night in an unforgettable way. After a long time of waiting before Him, I was given a vision of Christ upon the cross. I saw Him hanging there; saw the spittle of the soldier on his cheek, the blood running down His naked body. Suddenly the vision vanished and all that remained was an empty cross. Then the impression came that the cross I was seeing was one on which I should be crucified. Not in a literal sense, of course, but in the way the Apostle Paul refers in his writings to the Galatians: 'I have been crucified with Christ and I no longer live, but Christ lives in me. The life I live in the body, I live by faith in the Son of God, who loved me and gave himself for me' (Gal. 2:20).

The implication of this, it seemed to me at that time, was that, just as Christ had been crucified, I needed to be also, albeit in a much different sense. It was not that I had to atone for my sin – that had been accomplished once and for all by Christ's death for me – but the invitation now being presented to me was to place myself symbolically in His hands so that a deathblow could be delivered to the ruling passions of my life.

In my vision I saw myself nailed to a cross. There was no pain, just a sense of absolute surrender. When the vision vanished I was filled with an incredible peace. I spent the whole night in prayer and the next day, even though I had gone without a night's sleep, I felt as if I was walking on air. Over the weeks that followed I became aware that, as my previous encounter with the Holy

Spirit had given me a new sense of *power*, this had given me a new sense of *purity*. I do not wish to imply that the Holy Spirit comes only at times into a Christian's life. He resides in a Christian's heart permanently. However, I believe there are certain crisis moments in our lives when a special work needs to be done and He undertakes that work in response to our willing prayers.

Bible students, familiar with the doctrine of 'sanctification by faith', will say that is what happened to me that night – I was sanctified in one critical moment by looking to Christ in faith. Others will say it was an extension of the baptism in the Spirit, the Spirit working in another operation designed to deal a deathblow to the stirrings of sensuality in my life. I am not sure how to define it, and I do not share it here with the intention that others should follow my example. But that was how God dealt with me over the problem and for that I cannot thank Him enough.

This experience I must add did not place me beyond the possibility of a carnal thought, a stab of pride, or a trace of envy. It meant, rather, that I became more conscious of the Holy Spirit's presence than sin's presence in my heart. Evil was not eradicated in me (as some proponents of the theory of 'imparted holiness' believe), but I found the appetite for lust and sensuality was not there to the degree it was before. Temptation would still rise up to confront me, but I found that it did not dominate me in the way it once did. Something had happened inside me that, while not taking away my responsibility to say a flat 'No' to sin, reinforced my desire for God, for holiness and purity.

The year 1945 will ever be remembered by people of my generation as the year in which the war in Europe came to an end. On 8 May (later known as VE Day) it was announced that the war in Europe was over, and right across the land people rejoiced in different ways, some even dancing in the streets.

Celebrations in my village included tea parties in every street – despite the rationing – and in the evening a huge bonfire was lit on top of the mountain which every able-bodied villager attended. It was wonderful to see the street lights go on again and no longer to worry about whether our windows were blacked out. Before he went to bed that night, my father opened the curtains and left the lights on until the next morning, as did many others. He said there was something very gratifying about having no longer to worry about concealing the light after years of ensuring that not the slightest gleam could be seen from the outside.

In that same year, we had a new addition to our family. A young man, David Cecil Jones, who worked alongside my father in the mines, had lost his mother, and as he was not the sort of young man who could look after himself, he was invited by my father and mother to share our home. Both my sister and I also welcomed him as a brother and he became as close to us as we were to one another. Later, when his mother's small estate was wound up, he received a small sum of money that enabled him to buy a car – a Jowett Javelin with a two-stroke engine. At that time there were not many in our village who owned a car although there were quite a number who had a motorcycle, myself included. The car revolutionised our family's movements and made it possible for us to travel together more widely. I was thrilled when we took possession of the new car and quickly passed my driving test. David was very generous and allowed me to borrow the car for my own personal use from time to time. Neither David nor my father were able to drive and whenever they wanted to go anywhere and I was unavailable a neighbour would drive them.

Because petrol rationing was still in force at that time, my father was strongly against my using the car for my own purposes; he wanted to conserve the petrol for when the whole family wanted to go for a day out. When he worked on the afternoon shift I often managed to persuade my mother to let me use the car, with the promise that I would return it before my father got home. This arrangement worked fine until one evening when I was out in the car the half shaft snapped (a regular occurrence in the Jowett Javelin of that day) and I had to return home by train and report the incident to my father. Both my mother and I were in the dog house for days after that, I can tell you!

As there were just a handful of young people in my own church in Fochriw at this time, due to many finding work in other parts of the county, I formed relationships with a group of young people from a church in the town of Dowlais. There were literally dozens of young people on fire for the Lord in this church, and on nights when there were no activities in the building we would meet in different homes to sing and pray together. As you might expect, romantic relationships would develop in such a group from time to time, a notable one being that of my close friend, Ronald Lewis, who struck up a romance with one of the girls, Edna, whom he eventually married. Romance was out as far as I was concerned. I had already finished one relationship and was not quite ready for another.

Ronald worked for Great Western Railways as a trainee engine driver, something I very much wanted to do myself at one time, but when I applied for the position and was invited to go for some initial tests in Swindon, it was discovered that I was colour-blind. It has never proved to be a problem in everyday life, but the examining authorities felt the deficiency disqualified me from taking up that position. I have always been crazy about trains, and the disappointment of finding I was not suitable for training to become an engine driver was hard to bear.

Towards the end of 1945 my paternal grandmother died. Although I lived in a house opposite to my paternal grandparents I never developed as close a relationship with them as I did with my maternal grandparents. I think this was because I had spent the first six years of my life in the home of my mother's parents and visited my father's parents only occasionally. I did grow to have a strong affection for them, however, and was deeply saddened by her death. I remember my grandfather pounding on our door at around midnight crying out in Welsh that my grandmother had died. She had suffered a massive heart attack, and it was all over within a few minutes. I went at once with my father to my grandparents' home and had my first experience of looking upon a dead body. I was surprised at how inwardly calm I felt, seeing my grandmother lying there. I had always had a fear of death, but I think my faith in Christ had taken away that fear and replaced it with the certainty that the apostle Paul had when speaking on that subject in 1 Corinthians 15: 'O death, where is thy sting? O grave, where is thy victory?' (1 Corinthians 15:55 KJV).

In those days, as I said earlier, few homes had telephones. As I remember it, there were only three in the village – one in a telephone box outside the Post Office, another in the Post Office itself and the third in home of the village policeman. As it was necessary to inform the other relatives who lived in a village several miles away, my father didn't want to wait until morning. He asked me to walk with him to the local bobby's home to ask him if he would persuade the policeman in the next village to go to my father's brother's and sister's homes and break the sad news.

My father seemed fairly calm and composed as we walked to the officer's house through the darkened streets of the village, but as we were returning home he suddenly stopped in the street and started to sob in a way I had never witnessed before. Seeing him in such pain and weeping so much, I couldn't help sobbing, too. The depth and degree of my sorrow quite frightened me. I had shed tears many times before, of course, but never quite like this. My body shook as I stood there in the street and my father had to console me. He told me later that he was surprised at my tears, as he knew I was not as close to my paternal grandmother as I was to my maternal grandmother. I could not understand at that moment for whom I was crying – myself, my father or the loss of my grandmother.

Clarity came many years later, when reading the theological writer Frederick Buechner. He said that whenever you find tears in your eyes it is well to pay the closest attention to them, especially the unexpected tears. 'They not only tell you something about the secret of who you are, but more often than not God is speaking to you through them of the mystery of where you have come from and summoning you to where, if your soul is to be saved, you should go next.' [1]

The tears I shed on the street that night brought me in touch with something I needed to learn – empathy for someone whose heart was breaking. This is where I needed to go next in my development as a person and a follower of the Lord Jesus Christ. Compassion for others is, I believe, one of the qualities that God wants for all our lives but especially those who are called to counselling or helping others. The work that God had for me in the future would involve me empathising with the hurts and traumas of thousands of hurting people. That experience, in the middle of the night on the streets of Fochriw was, I believe, an important part of my developing discipleship. The value of it would be seen much later.

Notes

1. Frederick Buechner, *Whistling in the Dark* (Harper: San Francisco, 1993).

CHAPTER 6

FROM COAL PIT TO PULPIT

E arly in 1946 I was informed by HM Government that when I reached the age of 18 I would become eligible for two years' National Service. I was also told that because of the nation's need for coal I would be required to serve that time in a coal mine of my choice instead of the Armed Forces.

Under the Emergency Powers (Defence) Act, which was first drafted by Ernest Bevin in 1940 and remained in force for some time after the Second World War, many young men who were eligible for National Service found themselves serving their time either in a colliery near to where they lived or moving to a coal mining area. They came to be known as Bevin Boys.

Fortunately, living in a mining community meant that I did not have far to travel to the mine in the village of Bedlinog, about five miles away. It was a sad day when I said goodbye to my friends in the engineering shop at Dowlais, but I was assured by the representative of the Amalgamated Engineering Union, of which I was a member, that the two years I would spend in the mine, providing I worked in the engineering section, would be counted as part of my five-year apprenticeship.

Fortunately, my mother had a friend who was able to use his influence with the chief engineer of Bedlinog colliery and I was offered a position in the underground engineering section that involved, among other things, servicing the various pieces of machinery that were used to cut the coal.

From an early age I remember my father saying that no son of his would ever go down a mine. Most fathers who were miners did not want their sons to follow in their footsteps, if it was at all possible. Winning a scholarship was always important to any family, because it meant one could go on to college or university and then embark on a career other than mining. However, my father had no say in the matter and I duly found myself in the mine.

After a period of training on the surface at the colliery I eventually moved underground. Because the servicing of the coal-cutting machines could only be done when they were not in action, I was permanently allocated to the night shift. Work started at 10pm and ended at 6am the next morning.

I actually loved working in the mine. For one thing, there was a strong contingent of Christians there and it was wonderful to meet with them on the way to work, or coming back after the shift, and share together in the things of the faith. I formed some lifelong friendships with men like Robert Owen, Eddie Evans and Dave Evans, all of whom went on – like myself – to become preachers of the gospel.

It was in the mine that I heard God's voice calling me to the Christian ministry. I know that this question of being 'called to the ministry' is viewed with some suspicion by many modern-day Christians. They claim that the idea that God calls men and women to be preachers of His good news is nothing more than pious pretence or self-deception. If a man or woman has an ability to speak in public, they say, and they can clearly communicate the truths of the gospel, then they have a responsibility to do so without the necessity of a dramatic 'call'. Being called, according to this viewpoint, is just doing the work that lies nearest at hand.

There may be something in this argument, but Christian

history is replete with stories of people throughout the centuries who have heard God's call to leave their occupation and enter into full-time ministry in the Christian church. The divine summons has called them from the law courts, office desk, plough, mine and mill. Dr Martyn Lloyd Jones, one of the great preachers of the twentieth century, tells of a divine call which moved him from what could have proved a brilliant career in medicine to a pulpit in Aberavon, South Wales and eventually to Westminster Chapel, London.

A rich tapestry of several distinct, though interrelated, experiences preceded my call to full-time ministry, which culminated in a moment in the mine. It began when I attended a Saturday evening meeting in the little village of Crosskeys near Newport, Gwent. The speaker was James Salter, an Assemblies of God missionary from what was then the Belgian Congo. His theme that night was 'The Call of God.'

His message was based on the story of Mary and the Annunciation. He pointed out as he began that whenever God desires someone to do a special work for Him He does not leave them to infer it from circumstances alone, but breaks the news to them personally. He then declared: 'God did not allow Mary to infer her high motherhood from the changes that went on within her body, but broke the news to her beforehand.'

It was a very powerful, dynamic message. Even now, as I write, I can see him in my mind's eye, leaning over the pulpit and in a loud voice saying to the congregation, 'Before there was an Incarnation there was an Annunciation! Everyone has a work to do for God in this world, and although no one else will ever have to take on the mission that Mary undertook, of being the mother of Jesus, yet the principle is the same – if He wants you in missionary work or in the ministry then He will not suffer you to guess, to speculate, or conjecture. He will find a way of telling you so Himself.'

When he finished his message he invited all those who were willing to offer themselves to God in an act of surrender to go wherever He wanted to take them, to come to the front for prayer. As a number of people began to move forwards, the congregation started singing a chorus that was very popular at that time:

Lay your life on the altar for God;
He's calling for you today.
The fields of the harvest are white,
But labourers are scattered and few.
Lay your life on the altar for God;
He's calling for you today.

I had heard it sung many times before and each time I had always felt some apprehension rise in my heart. The issue of surrendering to God for service that would take me away from home greatly worried me. In the subterranean places of my heart lurked a very quiet, but very real fear that if I fully yielded to the Lordship of Christ He might send me somewhere I didn't want to go, and perhaps make me marry the most ugly girl in the world! I remembered the story of Jonah and how he rolled around in the whale's belly. Then there was Abraham. What if God asked *me* to take a knife to the things I loved most?

My biggest fear was that God would call me to become a missionary. Hacking my way through a jungle, swatting at mosquitoes, dodging snakes and wild animals was not my idea of Christian service! I remembered the Tarzan movies – the alligators, lions, boa constrictors, quick-sands. If I was to surrender my life to the service of God then it would be conditional – *no missionary service.*

Of course, what I didn't realise at the time was that when it comes to vocation, the will of God often lies along the line which brings us the most joy. How I wish I had been privileged at that time to have heard words like these preached by Idris Davies from Ammanford, Carmarthenshire, in a church I pastored in West Wales many years later:

> The voice that calls us to special ministry is a voice that usually locks in to our own gladness. The Spirit who searches our hearts and knows all things knows the things that bring us the greatest joy and He will move us along in that same direction. What brings you the greatest joy? I mean by that *true* joy. Is it making things out of wood, canvas or stone? Is it encouraging people? Or is it making something out of words?'

My greatest joy was putting words together and had I put more trust in the Holy Spirit I would have had no need to worry. He would call me to the thing that gave me greatest joy – speaking and writing for Him.

Despite all the negative thoughts that were running through my head that night, I found myself at the front with dozens of other young people, offering myself to God for full-time service. When I returned home that night I told my mother and father that I wanted to go up to the top of a nearby mountain to pray. As it was a beautiful summer's evening they didn't object. When I reached the top I sat there for some time, reflecting on what had happened and the message I had heard. I wondered to myself. Now that I had said to the Lord, 'My whole life is yours, what will you have me to do?', how would He show me His plan and purpose for my life? Would He call me to become a missionary?

By this time it was twilight, and I opened the pages of my Bible to see if God would speak to me through His Word. The pages fell open at the story of Abraham and Isaac in Genesis 22:1–14. I remember thinking to myself what utter abandonment to the will and purpose of God Abraham had demonstrated there on Mount Moriah. Didn't the New Testament say something about sacrifice? It was too dark to see the Bible at this point but my mind fastened on the words of Paul: 'I urge you, brothers, in view of God's mercy, to offer your bodies as living sacrifices' (Rom. 12:1).

A *living* sacrifice? What does it mean to offer that kind of sacrifice, I wondered. As I continued to think about that I began to gather together some stones and rushes and fashioned, as best as I could, an imitation altar and stretched myself full-length upon it. I stayed the whole night in that position and when dawn broke I knew that no matter what God called me to do, even if it was to be a missionary, I was ready. My life, I had decided, was to be a *living* sacrifice. Now I was fully and utterly committed to the Lordship of Christ in my life, no matter where He might lead.

The experience I had in the Crosskeys church, and on the mountain-top, was still reverberating within me a few days later as I made my way to the mine for my usual night shift. Somewhere around 2am everyone was entitled to a 30-minute break, and on this particular morning the break-time found me alone in a disused part of the mine. I took out my New Testament, which I always carried with me, and after a brief prayer began to read. I have no recollection of the reading but almost every other detail is ineffaceably imprinted on my memory.

I recall closing my New Testament and turning my thoughts towards the Lord in meditation and prayer. I also remember the strange, almost eerie silence that pervades the corridors of a coal mine in the dead of night. And I recall too the strange and peculiar sigh, known only to those who work underground, that the earth makes in the early hours as it seems to sink down into sleep.

Then I heard a voice – not audible, but thundering nevertheless in my soul. It was clear and strong: *'I want you in the ministry.'* It is impossible for me to convey in words the effect that moment had upon me. It is as real to me now as when I experienced it well over 50 years ago. I knew without a shadow of doubt that it would only be a matter of time before I would leave the coal pit for the pulpit.

Throughout the church's history it has always been understood that when a man or woman says they have been called to the Christian ministry the last word is not theirs. The church must confirm that call. Soon after the dramatic moment down in the mine, when I heard God calling me to the ministry, I sought an interview with my pastor, and when I told him what had happened he was overjoyed. 'I have felt for some time now that God would call you into full-time service,' he said, 'and I can't tell you how thrilled I am that at last it has come.'

Perhaps I should point out at this stage that in those days the term 'full-time service' was often used to identify those who left secular employment to take up full-time work in the ministry of the church. Today the term is rarely used – and rightly so. We have come to realise that really every Christian is in 'full-time ministry' and in that sense there is no such thing as a part-time Christian. Whenever he is asked about his work, a friend of mine makes the point in this way: 'My job is being a full-time Christian, but I work as a financial consultant to pay expenses.'

Uncle David pointed out during the interview that although I had given my testimony at many different meetings, it was time now to prepare myself to make and present a sermon. He also suggested that at some stage I would need to consider going to Bible college and prepare more formally for the work of the ministry. In the meantime, I should give myself to studying the art of preaching. 'I can give you two evenings a week for a period of six months, but you will need to set aside another two evenings for reading and homework assignments,' he said. I was eager to begin, and within a few days I was grappling with the basics of sermon construction.

I learned from my uncle that a well-constructed sermon has three parts: a commencement, a continuation and a conclusion. 'That's easy enough to understand,' I said, 'but how do you know what to say? How do you gather enough material to hold people's attention?'

'First,' my pastor said, 'you sit down with a blank sheet of paper before a text or passage which you feel drawn to, then prayerfully put down all the thoughts that come to you about it. Don't worry about the order of the thoughts – just get them down. Later you can give them structure and form. Whatever you do, don't consult a commentary until after you have exhausted your own thoughts. Commentaries are fine, but they can be terribly intimidating to a beginner. Get your own thoughts down first, then after that you can compare them with what experienced Bible commentators have said.'

After several weeks of study my pastor told me that he felt I was ready to attempt my first sermon. Nervously I agreed and a date was set for my debut a few weeks later. I prayed and agonised and spent long hours poring over the passage I had chosen to speak on, the story of the ten lepers in Luke chapter 17. Strangely, as the day for the preaching of my first sermon drew near, I lost a good deal of my fear. I think the many hours of prayer I had put in contributed to this sense of calm. My father's single piece of advice to me in the weeks I was preparing my sermon was simple, but one that I have never forgotten: 'Spend as much time preparing yourself as you do preparing the sermon.'

On the Wednesday evening that I was due to preach the little church started filling up with family members and friends. After some preliminaries such as a few hymns and choruses (we *always* began every meeting in our church with four or five choruses), my pastor introduced me by saying, 'It is my conviction, and also the belief of the leaders of this church, that God has called Selwyn to preach, and tonight we are privileged to hear his very first sermon.'

I clambered up into the pulpit, fully expecting to speak for 20 minutes, laid out my notes with the air of an expert and invited the congregation to open their Bibles at Luke 17. I began: 'The theme I have chosen for my first sermon is the well-known story of the ten lepers.' After reading the appropriate passage I plunged into my sermon with enthusiasm. I raised my voice at appropriate places, waved my arms as I had seen other preachers do, and delivered my message on the simple theme of how sad it was that so many of us receive the blessings of God but so few of us demonstrate an attitude of gratitude. After what seemed like an age I sat down bathed in perspiration. Then I looked at my watch.

I had taken just over seven minutes!

After the service, friends and family gathered round to congratulate me, but I felt deeply disappointed. I quickly made my way home and burst into tears. I felt I wanted never to preach again and begged the Lord to release me from my call. However, after a good night's sleep I arose the next day believing that a new chapter had opened in my life.

CHAPTER 7

'THE REVIVAL BOY'

In the months following my first attempt at a sermon, I had the opportunity to practise preaching in many different ways. I walked the hills alone and preached to the sheep, cows and horses. I preached to anything that moved on the mountainside and had life! Later, a Methodist superintendent minister invited me to join the Methodist Preachers' Plan and although I was not a Methodist I preached regularly in their churches. As a result, my sermons became more proficient and, I am glad to say, a little longer!

I particularly remember the occasion when I was present at one of the monthly meetings of the area's Assemblies of God churches in Dowlais. These were times of fellowship when usually one of the pastors would be scheduled to preach. It so happened that the speaker for this particular meeting did not turn up because of the bad weather and halfway through the service my pastor, who was leading the service, sent me a note about the predicament and asked if I would preach.

I gulped for a moment, as I had no notes with me, but some thoughts had been forming in my mind over the previous few days which were centred round the passage in Isaiah 6 where the prophet observed the angels around the throne of God saying, 'Holy, holy, holy is the Lord Almighty; the whole earth is full of his glory.' I had been particularly struck with the Lord's words, 'Whom shall I send? And who will go for us?'

I knew I had something to say on that subject, so I gave my pastor the nod. A little later the gathering was told that the appointed preacher had not turned up, so I would be taking his place. My pastor was careful to point out that I had been given only half-an-hour's notice so not too much should be expected of me. I got up into the pulpit and announced my text as Isaiah 6:8. Then, as I began in a somewhat rambling way, I felt what preachers describe as 'unction' – the supernatural ability given by the Holy Spirit that lifts one out of oneself.

Although I had only preached a dozen or so times before, never was I more conscious of the presence of the Holy Spirit. I had always known that the Spirit is with everyone who preaches the word (providing, of course, that their life is in harmony with the truths of Scripture), but that night He was there in special power. I spoke for 45 minutes without notes, something I had never done before, and after the service was over many of the pastors came to me and said, 'It is clear you are marked out by God to become a preacher. Our prayers are with you.'

Soon other churches began to invite me into their pulpits and within a short while I found my diary filled every Sunday for weeks and months ahead. The more I preached, the better at it I became, and it seemed for several months that my life was one sermon after another.

What did I preach about? Often it was on the theme of revival. On many occasions when I sat down to ponder what I should preach about, memories of my days sitting under the table in my grandmother's kitchen would come back to me and I would almost invariably find myself building a message around the theme that had so deeply impressed itself on me at that time. I read every book I could get my hands on that dealt with revival, especially those that recorded some of the events of the great outpouring of the Spirit on Wales in 1904–5.

I majored so much on the theme of revival in my preaching that some people used to refer to me as 'the Revival Boy'. One church secretary wrote to my pastor saying, 'We would like to invite the young man from your church to come and preach to us. We have forgotten his name, but he is the young man with the nice eyes and is always talking about revival. Ask him, please, to bring his accordion with him.' Whenever and wherever I would preach I would take my piano accordion with me and, before I began my sermon, would often teach the congregation a new chorus or sing a solo for them.

As time went on, I got more invitations from Methodist churches, and three Sundays a month were taken up with ministering in them. My travels to their churches took me far and wide to preach, from South Wales to West Wales and sometimes into Mid Wales. One of my favourite Methodist churches in which I often preached (and which has sadly since been demolished), was on the coast of West Wales. What used to intrigue me about it was that its pulpit was fashioned in the form of a whale's mouth. As the church was in a fishing community, I suppose it was somewhat appropriate. The first time I stood in that pulpit I jokingly told the congregation that as I came up its steps I was seized with a compulsion to sing. 'After all,' I said, 'everyone sings in W(h)ales!' No one laughed or seemed to see the point. I am afraid the joke died on the spot.

Honesty compels me to confess that there came a period in my early preaching career when I realised that I was becoming more interested in the mechanics of preaching than in the truths I was proclaiming. I began to love preaching for the sheer craftsmanship of it, rather than as a medium to portray the living Christ. I was to learn later that this is one of the occupational hazards of the Christian ministry. Many a preacher has told me that there were times in their ministry when he or she was more taken up with how a sermon was put together than seeing it as a means of transmitting the everlasting Christ.

I have held a high view of preaching ever since the moment I was introduced to the structure of a sermon by my pastor. It would be foolish to suppose that, because the work of preaching is divine in its origin, there is no technique to study or craft to learn. There have been many misguided zealots over the years who have thought of preaching as 'just opening your mouth and letting the Lord fill it'. Often, I am glad to say, the Spirit has spurned their superstitious sloth. The task of preaching demands that we be master craftsmen. I gave myself with all my heart to a study of its craft, but that did not stop me falling into the trap of becoming more interested in the *way* I said things than *what* I was saying.

Most of my preaching in those early days was evangelistic and I remember feeling a deep concern for those listeners who might be unconverted. At every service I would give an invitation for people to come to Christ and usually there would be several who would respond. Gradually, however, I seemed to lose that sense of deep concern for the souls of those to whom I was preaching and became more taken up with my style and structure of the sermon.

It was a dark moment in my life when I realised what was happening – that I was losing my passion for souls. I told no one about it but I wondered how it could be overcome. The problem was resolved for me in a rather dramatic way one evening while at work in the mine.

During the middle of a night shift I found myself working with a young man in a quiet and derelict part of the mine. Our job was to rescue some air pipes before that section was closed off because of the danger of the roof caving in. We worked quickly because of this threat, but talked about a number of things as we did so. He seemed a fine young man, somewhat worldly and given to swearing, but he had a good and kind nature.

As we worked together in the early hours of that morning I felt strongly impressed to share with him about his need to know Christ. But I put off doing so, telling myself that I could do it later on. I was wrong. About 15 minutes later a large stone (known to miners as a bell stone because of the way it was shaped) suddenly dropped out of the roof and crushed him to death.

It was impossible for me to move the stone and I raced through the mine to get help. It took six or seven men to lift the stone from the young man's body, and the sight that met us was horrifying and gruesome. It shocked me so deeply that I was unable to return to work for two whole weeks. I asked God to forgive me for failing to respond to His prompting in that moment when a soul stood between life and death. Out of it, however, came a determination never to disobey again a spiritual prompting of that nature. The whole matter added sharpness to my spiritual life in regard to witnessing for Him, both with individuals and with congregations – something that has remained to this day.

I think I need to make it clear what I mean by 'spiritual prompting'. I am not one who believes that we must witness to every person we meet, but I do believe that there are times when a person we are speaking with is not far from the kingdom and may be just waiting for an invitation to enter. At such times I believe the Spirit will prompt us to say the right thing, but that prompting will depend on our closeness to Christ and how prayerful and sensitive we are to the Holy Spirit at work within us.

Often when I am preaching to Christians, I will feel a prompting to depart from what I have prepared to say for a moment and stress the importance of making a first commitment to Christ. I have come to regard those promptings as extremely important, and there have been numerous occasions when people have come up to me and said, 'I think you may have been talking to me in your sermon today. I have never before given my life to Jesus Christ but I did do what you suggested. Am I now a Christian?'

Although I have never lost my interest in the craftmanship of preaching – not for one single moment – I am much more alert to the fact that I may be talking to someone who might be hearing the message of salvation for the last time. What happened deep in the coal mine, when a young man lost his life, brought the weighty matters of eternity sharply into focus for me – a sharpness I have better understood and cultivated from that moment to this.

A significant happening in relation to my entering the ministry was when my pastor invited a Scotsman by the name of John Wallace, who was the Principal of a Bible college in Bristol, to lead an anniversary weekend in our local church over Easter 1948.

I was deeply impressed with his abilities as a preacher and Bible teacher over that weekend, and I spent a good deal of time picking his brains, so to speak, on such subjects as homiletics (the science of preaching) and hermeneutics (interpretation of the Bible). Uncle David had already spoken to him about the possibility of my attending Bible college one day, so he told me about the courses and training offered at his own establishment, which was known as the BBC – Bristol Bible College.

'Our college has not been going long, but we could provide you with a couple of years' intensive training that would adequately prepare you for the Christian ministry,' he told me. 'We have a wonderful staff of tutors, godly men who have had great experience in the ministry and who have good minds.'

I already knew that the Bristol Bible College was gaining a high reputation in the Welsh valleys, and that John Wallace was regarded as one of the best Bible teachers of the day. He had preached in many of the Welsh churches and, although I had never heard him before, I was well aware of his standing. I warmed to him over that weekend and felt drawn to pursuing the idea of attending his college, subject to my parents' and pastor's approval, of course.

Soon afterwards I sat down with my parents and Uncle David to discuss the possibility of my entering Bristol Bible College the following year. After much prayer and discussion it was agreed that I would make an immediate application. Within a few weeks a letter came back from John Wallace's office saying that my application had been accepted and they would look forward to receiving me as a student in the following September.

There was just one difficulty – the college fees. My parents did not have much money, but they committed themselves to saving and sacrificing in every way they could, so that when the time came I would be able to meet the financial obligations. David Cecil Jones, the adopted 'brother' who lived with us also helped with the fees.

A few weeks after I made the decision to leave secular employment and head for Bible college, my pastor said to me, 'As it is likely you have just over a year before you attend college and after that I will not have very much input into your life, there is something I would like to share with you in the remaining months we have together. I want to teach you to steal, to drink, to lie and to swear.' Seeing my astonishment, he quickly went on: 'I want to teach you how to steal time out of every day to read something from a certain book in the Bible; to drink from its clear refreshing waters; to lie on your bed at night and meditate on its great themes; and to swear that by the grace of God you will put into practice its wonderful teaching. The book I refer to is Proverbs.'

His novel approach certainly grabbed my attention! He told me that he was introducing me to Proverbs because he believed that the principles contained in it, when put into practice, would contribute to my spiritual growth more than I could ever imagine. He drew my attention to Solomon's opening words in the book, which in the King James Version (the main version we used in those days) are:

> The proverbs of Solomon ...To know wisdom and instruction; to perceive the words of understanding.

Had the Living Bible paraphrase been available at that time we would have read this:

> He [Solomon] wrote them to teach his people how to live – how to act in every circumstance.

'What Proverbs is all about is acquiring wisdom for living,' my pastor explained. 'And what I long for you is that you will become a wise man and share that wisdom with many others. Multitudes know how to make a living, but not how to live. They know everything about life except how to live it. The more you understand the book of Proverbs and the more you put its truths and principles into practice, the more effective you will be in living. I guarantee it.'

I spent the next few months studying Proverbs, answering the questions my pastor asked me concerning the book and committing to memory many of its powerful principles. My study of Proverbs, perhaps more than any other book in the

Bible, has supplied me with the wisdom for living, and this has greatly empowered and undergirded my ministry.

Once I had devoured Proverbs, Uncle David said, 'Would you be interested in learning one more thing before you leave for Bible college?' When I said I would, he said, 'Then let me show you how to get the best out of the Bible. You may think you get the best out of the Bible by reading it, studying it and memorising it. While you can get much out of Scripture by those methods, the way to get the best out of the Bible is to *meditate* on it.'

I learned from my uncle that meditation is the art of taking an appropriate phrase, a verse or passage from the Bible and letting one's mind dwell on it until the spiritual energy contained in it deposits itself in the soul. It involves taking a phrase or verse from the Word of God, the Bible, and thinking about it until it begins to affect every area of your life. In a sense, meditation is really the digestive system of the soul.

I will ever be thankful to my uncle for introducing me to the concept of Bible meditation. I am convinced that my life and ministry would not have been half as effective were it not for the fact that I learned not just to study the Bible, but also to meditate on it.

CHAPTER 8

PREPARING FOR BIBLE COLLEGE

During the summer of 1948 my two years' National Service in the mines ended and, as I had just over a year before going to Bible college, I began to look for another job. Eventually, after spending several weeks going for interviews for various positions in engineering, I eventually found employment in the engineering shop of Aberdare Cables – about 15 miles from my home.

I continued to preach almost every Sunday and spent the week-nights in fellowship with young people from the Dowlais churches. I became friends with a young man called Derek Thomas, who was actually an apprentice in the very engineering shop where I had worked in Dowlais. During the summer we were drawn to the idea of attending two of the Christian holiday camps that had sprung up since the war had ended, one in Scarborough on the Yorkshire coast and the other in Bonsall, near Matlock in Derbyshire. We decided to spend a week at each. With us came Eddie Evans, another friend I had made when working in the mine.

The Scarborough camp was owned and run by George Oldershaw – a kind-hearted and avuncular figure who ran what we would call nowadays 'a tight ship' but still managed to create a very relaxed atmosphere. It was a wonderful week of sunshine and Christian fellowship. After breakfast there were optional Bible studies, prayer meetings and discussion groups. In the afternoon participants were free to go into Scarborough, or to do whatever they chose.

At the end of the week, having made so many new friends, Derek, Eddie and I were reluctant to leave for the Bonsall camp. And when we arrived there we found the atmosphere quite different. The man who had started it was a good but rather rigid type of individual who seemed to be more interested in campers keeping the rules he had made rather than trying to help them enjoy their stay.

We arrived in time for dinner, which was followed by the evening fellowship. We were feeling a bit playful, so we decided to walk into the meeting looking like clergymen. We turned our collars and waistcoats back to front, and with our Bibles under our arms we walked down the whole length of the marquee and sat on the first row. Everyone laughed except the organiser. After the meeting ended he came up to us and told us off in no uncertain terms.

Then we met two young girls who had been in the meeting, but it was obvious from their unease that they were not Christians. They told us they were from the village of Bonsall and someone had invited them to the evening fellowship. We talked to them about spiritual things and offered to escort them back to the village. We tried in vain to encourage them to accept Christ that night, and in our evangelistic eagerness we forgot that we had to be back in the camp by 10pm. It was actually around 11pm when we returned to find the gate leading to the field was locked. So we had to climb over a fence to get to our tent.

We made our way as quietly as we could towards our tent, only to find one of the supervisors standing at its entrance. He shone his torch on us and said to us, 'We thought after what you did in the meeting that you would not be up to any good. You will be expected to give an account of yourself first thing in the morning before breakfast in the organiser's tent.'

We duly presented ourselves to the 'camp commandant' early next morning. After listening to our explanation about why we were late getting back to the camp, he said he thought we were irresponsible young people and not the kind he wanted in his camp. 'You are no longer welcome here,' he said, 'and I want you to leave right away.'

As we still had a week left of our holidays, we wondered what we should do. Eddie Evans remembered that some friends of his in Walsall, near Birmingham, had often invited him to go there. A quick phone call confirmed the fact they would be delighted to accommodate us for the rest of the week.

It always amused us years later, when all three of us had become Assemblies of God ministers, to attend the same Annual General Conference as that camp organiser, who was also an AOG pastor. We heard that he often told people his firm action taken against us at his camp had helped to advance our spiritual life!

Some time after returning home I found myself attracted to a young lady from the Dowlais church. After several months of courtship we got engaged. But I made it clear to my fiancée that marriage would have to wait until I had finished Bible college.

Preparing to leave home and go to Bible college took a lot of my time, and before leaving there were lots of farewell parties to attend. The night before I went to Bristol was a rather sleepless one. I could not help wondering how my life would change and how it would all turn out. I thought about how influential my father and mother had been in my life, and the more I thought about them, the more compelled I felt to slip out of bed and write them a letter of appreciation, which I did. I left it under my pillow for them to discover after I had gone.

The Ten Commandments formed the background of my

parents' moral and spiritual conscience. The way they interpreted those moral laws, however, took them at times to the edge of the puritanical. For example, I was forbidden to cut my nails on a Sunday or read a Sunday newspaper. I could not even listen to anything on the radio that day, except the news. On one occasion, when Christmas Day fell on a Sunday, I was not allowed to go outside and kick the football I had been given as a present until the following day.

My father had his own list of what he called 'sins' among which would be dancing, smoking, drinking, and going to a cinema. My mother, however, liked the cinema, and when we lived in Birmingham she would sneak off with me to a late afternoon matinee and say, 'Don't tell your father.'

My father, as I said earlier, worked in the mines as a wireman for most of his life, except during his time in Birmingham when he worked the Metropolitan Vickers factory wiring trains. He often preached somewhere or other on a Sunday, and he had a great sense of humour. I used to love to go for walks with him, and I remember him saying to me on one of my mother's birthdays, 'Everyone else adds a year when they have their birthday; your mother takes a year off.'

But I cannot ever remember my father hugging me or telling me that he loved me. I have heard from others how, in later life, he would brag to them about some of my accomplishments and say how proud he was of me, even though not once did he ever tell me that to my face. My mother told me how much she loved me, often, but I longed to hear it from my father too. I remember when he died, standing at his grave and thinking, as the coffin was lowered into the earth, 'Well, Dad, you'll never be able to tell me now.'

Despite this, however, his stand for living life according to the Scriptures, although at times interpreted legalistically, had a profound effect on me. In my early teens I rebelled against almost everything my parents believed, but it was not an easy rebellion. Whenever I was engaged in wrongdoing, I would often hear my father's voice in my conscience, clear and insistent, speaking of the things I had been taught at home.

Were my parents deeply in love? I'm sure they were, although I cannot ever remember them showing outward signs of affection, like a hug or a kiss, or holding hands. It was part of the culture of their day to hide such signs and that may well be the reason I never once heard them say to one another 'I love you' or see their eyes light up with a loving glance. On the other hand, although they argued and fell out and sometimes wouldn't speak to one another for a day or two, I never saw any physical abuse. My mother could get angry at the drop of a hat but once she had her say and 'got it off her chest' as we say, there was no sweeter person to be found anywhere!

Both my parents were hard working and saw laziness as something to be deplored. I think my great capacity for work is down to their influence, too. My father used to say, quoting something he had read, 'Laziness grows on you; it begins in cobwebs and ends in chains.' Never once did I hear a swear word cross my mother's or father's lips. They were not perfect, as I have explained, but they had strong convictions about the Bible and the way life should be lived. I am a grateful beneficiary of their deep spiritual and moral convictions.

And so the day came, in September 1948, when I arrived on the doorstep of Bristol Bible College. As I rang the bell I half hoped no one would answer. I felt a sense of panic that I would find myself out of my depth. I had received a reasonable education, but would I be up to delving into theology and plumbing the profound depths of Scripture?

I wondered what the other students would be like. Where

would they come from? How many would be from a working class background like myself? Would they be easy to relate to? Later that evening, when I got to the lounge for the welcome meeting, the Matron, Mrs Wright, asked us all to identify ourselves one by one. One of the students, André Lemarquand, had come from Switzerland. He was a brilliant artist who had been headhunted by Walt Disney, but God had first claim on his life, he told us. Another overseas student was Miss Emily Dudgeon, from Kenya, whose parents, she told us, were plantation owners.

Most of the other students were from the UK, and one by one we gave a little potted history of ourselves. The orientation session ended with the announcement that lectures would begin the following day. I still remember the thrill that went through me at that moment as I contemplated delving into the Scriptures every day in the company of students who had as much of an appetite as I had for knowing more of God's Word.

It was a tremendous joy day by day to explore the Scriptures in a more in-depth way than I had experienced before, free from the restraints of daily work routines. As the studies intensified, I savoured every single moment, and was lost in wonder, love and praise. I realised within a few weeks that my pastor had prepared me well for the training I was receiving. My tutors were now fleshing out the things he had taught me in outline form in the most exciting ways. There were nights, especially during the initial weeks, when I could hardly sleep for the sheer excitement of what I was learning. My favourite subjects were pneumatology, hermeneutics and homiletics. Those were subjects taken by John Wallace himself. But if someone had asked me what was my favourite of all the subjects I was learning at Bible college I would, without any hesitation, have answered, 'Homiletics.'

Every Saturday morning students would participate in what was called 'The Sieve'. This involved one of us preaching and the others analysing the form, content and delivery – putting it through the 'sieve', so to speak. I looked forward to those occasions more than anything. Sometimes we would be harsh in our criticism of each other's preaching – mercilessly so, on reflection – and it was not unusual to find a student who had been 'sieved' walking alone in the garden in tears. But I can say that I certainly benefited from the critiques of my sermons. I learned three things that helped me to become a better preacher. Firstly, my Welsh fervour would lead me to say things at such speed that my words would tumble over one another. Secondly, I had a habit of pointing my finger at people as I spoke. This came across as threatening, I was told. Thirdly, I looked rather too serious when I preached ('grim' was a word one person used). Although the content of my sermon might be serious, someone said, it was not necessary to look as if my face would make a good frontispiece for the prophecy of Jeremiah!

One of the students, Charlie Rogers, a fellow Welshman who came from Abertyswyg, a nearby village to mine, preached a sermon at one of the 'sieves' that in terms of shape and form I have to confess was not impressive. Yet it proved to be so memorable that I can remember it vividly to this very day.

He took his text from the story in Mark 14 of the woman who poured perfume on Jesus' head. 'Leave her alone,' said Jesus. 'Why are you bothering her? She has done a beautiful thing to me' (v.6). I became conscious as I listened to Charlie that through his rambling presentation I was hearing the voice of God. 'What are we doing here in Bible college?' he said. 'Are we simply seeking to develop skills in teaching, preaching or communication? That's good, but surely that's not our main purpose. Are we looking for principles, for proof texts so that we can go out and preach about them? Or is it to know the Saviour more intimately, to see His face, to experience Him more deeply?'

When the 'sieve' was over I went out into the garden, where I could be alone, and had what might be called a numinous experience. God seemed to come so close to me that I felt afraid, and yet not afraid. I must have spent an hour in solitude asking myself the question over and over again: 'Am I more interested in learning the highways and byways of Scripture than in knowing the Christ who is concealed in its pages? Is it possible that I am more taken up with the words of the Bible than with the Word who is bigger than men's words?' I came to the conclusion that I was. But that sermon, and my time in the Bible college garden, brought about a paradigm shift in my thinking.

In the days that followed, the Spirit began to do a deep work in my soul. I had been in danger of putting doctrine before devotion. I loved the time we spent in the classroom studying all the different subjects, but I knew I must not lose sight of the One who was behind the book.

The more I pondered the story of Mary of Bethany, the more I began to realise why Jesus said that wherever His gospel would be preached her loving deed done that day would always be told, because she had done 'a beautiful thing' for Him. The story of the outpoured perfume would be told everywhere, because the Spirit wants to draw our attention to the fact that the most important thing in our lives is not our grasp of doctrine (although that is important) but how passionate we are in our love for the Lord Jesus Christ.

From that time, my whole approach to the Bible changed. I began to look at the Bible in a new way. I believe I have come to a more intimate place with the Saviour as a result of my fellow student's sermon. Often when I am interviewed, people ask me,

'How did you come to place such an emphasis upon reading the Bible devotionally?' I respond by taking them back to the work of the Spirit in my heart so long ago. And when an interviewer asks, 'What are some of the most important lessons the Lord has taught you in your 60 years as a Christian?', I always include in my list the realisation that Jesus is not simply seeking a personal relationship with me, but an intimate one.

CHAPTER 9

MY DAYS AT BIBLE COLLEGE

One of the most wonderful and memorable experiences I had within the first few months of my Bible College training was being introduced to a man who at that time was one of Britain's finest preachers, Dr W.E. Sangster. It came about after John Wallace happened to mention at lunch that a famous preacher was in town and it would be well worthwhile for students to go and hear him.

William Edwin Sangster was the pastor of the famous Westminster Central Hall, across the road from the Houses of Parliament. He was in Bristol to speak on the subject of preaching and, as that was one of my favourite subjects, I went along to hear him. As I listened, I marvelled at the craftsmanship of his sermons. I had listened to many great Welsh preachers since I had become a Christian, but I had never heard anyone with such homiletical skill as Dr Sangster's.

John Wallace had taught us that whenever we listened to a preacher it would be useful for us novices to try to anticipate him. 'Whenever a preacher announces his text, think to yourself, How will he handle it? How would I handle it? Then anticipate where he will go with his theme. What will be his divisions? In this way you will learn a lot more about the art of preaching and communication.'

As soon as Dr Sangster announced his text, 'It is a good thing to give thanks unto the Lord' (Psa. 92:1), I tried to follow my

Principal's advice. But I was so taken up with what he was saying and the way he was saying it that I quickly gave up all thoughts of analysing the sermon and became transfixed by the sheer dignity of the man in the pulpit, his unforgettable delivery, his dramatic gestures and, above all, the substance of his message.

When he had finished I stood in line to talk to him. There were dozens of people ahead of me and when I was eventually able to speak with him my opening question was, 'How can you help me preach like that?' He told me that he had just published a book entitled *The Craft of Sermon Construction* and when he found out that I was a Bible college student he offered to send me a copy free of charge. There began that day a relationship that developed by letter and occasional visits to Westminster Central Hall, and had a tremendous impact upon me, both personally and in relation to my preaching.

Whenever I was on holiday or had a free weekend I would make my way to London from whatever part of the country I was in, to listen to Dr Sangster. On Sunday nights one had to be at the church half-an-hour before the service began to get a seat in the 3000-seat sanctuary. I learned so much from those visits. Though there were several people such as my pastor and my Principal, John Wallace, who taught me much about preaching, I regard W.E. Sangster as my mentor-in-chief on the subject. I am grateful that I had the privilege of sitting at the feet of a man who has been described as one of the greatest preachers Methodism has ever produced.

Each Sunday we students were required to attend the church that John Wallace pastored, called the Mount of Olives Assemblies of God church on Blackboy Hill, which was no more than a quarter of a mile from the college. On some weekends, however, a small group of students would be invited to take a service in some of the churches in Bristol or the surrounding area.

There were numerous talents among the students chosen to do this; mine was playing the accordion or preaching.

At the end of each term, Christmas, Easter and the summer holidays, we returned home. Although it was wonderful seeing my fiancée, family and friends again, I just couldn't wait to get back to college. There was something magnetic about the place, and nothing gave me greater pleasure than when the train pulled in at Temple Meads station and I got on the bus to the top of Blackboy Hill and walked the few yards to the college. Every time I did it I had the feeling of coming home.

Bristol Bible College, though its teaching and training programme was excellent, did not have an academic diploma or degree programme. In those days it was considered 'worldly ambition' to strive toward academic degrees. Over the years things have changed considerably and today there are few Bible colleges that do not have a certificate, diploma or degree programme.

Although I was well satisfied with the standard of tuition, I was a bit disappointed that nothing was taught on the subject of revival or Christian counselling. When I asked the Principal about this he said that he could not find anyone qualified to teach on these subjects. When a student asked one of the tutors, who was a pastor, about the place that counselling should have in the local church, the reply was, 'If people pray, read their Bibles every day and faithfully attend all the services of the church then they won't need counselling.' When I tried to take the point further and asked how he dealt with someone who came to him with a spiritual problem, he said, 'I find an appropriate text, read it to the person concerned and tell him or her to obey what the Scripture says.' This low view of counselling, and the lack of training in that area would affect me later in a way I could never have contemplated.

With these caveats, I regard my time at Bristol Bible College as richly rewarding and have no doubt that it was the right place for me to be. The days there were not all study; there was fun, too. Although I was growing in my knowledge of the Scriptures and was beginning to settle down and have a more serious approach to life, I had not lost my mischievousness and always had an eye for some harmless prank. One Saturday, the students were invited to lead an evening youth rally at a church about 40 miles from Bristol. A coach had been hired and John Wallace's son and his fiancée asked if they could travel back with us. I said to the other students, 'Most of us one day might have to conduct a wedding, so why don't we get some practice in right away? Here are a couple who are soon to be married, so I suggest we take them through a rehearsal right now.'

Everyone thought it was a good idea so, wedging myself at the front of the coach with John Wallace's son and a 'best man', I asked one of the students to walk the girl down the aisle of the moving vehicle so that I could conduct a 'wedding' as best as I knew how. It was all good fun, but when John Wallace heard he was not pleased. Just before lectures started the following Monday morning he summoned me into his office and severely reprimanded me. He said, 'When my son told me what had happened I could not believe that it was you who engineered it. You made light of a very serious issue and I hope that you will never do anything like that again.' I apologised right away. The Principal responded very generously by saying that what had happened would not affect his regard for me personally and that I need not have any fear of my misdemeanour hindering my progress in the college. But for several days I felt very chastened. It was not easy coming to terms with the fact that I had earned the Principal's displeasure.

I don't think I have ever known time to go so quickly as it did when I was in Bible college. They were truly halcyon days. The Bible became more and more precious to me day by day. I would approach every lecture with eager expectation. I drank in every word, made copious notes and followed up by reading everything that was available in the college library on the subject for the day. I have always had a thirst for knowledge, something that has remained with me to this day. I would sometimes study late into the night but eventually I began to feel physically run down. Ideally, I would have liked to have spent three years at the college but my parents could not afford a full three-year course. I persuaded the Principal to let me have the material I would miss, but giving myself to the study of that material took its toll on me physically. For several weeks I suffered from a series of boils, a sure sign that I was below par physically.

There were many defining moments in my time at college: the way God spoke to me through Charlie Rogers' sermon, talks with John Wallace. But there was one that came several months before the course finished which has affected my life in a most wonderful way.

It happened after a morning lecture by Spencer May, a local pastor and a fine Bible teacher. One of the subjects he taught was New Testament Greek, which was optional. He had been a missionary in India, but had returned to this country because of ill health and had become the minister of a church in one of Bristol's suburbs. It was a sunny day and several of us were sitting in the garden after lunch, when Spencer May joined us. As we talked together, one of the students asked him, 'How do you spend time in the Bible yourself? What is your approach to Bible study for your own soul?'

He told us that that he had three approaches to Scripture. One was to read through the whole of the Bible in a year. He had done this for most of his life. Another was to look up all the Scriptures on a particular theme. An example he gave was the bloodline in the Bible – examining the Scriptures that spoke of the place of blood in the Old Testament sacrifices and its corresponding emphasis in the New Testament. Yet another way was to 'live in the Bible' – to slip into the skin of a Bible character and imagine being that person. I had come across this before and had practised it to a small degree, but when we asked him to share more about it he said, 'I am afraid that I have probably said too much already because it is not something that my colleagues would necessarily agree with, and out of respect for them I don't think I ought to say more.'

His remarks made me even more curious, and later I asked him if I could see him privately away from the college to discuss the issue he had raised about living in the Bible. He invited me to his home where he expanded at length on the subject. I can't remember word for word the conversation we had, but in essence this is what he said:

> This is something I practise but rarely mention in my preaching or teaching because some often regard it as suspect. Through the reverent use of the imagination there can be rich spiritual rewards by slipping into the skin of a Bible character and looking at life through that person's eyes. In that way the Bible comes alive in a way that is utterly fascinating. I have never taught this because some people are afraid of the use of the imagination and are sceptical about it, but it is something I often practise. There are those who speak disparagingly of the imagination and classify it in their minds with whimsy and speculation. But every great feat has to be imagined first before it can be turned into reality.

I was so intrigued with this idea that I began to read everything I could lay my hands on that talked about the imagination. I saw that many great achievements belong first to the imagination, and that it is one of God's greatest gifts to us. So why shouldn't we utilise it in the interests of our soul? It can help us not only run into the future but also to run back into the past. I began to practise it. I learned how to run back through time and jostle with Peter, James and John when they walked with the Saviour; I imagined myself in Zacchaeus's shoes as he hid in the sycamore tree and found Jesus looking up at him.

I have been amazed how easily Bible characters come to life through the reverent use of the imagination. Over the years, I have studied the subject of the imagination at great length. Dr W.E. Sangster, someone who also practised 'living in the Bible', said, 'The proper use of the imagination is not to conjure up things and foolishly believe them to be true, but to take true things and make them vivid in the life of today.'[1] He also points out that you can read the Bible with or without imagination. You can come to it in a detached fashion, and always be external, or you can slip between its covers and make it autobiographical. The latter practice has done a lot for me spiritually. I have rarely talked about it in my ministry because many view it as controversial, but I would not wish to omit this from my autobiography without at least saying how meaningful it has been for me.

Towards the end of the course I began to become preoccupied about my future. Talking with other students, I found that they had similar concerns. It was interesting that the prayer room at the top of the building was more and more in demand as our days at the college drew to a close. Anyone who wanted to use the prayer room needed to pre-book the required amount of time. Usually there was no limit to the number of hours one could spend there – it was a matter of first come first served. A few months before the course ended, however, there were so many wanting to use the room that everyone was limited to just one hour.

The prayer room was about twelve feet square and had been a bedroom at some stage. There was still a single bed at one end because students had asked for it to stay there, as it was more comfortable when praying to kneel at the side and place one's elbows on it. In the corner of the room was a full-length mirror, left over from the days when it was a bedroom. I had hardly noticed the mirror before, but as I became more and more anxious about my future in the Christian ministry, I began to use that mirror, not out of vanity, but as a device for questioning what was going on in my heart.

On one occasion I remember looking into the mirror and saying out loud, 'Selwyn Hughes, you have come a long way since the moment you were converted. Now that you have a basic grasp of Scripture and some understanding of what will be required of you in the ministry, what is going to happen in the months ahead? What will you do when the course ends? At the moment nothing is definite. Will you go back to work and see how the Lord leads from there? Or will God leave it until the eleventh hour before He opens the door for you into the ministry?'

One day I shared my concerns with John Wallace. His response was: 'Whatever God wants you to do for Him He will guide you into. You may not know where He wants you to go and what He wants you to do until you are just weeks away, or even days away, from the end of the course. Don't worry about it. Just trust.' I found his words reassuring, not just for their content, but also for the confident manner in which he spoke them. So often the power of what we say is not in the words but in the way they are said. I heard something of the comfort and encouragement of God in his remarks that day. Reassured that whatever God had for me would work out in His way and in His time, I concentrated on the remaining part of the course.

About two months before the end, a group of us were sitting around talking about what we might do at the end of the term. Someone (I cannot remember who) came up with the idea of trekking from Bristol to Land's End and back, following as much as possible the route that John Wesley travelled when he visited the Methodist churches in the West Country a century or so before. Our intention was to share the gospel with whoever we met on the way, preaching in different churches, open-air meetings and distributing evangelistic literature. Five of us warmed to this idea and within a few days, after talking to the Principal, Charles Rogers, André Lemarquand, Maurice Paine, Herbert Agar and I started to make plans.

We prepared our itinerary, contacted the churches and soon everything was set. We bought a cart to carry our equipment – tents, cooking utensils, a couple of musical instruments and evangelistic literature. Herbert, a Yorkshireman who was useful with his hands, made a curved aluminium top to the cart to keep out the rain. André painted the words 'Bristol Bible College' on it, together with a beautifully drawn image of a cross. Someone gave us a bicycle so that we could get around quickly in an emergency. We agreed to start the trek the day after the course finished. When all the arrangements had been made we settled down again for the last days of our studies and our final examinations, and eagerly awaited the day when we would set off on our travels.

Notes

1. W. E. Sangster, *The Secret of Radiant Life* (London, Hodder and Stoughton, 1957).

CHAPTER 10

TREKKING – AND MY FIRST CHURCH

few weeks before my time at Bristol Bible College ended, John Wallace called me into his office one morning and said, 'I have received a letter from a thriving church in the north of England, which I happen to know very well, and they have asked me if I can recommend someone to them as their pastor. I am prepared to recommend you for that position, but before I do I have had another letter from a small new church in Helston, Cornwall, a place you will be passing through on your trek. They have also asked me to recommend to them one of our students to become their pastor. I am prepared to recommend you to either; you make the choice.'

I thought about it quickly and decided that there was no comparison between a thriving church and one that is small and new, so I said, 'I'd like you to recommend me to the one up north.' The Principal appeared to be disappointed at my conclusion. I could not help but see the sadness in his eyes. This was confirmed when, leaning heavily on the mantelpiece, he said, 'I am surprised that you would go for the church up north. The way I have read your temperament I thought you would have preferred the challenge of starting small and working your way to bigger things. You will need to be on probation for a year before you can be accepted as an Assemblies of God minister, and a year in this small church, learning the ropes, so to speak, would be an ideal situation for you. You will probably want to move on after a year. It is my belief that a church ready-made and well established will never satisfy your adventuring spirit.'

I said, 'Let me go to the prayer room and pray about this.' 'Take your time,' he said. 'I will have to get back to both these places in a few days, but in the meantime I will also pray that God will lead you to do the right thing.' While I was in the prayer room, John Wallace's words reverberated in my heart: 'A church that is ready-made will never satisfy your adventuring spirit.' Was this a word of wisdom from a man of God? Could this experienced pastor see something I was failing to see? The more I prayed and pondered the situation the more his words burned into my soul. The following day I went to John Wallace and told him that I now felt it right to make the little church in Helston the focus of my first year in the Christian ministry. That appeared to please him a great deal.

The final examinations involved a lot of reviewing and other work. The last thing every student had to do at the end of term was to preach a trial sermon before the full team of tutors and an invited audience – an event that lasted several days. Unknown to me, there was an Assemblies of God evangelist, Howell Harris, in the audience. He was a man greatly used by the Lord to open up new AOG churches. As he happened to be in Bristol, and heard that the BBC students were preaching their trial sermons, he came along for one morning only – the morning it was my turn to preach. Little did I know then what an important part he was to play in my life.

The college course came to an end on a Friday in July 1950 and the next morning the five of us participating in the trek were awake early, packing the cart with all the things we needed, such as cooking and eating utensils, evangelistic literature, clothing, tinned foodstuffs, clothes, a bicycle and, of course, my piano accordion.

At 9am the staff and some of the tutors joined us at the college gates to bid us a prayerful farewell and soon we were threading our way through the Bristol traffic en route for our first stop – Weston-super-Mare. We were scheduled to take the Sunday services in a church in the town and we reckoned on the first leg of our journey taking between ten and twelve hours. Our strategy for pulling the cart had been worked out and practised beforehand. Two of us would pull it from the front for about half-an-hour and then change over. When we came to a hill two would push from behind as well while one would direct overtaking traffic.

Everything seemed to go well until we were about halfway there. Then the weight of the contents of the cart caused one of the wheels to begin to buckle. It was impossible to continue with the cart in this condition so we pulled in to a lay by and held an emergency conference. Should we return to Bristol, get the wheel reinforced and set out again a few days later? We were all reluctant to do that as we felt it would be like ordering a retreat. Should we stay where we were and see if the problem could be sorted out locally? That was uncertain as we were in a sparsely populated area and had no way of knowing how long it would take us to find the kind of help we needed, if at all.

As we prayed together, our leader, Herbert Agar, said one solution would be to unload the cart, take what we were carrying to Weston-super-Mare, pull the empty cart to Weston and then on Monday look around for someone to help us reinforce the damaged wheel. But how could we transport the contents of the cart to Weston? It would be far too much to take on a bus. Then I remembered about a friend of mine in Bristol – a Christian building contractor who had several vehicles and for whom I had driven sometimes when he was short-staffed. I telephoned him and he readily agreed to loan us one of his vehicles.

I caught a bus back to Bristol, got the van, returned to the spot where we had broken down, put all the contents of the cart into the van, drove to the church in Weston where we were due to take the Sunday services, returned the van to Bristol, then got the bus back to Weston. This all took about four or five hours and, by the time I finally got back to Weston, the rest of the team had arrived at the church where we were due to spend the night. After we had taken the services on Sunday we made enquiries and found someone who could help us with repairs. It took just a few hours on Monday morning to complete them and by the afternoon we were on our way again, with the wheel strengthened, to our next destination – Taunton, in Devon.

After Weston, it took us a couple of days to reach our next stop, Taunton, and this gave us the opportunity to taste the real joys of trekking – sleeping in a field, cooking on a small stove, searching the villages for fresh bread and washing in rivers. After a service in a church in Taunton we headed for Exeter, stopping at villages on the way to give out evangelistic literature, hold an open-air service and witness to whoever we met. Sometimes people would stop their cars after overtaking us and ask us what we were doing. This always gave us an opportunity, as John Wesley would put it, 'to say a good word for Jesus Christ'.

We stayed at the Assemblies of God church in Exeter for several days, conducting evening meetings, and from there we headed for Newton Abbot. The church members there were very welcoming, and gave us the exclusive use of their small hall in which to prepare our meals and sleep.

We spent a few days in Newton Abbot, ministering in the church, and it was there that we reviewed the progress of our journey so far. Our greatest joy was the way our ministries had been received by the churches we had visited. We took it in turns to preach and give our testimonies, and although we didn't keep a record of those who committed their lives to Christ for the first time, there must have been well over 20, most of them young people.

It was in Newton Abbot that I left the team to go to Helston. An induction service for me had been arranged at the church on the last Sunday in August. It was the only date available for the minister conducting that service, so I had to end my participation in the trek. I took the train from Newton Abbot to Falmouth on the Friday and stayed with the minister who was to conduct my induction service. When we met he told me that, as far as he knew, no accommodation arrangements had been made for me in Helston and that I would have to find somewhere myself; but I was welcome to stay at his home until I did so.

It was from him I learned a little about the church I was about to be inducted into. It had been founded a few years previously after Simeon Dunstan, a young evangelist attached to the Assemblies of God, had held a crusade there. The crusade organisers had taken over an old Salvation Army hall that had closed down through lack of support. It seated about 100 people and I was told that during the crusade it had been packed to capacity. The Assemblies of God then appointed a young pastor, William Roy, to establish the converts in the Christian faith. When he left, another student from the BBC, Walter Cowell, had spent a year pastoring the group.

We made our way by bus from Falmouth to Helston on the Sunday morning of my induction. Helston, lying midway between Falmouth and Penzance is a quaint and bustling town with narrow, winding streets and cobbled alleyways. Nowadays it is known the world over for its spring folk festival, called the Floral Dance, which is one of the oldest surviving customs in England. When we arrived at the church for my induction we found 12 people there. Six of them were visitors on holiday!

Before the actual induction ceremony I preached my first sermon in the church from Paul's words to the Corinthians: 'For I resolved to know nothing while I was with you except Jesus Christ and him crucified' (1 Cor. 2:2). After that I was then inducted to the ministry of the church, and when the minister taking the service prayed for me, he not only asked God to make my ministry profitable there, but added a bit of practical concern: 'And, Lord, please help Selwyn to find suitable accommodation.'

At the end of the service a lady came up to me and asked, 'Is it true that you don't have any accommodation in the town?' When I replied in the affirmative, she gave me the address of a Miss May Lukies who, she said, would be only too glad to help. Miss Lukies attended a church in Porthleven, a nearby fishing village, but was well known in Helston for her kindness and generosity.

After lunch in the home of one of the members, I called at Miss Lukies' home. When I explained my predicament she told me that she had a room that was not being used. 'You are most welcome to it and it will cost you nothing. You can move in at any time. Today, if you wish.' She was out at work on weekdays so I would have to make my own meals, but she said she would cook for me at weekends. I gladly accepted her offer, returned with my minister friend to Falmouth, picked up my belongings and was safely ensconced in my new 'home' by late that evening.

My first task as pastor was to arrange for the arrival of the trekkers, who were due to hit town several weeks later. I put up posters all over the town, talked to the editor of the local paper and did everything I could to make their visit as widely known as possible. When the team arrived it was such a joy to see them again. They had some wonderful stories to tell me about what had happened since I left them at Newton Abbot. After a few nights of very successful meetings, which drew back quite a number of those who had left the church, the time came for the team to move on again.

I felt somewhat saddened as I watched them leave. Despite our occasional relationship problems we had grown very close over the weeks that we had trekked together. Now I was on my own, faced with performing as a pastor without showing myself up to be a complete idiot!

As a result of the few evenings of meetings with the team, I was assured of a regular congregation of between 30 and 40 people. However, as the church could seat over 100, I set myself the goal of increasing that number to at least 50, which I felt was realistic. I decided to visit 100 homes each day, ask people if they attended a church, and if they didn't, then I would invite them to mine. I planned a brief doorstep introduction that was meant to go like this: 'I am a Bible student from Bristol and I have come to take charge of the church which meets in the old Salvation Army hall. If you don't go to any church I would like to invite you to mine.'

I remembered feeling strangely nervous as I approached the first house, wondering what kind of reception I would get. After I had given my short speech the lady looked rather quizzically at me and said, 'What is a student Bible?' Instead of saying 'I am a Bible student from Bristol' I had been so nervous that it came out as 'I am a student Bible from Bristol.'

As a result of knocking at the doors of hundreds of houses, about ten new people started coming to the church. We were now close to my initial goal of 50 meeting together on Sundays. My mistakes were not confined to the doorstep; I made some foolish ones in church as well. One Sunday morning I decided to recite the well-known passage on the Communion from 1 Corinthians 11, which I knew by heart. Honesty compels me to admit my reason for doing this was to show off to the congregation my ability to memorise scripture.

I paused before the Communion table and said, 'We will now hear the apostle Paul's words relating to the Communion, words which I regard as so important that I have memorised them.' I continued, 'The apostle Paul said, "For I have received of the Lord that which also I delivered unto you, that the Lord Jesus"...' Then my mind went blank. I was in a complete state of panic and, rather than climb down from my pride and get my Bible, which I had not even taken out of my briefcase, I decided to cover up by asking everyone to bow their heads for prayer. But I couldn't remember the special prayer I had memorised either, and I found myself saying as I took the bread and Communion cup in my hands, 'For what we are about to receive, may the Lord make us truly thankful'!

A few Sundays later I preached on Judas Iscariot's betrayal of Christ. As I was drawn towards the dramatic when preaching at that period in my life, I had prepared a bag with a handful of heavy coins in it, which I intended to throw down from the pulpit on to the floor of the church to illustrate Judas' remorse. But as I came to the point in my sermon where Judas became remorseful about his betrayal of Christ I decided to throw the bag of coins at the wall of the church instead of on to the floor. I did it with such force that the bag burst open and one of the coins hit a woman on the side of her face, bruising her cheek quite badly. I swiftly apologised and she was very forgiving about it, but someone did tell me later that she overheard her saying to a friend that the new preacher in the Assemblies of God church was 'quite mad'!

I made so many mistakes that I wondered whether I was cut out to be a pastor or not. Perhaps I had made a mistake about hearing the voice of God speaking to me in the mine. For a while I was on the verge of quitting what up until then I had thought was a clear call to the Christian ministry.

CHAPTER 11

A TIME OF SPIRITUAL CRISIS

A few months after I had taken over the pastorate of the little church in Helston, I found myself in an increasingly depressed mood, wondering whether I was really called to be a pastor. It was as if I was living in a room where the blinds were drawn and all I could see were the sun's rays peeping through the cracks in the curtain. Then came a startling moment of sun-drenched grace. The curtains opened and I received a word from God. It was a word so precious that, had it not been given, I do not believe I would have continued in the ministry and my life would have been vastly different.

The man who brought me this word from God was a veteran Christian who was known to us as 'Brother Goldsworthy'. He was not actually a member of the church I pastored, but he attended services as regularly as he could. One Sunday night, after everyone had left the church, he remained in his seat. When I jokingly said, 'Aren't you going home tonight, Brother Goldsworthy?' he responded, 'Come and sit down, Pastor. I believe I have a word for you from God.'

As I sat beside him, he opened his Bible and began by reading me the words found in Jeremiah 33:3: 'Call to me and I will answer you and tell you great and unsearchable things you do not know.' This was the same text that was given to me by my pastor on the night of my conversion. 'God has shown me,' he went on, 'that you are feeling somewhat discouraged at this time, and as I have been praying for you the Lord has given me this word for you in Jeremiah. Also, He has given me a little glimpse into your future.' Then he proceeded to outline the direction that he felt, under God, my life would take. 'You are going to be a writer one day and the Lord is going to take you to many countries of the world. You will not always play the role of a pastor, but after the Lord has taught you the lessons you need to learn in the pastoral life He will guide you into a ministry that will be beyond anything you can imagine. Keep calling on Him, keep close to Him in prayer and step by step He will reveal to you His deep purposes for your life.'

Without another word he closed his Bible, put his coat on and went out into the night. I sat there dumbfounded, with tears running down my face. As I stood up I literally felt my spine straighten up, my shoulders go back as though what was happening in my body was a reflection of what had happened in my soul. I knew that in the mercy of God and in the Lord's own good time something big and beautiful lay up ahead.

The encouragement I got from Brother Goldsworthy that memorable night flowed out of the fact that, as the Psalmist put it, my times are in God's hands. I was reminded that the Almighty had mapped out a purpose for me that nothing could destroy. The words he gave me on that occasion were so powerful and precious that it would be worth the most arduous of climbs to hear the least audible of its echoes.

After that I went back to my work as a pastor with renewed energy and enthusiasm. By now, a fine group of young people was attending the church, who were always ready to take part in any evangelistic activity I organised. Our favourite form of evangelism was holding open-air services in the centre of town. Cornish people love music, and whenever I played my piano accordion outside it was always guaranteed to bring a small crowd. Many, of course, would drift away when the music stopped and the preaching began but there were others who stayed and listened to what we had to say.

Three months after I became pastor the church offerings had increased considerably from what they had been in the first few weeks of my arrival. During those early weeks the congregation gave a total of just twelve shillings and sixpence a week, out of which I had to pay ten shillings to the Salvation Army regional headquarters in Falmouth for the rent of the hall. That left me with two shillings and sixpence to live on! I survived on this menu:

Breakfast: two slices of toast.
Lunch: a cup of beef tea and bread.
Dinner: a bag of chips.

On this diet I studied hard, and prepared two new sermons every Sunday, and a midweek Bible study.

Two miles from Helston is the Royal Naval Air Station, Culdrose, one of the largest helicopter bases in Europe. A young woman in the church, Enid Osmand, was the manageress of the NAAFI (Navy, Army and Air Force Institute) canteen and she used her influence to get me on to the station to conduct meetings in the chapel. Although hundreds of naval personnel served there, I was disappointed to see only 20 or 30 men come to these services.

Enid was exceedingly kind to me and would often help me out with 'little extras' that she was able to buy from the canteen at very low cost – things like biscuits, bars of chocolate and cakes. After a few weeks I began to feel myself becoming emotionally involved with her. Although I did not say anything to her, I realised that this was an issue that I had to handle very carefully.

Although I wrote to my fiancée regularly while I was in college, and had seen her when I returned home during the term breaks, I had begun to realise that my feelings for her were changing. Without realising it, this had begun to reflect itself in my letters. As I had not gone home during the college midsummer break my next homecoming would be at Christmas. I knew I had some hard thinking to do in the weeks coming up to it.

I did not want to be away from the church too long over Christmas, so I arranged to travel back home on Christmas Eve and return before 1 January so that I could lead a New Year's Eve service. I thought that my return home would clarify my feelings one way or the other: either I would make up my mind that my fiancée was the girl I would marry, or I would decide it would be someone else. The days I spent at home with my family and seeing my fiancée helped to clarify my thinking to some degree. It was clear that my feelings for my fiancée had changed but I dreaded the thought of making this known to her. I decided to give it a few more weeks before coming to a definite conclusion.

When I returned to Helston I knew after a few weeks that, regardless of whether Enid would be interested in pursuing a romantic relationship or not, my feelings for my fiancée had changed to such a degree that it would be wrong to continue with the engagement. I had talked over this possibility with my mother and father over the Christmas break and my father had simply said, 'Better a broken engagement than an unhappy marriage.'

Just a few days into January I wrote my fiancée telling her of my decision to break off the engagement. It was one of the most difficult letters I have ever written in my life. I knew the hurt and misunderstanding it would create, not only to her and her family, but also to the people in the church. Although she did not reply to my letter, her mother and father did, in an understandably concerned way. They accused me, among other things, of making a mockery of their daughter and said that I was not fit to be a minister of Jesus Christ. Those words cut deep into my soul. I consoled myself with the fact that though I was the cause of much grief and hurt, it was better that way than to go ahead with a marriage that was not based on true love.

A week or two later I arranged a quiet meal with Enid in a restaurant in Porthleven and told her what had been happening in my heart. She said she felt great sympathy for my fiancée and the broken engagement, but agreed that no marriage ought to be entered into unless there was a total commitment of true love. When I asked her if she was interested in going out with me, she said she was, but pointed that my position as pastor meant our relationship would have to be managed very carefully. We decided to keep things to ourselves for a few weeks. Then, when we saw things more clearly, we would take the church into our confidence.

Enid was born in Helston on 10 August 1929, the youngest of James Henry and Annie Osmand's four children. Because she was so petite and pretty she was rather doted upon as a young girl. Her childhood and early teens were extremely happy, except when she was run over by a car and spent several months in hospital recovering from some serious injuries to her legs. Then her mother died when she was 13 and the shock affected her so much that she lost her voice for several months. Enid had been converted through the ministry of William Roy, the first pastor of the new church in Helston, and although she had sought to taste most things the world has to offer, once she committed her life to Jesus Christ she had become a strong and deeply committed Christian.

After a few weeks of courtship we felt it was time to take the church into our confidence. So one Sunday night after the service had finished I invited all those who had committed themselves to membership to stay behind as I had an announcement to make. I explained about the reason for my broken engagement and my feelings for Enid and asked if there was anyone who might see the present situation as interfering with my role as pastor. Everyone seemed to appreciate my taking them into our confidence on this issue and there was not one dissenting voice. Some even said how happy they were that one of their Helston girls might marry a pastor. They seemed to see it as some kind of spiritual achievement!

As the weeks went by I began to feel a little concerned about the whole situation, as I knew that it would not be all that long before the year I had committed to looking after the church would be up. I did not want to move away from Helston and have to continue a courtship by letter. Enid and I talked about this and decided that, as we were fully committed to each other, we would get married in April that year, 1951, and face whatever the Lord had for us in future ministry together.

One of my friends in the area, the Revd Philip Anstey, a pastor in Falmouth, agreed to conduct the marriage service and we were married in the Bible Christian Chapel in Meneage Street, Helston, on 10 April. My parents, sister and David Jones travelled down from Wales. As it was the first time they had been in Cornwall, they stayed for a few days after the wedding and got to know their new in-laws. Enid had two sisters, Dorothy and Joan, and a brother, Jack. Dorothy had become a Christian in the days when the Salvation Army were active in Helston and Joan was to become a Christian many years later.

Enid and I spent our honeymoon in Torquay, Devon. I had developed a special friendship with the minister of Newton Abbot since the time we were at his church on the trek and had preached there several times in the months since, so when I telephoned him to say Enid and I would be spending our honeymoon in nearby Torquay and we would like to come along to his church, he said, 'In that case, we would like you to speak to us, so be prepared for that.' My interpretation of his remarks was that he would like me just to say how Enid and I had met and to introduce her to the congregation.

I was mistaken. When we arrived at the church on the first Sunday of our honeymoon I saw a poster on the church notice board that said: 'Preacher for this Sunday is Selwyn Hughes from Helston. Both services – 11am and 6:30pm.' When I pointed out to the pastor that I thought his invitation to speak was to say a word about my new wife, he was horrified. 'I have not prepared a message because I was relying on you to bring it. What shall we do?'

Fortunately, one piece of good advice I had absorbed at college was, 'Whenever you go to someone else's church keep in mind that it may fall to you to preach. The appointed preacher might be taken ill or hindered from arriving and people, knowing you are a preacher, will look to you.' I had got into the habit (something I have continued to this day) of going into a church where I am not preaching with one or two sermons in mind that are so familiar to me I could preach them without the help of notes. So I reassured my friend that it was not a problem and spent that day preaching the gospel in two services at the Assemblies of God church in Newton Abbott. I have often wondered how many preachers there are who can say that they were booked to preach on their honeymoon!

After our honeymoon we returned to Helston, and a little time later we said farewell to our church friends and Enid's family. In due course, after some preaching engagements in the west country, we went to Wales to stay with my parents for a few weeks.

I had a number of preaching appointments in Wales and our plans were to wait on the Lord for the next stage of our ministry.

About a month after we had set up temporary home in my parents' house, I received a telegram from the evangelist, Howell Harris, who had just finished a crusade in the little town of Llandeilo, West Wales. He asked me to telephone him immediately. When I did I learned that his crusade had resulted in a large number of converts who wanted to start a church of their own. He asked if I could come and talk with him about establishing the new converts in the Christian faith. 'You may wonder why I contacted you when we don't really know each other,' he said, 'but I was present when you preached your examination sermon at the Blackboy Hill Assemblies of God church last year. I said to myself, 'That is the young man I would like to follow me whenever it is appropriate to turn the converts in my crusades into disciples.'

Llandeilo is only about 50 miles from my parents' home. Borrowing David Jones' car, Enid and I drove over there and spent a day talking with Howell about plans for the future. A Christian pharmacist, Ernest Griffiths, and his wife, Lilian, had sponsored the crusade. They had been sent to the town by the company they worked for, only to find that all the churches were Welsh-speaking. Although Ernest spoke Welsh, his wife did not, and they thought it would be helpful for the non-Welsh speaking community in the town to have a church where the services were conducted in English.

As we talked in Ernest and Lilian's home, we were told that a problem had arisen during the crusade which had upset the local ministers. Because there was no support for the evangelistic crusade from the other churches, Howell Harris had made an off-the-cuff and rather inappropriate statement one night from the platform in which he criticised the ministers for their noncooperation. Ernest said that if I came to help establish the new converts in the faith I would have 'to win over every minister in this town' – not an enviable task.

I asked for a day or two to pray about it and think it over with my wife. We talked at great length about everything as we drove back to my parents' home and we wondered if this was the next door opening to us in the ministry. I remember saying to Enid, 'We have just come from the small town of Helston. I was rather hoping that the next step would be to a larger town, a place where I could really flex my spiritual muscles, so to speak.'

At this point, Enid, who was always a lover of poetry, took out something she carried in her Bible and read it to me. I had never heard it before, but as soon as she read it the Holy Spirit witnessed to my heart that Llandeilo was to be the next stopping place on my spiritual journey:

> I said, 'Master where shall I work today?'
> And my love flowed warm and free.
> And He pointed to a little plot and said,
> 'There, tend that for me.'
> I said, 'Lord, no not that, not that little place for me.'
> And His gaze when He turned was so sweet, yet so pained.
> 'Remember, my child, please remember this fact:
> Bethlehem was just a little place,
> And so was Galilee.'

CHAPTER 12

MY TIME IN LLANDEILO

Llandeilo is a town rich in history. It sits prominently on the north bank of the river Towy in the county of Carmarthenshire and in medieval times was regarded as the capital of Wales. It has the reputation of being one of the cradles of Christianity in Wales and is named after St Teilo, a contemporary of St David. Surrounding the town is some of the most beautiful and unspoilt countryside in the United Kingdom. Just 20 miles away one meets the fringe of the lovely Brecon Beacons National park. Today Llandeilo is a thriving market town and a focal point for the neighbouring villages and the agricultural community. It is, without doubt, the most beautiful place in which I have ever lived.

After a few weeks living with a couple who had been converted in the Howell Harris crusade, Enid and I found an excellent furnished flat to move into. Week after week we strove at the task of establishing the new converts in the Christian faith. We met in a rented building that belonged to one of the local pubs three times a week and twice on Sunday. There is something very stimulating about discipling new Christians with their probing questions and childlike expectations. 'God just answered a prayer of mine,' said one. 'Does that mean He will answer every prayer I pray?' Others asked, 'How often do we have to pray for something? Is once enough?' 'Do we really have to give a tenth of our earnings to God and does that mean a tenth of our gross income or net?' 'What does circumcision mean and what has that got to do with the Christian faith?' 'Do we have to stop smoking and drinking and swearing?' 'What happens if we sin? Does that mean we lose our salvation?' And so on.

My first major task, after settling in the town, was to visit all the ministers and see if I could mend some fences, so to speak, following Howell Harris's public criticism of them. When I visited them in their homes I discovered that Howell Harris's pejorative statement had offended them much more deeply than anyone had realised. In theory they said they were willing to forgive him for his inappropriate remarks, but it was quite different in practice. They certainly showed no brotherly warmth or friendliness toward me. During the whole time I ministered in the town I was never once invited to the bi-monthly ministers' fraternals. When I asked why, one of the ministers told me that they did not feel there was a need for another church in Llandeilo. They believed there was a big enough variety of churches for people to choose from and 'we all felt starting a new church was entirely unnecessary'.

When I pointed out that most of the converts were English-speaking and would find it difficult to attend services conducted entirely in a language they couldn't understand, I got this astonishing response: 'Let them learn Welsh!' That, in my opinion, was about as helpful as the famous remark Marie Antoinette was supposed to have made when the French peasants complained that they had no bread: 'Let them eat cake!'

The converts I was discipling grew by leaps and bounds. I taught them how to get into the Bible on a daily basis, how to witness to their friends and neighbours, how to pray, how to practise Christian principles, such as forgiveness, putting others first, and so on. There were baptisms in the river, open-air services in the market square, and slowly the church began to

My maternal grandparents

My parents

A view of Fochriw, my home village, taken in the early 1920s. South Tunnel Terrace was off to the left on the hill from which the picture is taken
(County Library, Dowlais)

Fochriw railway station looking towards Bargoed (early 1920s). I daily rode the train there after winning a scholarship to Bargoed Grammar School in 1940. There was great excitement among schoolboys at their free rail passes: they were often used to make evening visits to the town after homework was finished!
(County Library, Dowlais)

Inside the Mission Hall, Fochriw, where I was converted

At Bristol Bible College,
playing the accordion with
Walter Cowell (ukulele) and
Maurice Paine (clarinet)

The Trek – following John Wesley's route to Cornwall – at the end of our time
at Bristol Bible College. Left to right: Me, Maurice Paine, Herbert Agar,
André Lemarquand and Charlie Rogers

Our wedding in Helston, Cornwall, 10 April 1951

With Enid, David and John

*Enid with my father and sister
Pamela at an evangelistic dinner*

David and John in the garden

Enid and I celebrate our 30th wedding anniversary, 10 April 1981

Ministering in Colchester, 1959–1961

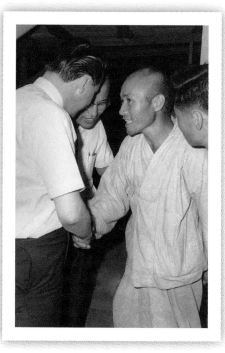

Buddhist priest receives Christ, Pusan, Korea, 1968

Ministers' Seminar, Madras, India, early 1970s. On my left are Eric Bowtell and Henry Joseph (for many years our distributor of EDWJ in India)

1965

1970s

The growth of Every Day with Jesus from postcards to a bimonthly periodical

1980s

1990s

2000s

Waverley Abbey House, as purchased in 1983

Renovations to Waverley Abbey House, 1985
(Mick Rock)

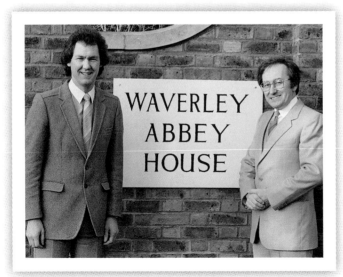

Trevor Partridge and myself outside CWR's new headquarters

grow, not only in terms of spiritual growth, but in numbers as well. Although we did not encourage people to leave their churches to join us, several people did this because they said they were not being fed spiritually. It's always a difficult situation for a pastor when this happens, but in most cases there is very little that can be done about it.

One of those who came to us on this basis was Mrs Wendell Thomas, a town councillor who, a few weeks after joining us, became Mayoress of Llandeilo. It was customary when a new Mayor or Mayoress was appointed that the occasion be celebrated with a special religious service and, as I was now her pastor, she asked me to lead such a service and to give the mayoral address. 'In that address,' she said, 'I want you to preach a clear gospel message, because there is so much religion in the town and so little emphasis on the true gospel. Preach Christ and let the chips fall where they will,' she insisted.

The service was held in one of the local churches. At the beginning of my address I drew the attention of those present to the moment in Christ's ministry (John 6) when, because of His hard sayings, many turned away from Him. Sensing the mood of His disciples as they watched the crowds departing, Jesus brought the issue out into the open and startled His disciples with the blunt demand: 'Will you also go away?' Simon Peter replied, 'Lord, to whom shall we go? You have the words of eternal life.'

I made the point that in all the realms of fact and force there was simply no substitute for Jesus. He is the incomparable Christ. No one else could provide life for the soul, power to live life the way it should be lived, and forgiveness for sin. It was a sermon packed with gospel assertions from beginning to end. It triggered a lot of discussion in the local newspaper in the weeks that followed. One of the letters published said the occasion was more like a gospel crusade than a mayoral service. But another said,

'Why don't we hear more about the gospel in our churches, rather than clever little talks on current events?'

Most of the letters, I have to say, were critical of the emphasis on the gospel, but the Mayoress brought the discussion to an end when she wrote to the paper explaining that the message I preached had been at her request. She pointed out that the most important aspect of the service was not to draw attention to herself or the work of the town council, but to put the focus on Christ, whose follower she was and whom she served. 'If Jesus Christ is not at the centre of things,' she said, 'then they will not work properly, and as long as I am Mayoress I intend to follow Christ's principles in everything.'

It was in Llandeilo that I started my writing ministry. I saw an advert for reconditioned typewriters on hire purchase at two shillings and sixpence per month. I knew that if I was to become a writer it would be an advantage for me to teach myself to type, so I paid the deposit and duly set about gaining the necessary skill. I would get up early every morning to practise and, though I never became a touch typist, I soon developed both skill and speed with the use of one finger on each hand. Soon I began to write articles for Christian magazines, and the money I earned helped me to quickly pay off the hire purchase balance on the machine. I have always considered teaching myself to type as one of the best things I ever did.

One of the things I have observed in my long life is that often the people we meet are part of God's purpose for our lives. As I look back over the years, I often wonder how different things would have turned out for me if I had not met a certain person at a particular time or if a situation had not developed the way it did. One Sunday afternoon in Ernest Griffiths' home we were talking about church matters in general when he handed me a book by a writer I had never come across before – E. Stanley

Jones. The book was entitled *The Way*, and was a series of daily devotional writings that followed a theme through the whole year. E. Stanley Jones was a Methodist, born in the United States, who became a missionary to India. He became known internationally through a landmark book, *The Christ of the Indian Road*. He did a great work for God in India and spent a good deal of his life debating with educated Indians about the supremacy of Jesus Christ over other religious ideas and practices.

The moment I opened the book something strange happened to me. It was something that I can't quite put my finger on, let alone find words for. Maybe there are no words for such moments in a person's life. What I experienced that day was profoundly moving, and one of the things that it did for me was to make me wonder whether the writing ministry that God would lead me into might be in the realm of the devotional. More and more I felt myself being drawn into that kind of writing and *The Way* was precisely that to which my heart warmed.

I thought to myself: 'I wonder if there is a place for a devotional that follows a biblical theme or topic which does not have to be sustained over a year, but perhaps a month or even two months?' I asked Ernest to lend me the book, and, in the weeks that followed, I came to the conclusion that if I ever became a writer this would be the style I would want to emulate. I knew I was not experienced or knowledgeable enough about life in general or the Scriptures in particular to write a daily devotional at that time, but perhaps one day. Looking back on that moment which, 50 years later, is still undimmed in my memory, I think that too was another moment when a door opened and let in the future.

Another person I came to know when I pastored the Llandeilo church, and whom I regard as part of God's purpose for my life, was a young seed salesman, Mordecai Price. Mordecai attended an Apostolic church outside Llandeilo but he was often seen in the town, especially on market days. In his youth he had been struck down by polio and because he couldn't use his legs his car was fitted with hand controls. The accelerator and brake were on the steering wheel, which he operated perfectly safely. To open the gate when visiting farms he would put out his crutches, lever himself up, hobble to the gate, open it, then get back to his car, drive through and then repeat the process to close the gate. Sometimes this took him 20 minutes or more. I don't remember ever meeting anyone with such courage and indefatigability.

Mordecai was a most effective personal evangelist. As he drove to the many farms throughout West Wales he would often give a lift to someone walking along the road. Before the person got out of the car he or she would be gently confronted with the importance of receiving Jesus Christ as Saviour and Lord.

He had built up a reputation in Wales of being one of the greatest personal soul-winners of his day, and on several occasions I travelled with him to see him at work. Every month he would buy 100 copies of the New Testament from the Pocket Testament League, because in the back of each one was a clear step-by-step procedure on how to become a Christian and how to grow in the faith. One day when I travelled with him he gave a lift to three different people. Before they departed each one of them bowed his head and received Jesus Christ as Lord and Saviour. Each was then given a copy of the New Testament and encouraged to join an active evangelical church.

Mordecai became a firm friend and was a great inspiration in my own personal evangelism. As he was one of the top salesmen for T.B. Lock and Sons of Yeovil, Somerset (Seed Merchants), it meant he had a lot of paperwork. I used to help him type out his orders in my spare time, for which I was paid generously.

It was also in Llandeilo, in the spring of 1951, that I conducted my first funeral service. The granddaughter of one of the new converts, a beautiful little girl of just two years of age, was struck down with a fatal liver disease and I was asked to officiate at her burial. After the service was over and I returned home, I sat down with Enid to drink a cup of tea when I was suddenly overwhelmed with tears. I just couldn't understand why I was convulsed with such deep sobs. Was it the emotional effect of conducting my first funeral? Was it because I had put up defences to ward off my deep feelings of sadness at the situation and now that the funeral was over those defences had come down and reality was sweeping over me?

I reflected for a while on the emotion I felt, and came to the conclusion that I was beginning to see, albeit faintly, the pain the Father bears as He looks down upon the world He created torn apart by sin and death. This is where I was next being taken in my development as a person. Looking back I am certain those tears took me to a another place I needed to go, to see a little more deeply into the human condition and feel something of the pain that lies in the heart of God.

But Llandeilo will be remembered best for the birth of our first child. About midday on 15 March 1952 David Selwyn arrived, a bonny bouncing baby. My mother had come to stay with us a few days before David was due and after we had been up all night while Enid was in labour, my mother said, 'You go and lie down for an hour. The midwife said it might be a few hours before the baby arrives.' I did so, and while I was asleep David made his entrance into the world. In those days fathers did not attend the birth. I am always glad when I see from films and television what is involved that I was a father in those days and not today!

David was such a darling child; everyone loved him and he

was doted on from the moment he arrived. A few weeks later my father took him in his arms in our new church and dedicated him to the Lord. This was the first dedication in the church, and the event was celebrated not only by my family, my father, mother, sister and our adopted 'brother' David Jones, but also by everyone in the congregation. They seemed delighted that their pastor had now become a father.

CHAPTER 13

TAKING ON TWO CHURCHES

After nine solid months of discipling the new converts in Llandeilo and attempting to deepen my understanding of the word of God, my work came to the attention of the Assemblies of God church in Pontardulais, a town about 20 miles away.

A deputation from that church visited me one evening and told me that they were without a pastor. They wondered whether it would be possible for me to lead their church along with the one in Llandeilo. They pointed out that an excellent bus service meant that I could easily travel between the two towns to conduct a week-night prayer meeting and Bible study, preach at one of the two Sunday services and be available to conduct dedications, marriages and funerals, as well as visiting the sick. The church was not large, with about 60 members, but because they did not have a pastor, they told me, a number of people had stopped attending. They were confident that once a pastor was appointed many of them would begin once again to attend the fellowship. My visitors also pointed out that, as a young pastor with a family, I would find the additional salary very helpful – a point that was certainly taken!

They gave me a month to pray about the matter. First I talked to Enid about the proposition. She thought it would broaden my experience. Ernest Griffiths, the Llandeilo church elder, was also positive when I told him about it. I put the matter to the church members and there was not one dissenting voice. So when the Pontardulais church deputation came to see me a month later I told them I was ready to take up their offer, but on one condition: I did not want to be pinned down to staying for a particular length of time. This was because I felt there were other fields that I needed to explore to gain the experience and understanding that would help me reach the goals I had set myself.

Pontardulais is a town with a great spiritual history. During the 1904 Welsh revival all the churches and chapels were packed to capacity and some of the town's notorious drunkards were transformed overnight through the power and presence of the Holy Spirit. One of them, Jack Davies, was the secretary of the Assemblies of God church. At the time I knew him he had been a Christian for 50 years, but revival fire still blazed within him. It was he who had spearheaded the move for me to take charge of the church, which was known then as Noddfa, the Welsh word for 'resting place'.

On the day of my induction to this new field of opportunity the church was packed with friends and loved ones from different parts of Wales. My uncle, David Thomas, brought a coach full of people from Fochriw. He had a significant role in the service by praying a wonderful prayer and giving a short, but humorous talk about my life before I became a Christian. 'Little did I realise when I took him in my arms as a baby of just six weeks old, and asked God to make him a preacher, that I would be standing here today taking part in this induction,' he declared. I remember thinking to myself as he said those words, 'Wow! My whole life has been the answer to a faithful pastor's prayer!'

With two churches to take care of my workload doubled. The extra salary enabled me to buy a motorcycle, which made a world of difference to the travelling. I was also appointed secretary of the Assemblies of God District Council. There is an old saying that 'if you want something done give it to someone who is already busy'. I found that the busier I became the more I was forced to organise my life more efficiently and to develop stronger self-discipline.

I read an article in the *Readers Digest* around that time entitled 'Save Time Tomorrow by Planning Today'. It made the simple but telling point that no one plans to fail, but often our lack of success is due to the fact that we fail to plan. 'Make a list of the things you have to do tomorrow, the night before and the difference it makes to your day will surprise you, perhaps even stagger you,' the article said. I followed that suggestion and found it transforming.

Eventually the Pontardulais congregation, being the larger one, became more demanding than the Llandeilo church and it was suggested that we should live nearer to it. We found a lovely bungalow within walking distance of the church and one of the members helped us to arrange a mortgage. Within a few months we were settled in the first home of our own.

It was while I was in Pontardulais that I decided that if I was to become a writer then I needed some more formal training. I enrolled for a correspondence course in journalism and after I had written several things, those responsible for marking my work said I showed an aptitude for short story writing. They pointed out that there was money to be made in that market and I had the potential to break into it.

I sat down one day at my typewriter to write my first short story. Perhaps other short stories would follow and in time I might be able to earn a living just stringing words together. I decided to write under the pseudonym of Adrian White. I had come across the name somewhere and thought it rather classy. The idea I had for a short story was about a woman who committed what she thought was a perfect murder but unwittingly left a clue that enabled a clever detective to bring her to justice. The clue, of course, had to be in the last sentence.

The more I wrote the less I liked it. There was something about making up a story in this way that seemed foreign to my nature. What might seem right to others just didn't seem right for me. I was reminded of what Henry Thoreau, the great American writer, said: 'A man had better starve at once than lose his innocence in the process of getting his bread.' Was I in danger of losing my innocence? The story I had written wasn't my story; it was a story I had made up. But people want stories, thrilling stories, I had been told. What harm was there in giving them what they wanted? It was honest money.

I finished the story of about 3,000 words, took the last page out of the typewriter and tore the whole manuscript up. I decided that if I was going to write then it would be about something I believed in, something that would provide much more than an interesting distraction in life. It would be something that would help people understand what life is all about.

This must not be seen as a criticism of Christians who make a living or add to their income by writing for a secular market. I am simply saying that writing for a secular market was not right for me. It was not what God had called me to do.

I began then to focus on writing for the Christian market. At first I wrote articles on subjects such as 'How to turn the tables on the Jehovah's Witnesses', 'Evangelise or fossilise', 'Ten words to change your life', and, of course, 'Revival'. Most of these were snapped up by Christian magazines that didn't pay for unsolicited articles, but it was a tremendous pleasure nevertheless to see my name in print. Sometimes papers and magazines would pay me expenses to cover the costs of paper and postage, but this never amounted to much.

In the church at Pontardulais there were a number of young

people who were budding preachers and I began a Friday night Bible school during the winter for them and other young people from congregations in the town. My teaching was mainly on homiletics (the art of preaching) and hermeneutics (interpretation of Scripture). These sessions became very popular and helped provide a flow of good preaching for the congregation in Llandeilo. The more the church in Pontardulais developed, the more of my time was taken up by it, which meant my Llandeilo visits were reduced to once a month.

Not far from Pontardulais is Swansea, home of the well-known Swansea Bible College. Many Christians have heard of Rees Howells, the great intercessor and man of faith. I spent every available opportunity at the college researching on revival and learning as much as I could about the subject of faith. During the summer months the Pontardulais church was a major supporter of children's missions on the Swansea and the Gower Coast beaches. Sister Williams, a well-known children's evangelist, spent the whole of the summer leading the Gower events and, as secretary of the West Wales AOG District Council, it fell to me to organise as much support as possible for her from the churches in the area.

As the months went by and I became known in West Wales, more and more preaching appointments came my way. I found myself booked up for a number of conventions and anniversaries in churches from Cardiff in the south to Aberystwyth in the north. A young man making a name for himself as a preacher at that time was Eric Dando, pastor of an independent church near Bridgend. I first met him when we were invited to preach together at an Easter convention in Swansea and we quickly became close friends. Eric was a fine preacher and he became very interested in the Friday night Bible school, so much so that he became a regular and greatly appreciated visiting lecturer.

Our preaching ministries dovetailed together so effectively that we found ourselves being booked to preach together at more events than we could manage. Someone said, 'You have preached together so many times that by now you ought to be able to preach each other's sermons.' One night, in a church we had not preached at before, we did just that!

One of Eric's favourite sermons was based on three verses from Hebrews which state, firstly, that Christ appeared to take away sin (Heb. 9:11), secondly, that He now appears in the presence of God for us (Heb. 9:24) and, thirdly, that He will appear once more to the world at his second coming (Heb. 9:28). One of my favourite sermons was called 'God's wonderful time clock'. It was based on three texts: Galatians 4:4, which shows that Christ came right on time at Bethlehem; Romans 5:6, which states that Christ came to Calvary right on time; and Matthew 24:36 which tells that Christ will return to this world at the right time.

In an Easter convention which we both attended we decided to preach each other's sermon. Eric went first and preached my sermon on 'God's wonderful time clock' and I followed with his sermon on 'The three appearances of Christ'. We did not use precisely the same words or language that was characteristic of us as individuals, but we did keep to the main thoughts. At the end of the service a lady came up to us and said she had heard the messages the previous year at a convention. 'I enjoyed them then, but even more tonight,' she said, 'but I could have sworn the messages had been the other way round. I guess I must be getting old!' We didn't let on what had happened, but we agreed never to do it again.

My friendship with Eric was an important one and I believe it was used by God to steer us in different directions in our ministries. I felt Eric's preaching and teaching gifts could be better and more widely used if he switched from being pastor of a small independent church in a Welsh valley to being an Assemblies of God minister, so I used my position as secretary of the West Wales District Council of the AOG to gently push him in that direction.

Others also encouraged Eric along these lines and eventually he became an Assemblies of God minister in Glyn Neath, a village nestled in the valley that leads from Swansea to Merthyr Tydfil. That set him on the road to becoming a key figure in the AOG movement, serving as an Executive Council member and then as Chairman. He moved from Glyn Neath to Bethel Temple in Newport and built up the congregation to become one of the largest and most influential churches in the town. He remained pastor of it until he went home to be with the Lord. It seems somewhat ironic that not long after Eric was appointed to the Executive Committee I left the movement – but that's a story I will come to later.

Eric hailed from Thurnscoe, a mining village in South Yorkshire, not far from Barnsley. His family lived there and were very active in the community's church life. Eric would often visit them. After returning from one such trip, he telephoned me to say that an Assemblies of God church in South Kirkby, a village near Thurnscoe, needed a pastor and that he had recommended me for the position.

Although I was very happy in West Wales, immediately he told me what he had done I sensed that another move was impending. I knew in my heart that there were many lessons I needed to learn as I moved towards whatever the Lord had planned for my future, and they involved meeting and ministering to people of different backgrounds and perspectives.

After talking it over with Enid and spending much time in prayer, I told Eric that I would be interested to meet with the church. Within a few weeks I received an official invitation to visit the South Kirkby assembly (AOG churches are often referred to as 'assemblies') for a week of special meetings. The letter made clear that it was with a view to becoming their pastor. I was particularly intrigued with the PS the secretary, Bert Hobson, added to his official letter of invitation: 'We hear you play the accordion and sing. Please try to bring it with you.'

CHAPTER 14

FIRST DAYS IN YORKSHIRE

'Need help with your luggage, Guv?' asked the porter at South Kirkby railway station. I had arrived there on what proved to be one of the foggiest nights in living memory – a real 'pea-souper' as they say. It was impossible to see more than a yard in front of my face.

The kindly question was prompted by the fact that I had two large cases, one containing my piano accordion and the other my clothes. The porter asked me where I was headed for. When I gave him the address of the family with whom I would be staying, he said, 'Let me take you to the bus stop which is right outside the station. There'll be a bus along in a few minutes. It's only three or four miles.'

'But someone is supposed to be meeting me here,' I said. 'I certainly don't want to miss them.' 'That's OK, Guv,' he replied. 'I'll take you into the car park – that's where people wait for passengers coming off the train ... though how people will be able to find each other on such a night as this is beyond me.'

In less than a minute the porter had steered me through a side exit to the bus queue outside the station and promptly disappeared into the fog. Now I had a dilemma. I was not sure if the person who had been sent to meet me had been able to make it because of the fog and if I left my place in the queue and went searching for him or her it might be a long wait for the next bus. I decided to stay where I was.

The bus soon arrived and I clambered aboard for a 20-minute crawl of a journey that normally, I gathered, took just five minutes. A young woman who got off at the same stop as me helped me to my host's door.

'Didn't you see our son, Harold?' asked a surprised Bert Hobson as he helped me inside, 'we sent him to meet you'. After I freshened up and was sitting down to a much-needed cup of tea Harold, their teenage son, arrived. He was surprised and embarrassed to see me sitting in front of a roaring fire. He couldn't understand how he'd missed me after watching everyone come out of the main station entrance and had stayed for a few minutes after everyone had gone. I then explained what had happened.

The next morning, a Saturday, the fog had cleared and Bert Hobson gave me a tour of the village. South Kirkby is situated in what was then known as the West Riding of Yorkshire, about halfway between Doncaster and Wakefield. The Doomsday Book of records of 1086 showed it at that time to be a small settlement, probably no more than a few farmsteads, and that was the way it remained for centuries. The opening of Frickley colliery in 1903 turned it from a quiet backwater into a mining community, and the population grew rapidly as the pits flourished. Estates were built, schools were established, and so were churches.

We called in at the Assemblies of God church, known as 'Carmel', and sat there for a while as Bert, who was the church secretary, gave me a potted history of the rise and development of the Pentecostal community in South Kirkby. There was a congregation of about 70 people, most of the men being miners. It seemed the church had gone through a chequered history, having had several pastors since it started just before the Second World War.

The most successful period of the church, in terms of conversions and increasing membership, was just after the war ended, when Ron Jones was the pastor. Ron was also a Welshman. He later left the Assemblies of God and became well known in the Elim Pentecostal churches. I was told that my immediate predecessor, Jim Pears, had not enjoyed a good deal of success and this, plus health problems, had made him decide to move on.

I met the congregation for the first time on the Sunday when I preached at the morning and evening services. It was also the first time – the only time, it has turned out – that I found myself 'on trial'. It was a strange feeling, knowing that everything I did was being evaluated – my personality, the way I led the services, my preaching ability, my jokes – and that later a vote would be taken on whether I was to become their pastor or not.

Yorkshire people have the reputation for being blunt. They don't stand on ceremony, and they call a spade a spade. But at the same time they are wonderfully friendly and extremely hospitable. Some of the older Christians in the church had a quaint way of speaking and I shall never forget a dear old woman standing up in a prayer meeting and saying, 'Eee, Lord, we do luv thee!' I quickly learned some of the Yorkshire colloquialisms, a popular one being 'Put wood in ole', which meant 'Please shut the door.'

Every day of my week 'on trial' I was invited to tea in people's homes. 'Tea' took place around 4pm and consisted of sandwiches and cakes. Soon after I had arrived at the Hobson home, Edna asked me what food I liked and disliked. I happened to mention that I was very partial to John West's tinned salmon, something that was not easy to get at that time, as the shops had not quite got back to normal even though the war had been over for nearly a decade. Word quickly got around, so that every house I went for tea at I found (guess what?) in the sandwiches – John West's tinned salmon! Some of my hosts even left the empty tin in sight so that I could see I was eating the real thing.

I thought the trial week went well. I felt quite comfortable in a mining community, having come from that background myself. I was familiar with the miners' lifestyle and the way they thought and talked. When I told the congregation that I had worked in the mines myself for two years, the door of acceptance seemed to open a little more.

Towards the end of the week, Bert Hobson asked me what I thought of the people. I told him that I believed the congregation had much potential. Many of the members were young men and women with families, but few of them appeared to be active in the work of the church. To me they appeared to be like sheep without a shepherd. I knew that one of my first tasks, if the Lord opened the door for me to be their pastor, would be to harness their tremendous potential for active service in the cause of Jesus Christ.

I have always believed that no one should be unemployed in our Lord's service. Everyone has at least one gift, and part of the art of shepherding is to help people discover that gift (or gifts) and put them to work for the Master.

As I said farewell to return to Wales on the following Saturday, Bert told me that there seemed to be great enthusiasm among the congregation for me to become their pastor. This was confirmed after I had been home for a week, when I got an official letter from Bert saying the vote had been taken and the church looked forward to me accepting the position at the earliest opportunity.

Now began the difficult task of telling the congregations in Pontardulais and Llandeilo that I was moving on. I felt it fair to give them three months' notice and to do my best to help them find a successor. I had to withdraw from a number of committees, but I found that my ministerial colleagues readily accepted that as I was moving to take charge of another church.

One of the biggest concerns I had in leaving Pontardulais was more for my wife, Enid, than for myself. We were giving up a beautiful and fairly new bungalow in a cul-de-sac for a terraced house on a main road in a rather grim and grimy area of South Kirkby. Enid was a good homemaker and although I think she had a sense of loss at moving, she said she looked forward to the task, however difficult it would be, of turning our new place into a home.

The South Kirkby church paid for our removal costs and while the removal van made its way up north, Enid, David and I (and our dog, a Chow called Prince) went by train. We made the move early in the week so that we would have plenty of time to get ready for the induction service due to take place on the following Saturday.

Whenever a new Assemblies of God pastor is inducted, it is usual for nearby churches belonging to the Fellowship to give their support. On this occasion people came from South and West Yorkshire, including Royston, Barnsley, Wakefield and Doncaster. It was a memorable evening, with a packed church, a powerful induction sermon delivered by the minister from Royston and, of course, welcome speeches from several members of the South Kirkby congregation.

The following day, Sunday, I began the task of leading my new congregation. It was rather strange at first listening to the people singing old and familiar hymns such as 'Blessed assurance, Jesus is mine' with a Yorkshire accent. I told the congregation about this sense of strangeness, adding that everyone seemed to have an accent except my wife and myself! My son, David, was just three years old at this time and was an extremely 'taking' child in the sense that people were easily drawn to him. At the end of the services people made a beeline for him, and he was showered with sweets and little gifts every time he attended church.

After a few weeks, I was invited to preach at an anniversary service in a church in Hull, which meant that I had to arrange for someone to preach in my place at South Kirkby. That Sunday one of the members asked David, 'Where is your father preaching today?' 'I think he is preaching in hell,' said my little boy. You can imagine how that story was told in many homes and on the street during the following week!

A sad event happened shortly after I became pastor at South Kirkby which caused me a good deal of heart-searching and considerable personal pain. One dark winter night an unkempt and distressed man came into the church just as I was about to leave and asked if he could have a few words with me. He told me about an emotional problem he had which, as I listened to him, I realised was quite beyond me. I remembered what I had been told at Bible college. If someone has a physical problem, encourage them to go to a doctor. If they have an emotional problem get them to see a psychiatrist. If they have a spiritual problem then that is where you can intervene. Anything else you are not equipped to deal with.

I suggested that he saw a local doctor the following morning so that he could be referred to a psychiatrist. I said a quick prayer with him and sent him on his way. The next morning I heard that he had committed suicide by throwing himself into the colliery reservoir. I fell on my knees in my study, overwhelmed with grief. I remember thinking to myself, 'Surely a pastor can help deal with people's emotional problems, given the right training? There must be some basic principles one can learn without having to go through years of psychiatric education.' It took me several weeks to get over the shock and I kept going over in my mind what I could have said to him if only I knew more about how emotional problems arise. Eventually I consoled myself with the fact that good would come out of that bad situation, because it made me determined that, at the right time, I would pursue every means possible to acquaint myself with how problems arise in the personality and what could be done to correct them.

'Evolution is better than revolution' was one of the helpful things I had been told at Bible college in relation to taking up a new pastorate. Make changes quietly, we were advised. Don't be radical unless it is absolutely necessary. I began to form a strategy within weeks of arriving. It was built on prayer and evangelism. It had soon become clear to me that apart from the evangelism conducted through the Sunday school and the regular Sunday night services, the church lacked a vigorous policy of reaching out to the community to seek to win the lost to Christ.

I decided that before I began to emphasise and encourage this kind of evangelistic outreach, I first needed to lay down a strong foundation of prayer. It was not that the church did not pray, but that its prayers were not focused enough on the unconverted. I began to concentrate my midweek studies around the subject and occasionally preached on it on Sundays.

It soon became obvious that my emphasis on prayer was touching people's hearts. More and more of them came to the prayer meetings. I quoted the words of John Wesley who said that 'God does nothing redemptively except through prayer.' I organised extra prayer meetings, sometimes half-nights of prayer. After a few months of this emphasis I switched to the issue of evangelism. I encouraged people to pray for their unconverted neighbours. I invited those who were still in school to pray for a friend by name every time the bell rang for lessons. I called it 'the bell prayer'. I preached and conducted Bible studies on evangelism until I sensed that people were becoming more and more conscious of the need to win people to Jesus Christ.

I have always believed in the power of the pulpit. It has been said that the low level of Christian living and practice stems from the low level of Christian preaching. My Bible college principal, John Wallace, used to say, 'If the congregation goes to sleep it's time to wake the preacher up.' I preached my heart out on prayer and evangelism and one Sunday morning I preached on the parable of the Prodigal Son. It obviously hit home, for people kept coming up to me the following week telling me how much they had been stirred into reaching out to the community. I took the text from Luke 15:17 in the King James Version, which reads: 'There is bread enough in my father's house and to spare.' I made the point that the thing that drew the prodigal back to the father's house was not that he knew he would be welcomed back by the whole family (of that he was not quite sure), but he knew for a fact that there was enough bread in his father's house *and to spare*.

I challenged the congregation: 'When poor, famished prodigals look to this church, do they see us as a bunch of smug, self-satisfied Christians whose main purpose in life is to come to church to enjoy ourselves? Or do they see that what we have is more than enough for us, and we long to give it away? In other words, do we have enough to spare? What are we doing to show people that we care for their soul's salvation? Are we knocking at their doors telling them about Christ's love? Are we doing everything we can to let them know about the Good News?'

After months of emphasising prayer and evangelism it was clear that the spiritual tide was rising. The sowing of the seed had been done, but when would the harvest come? I did not have to wait long before the answer came.

CHAPTER 15

BREAKTHROUGH IN EVANGELISM

Many people have been key influences in my life, but the man who inspired me most to reach out and win people to Jesus Christ was John Nelson Parr of Bethshan Tabernacle, Stockport. He was known in the Assemblies of God fellowship as 'Mr Evangelism' because of his constant emphasis on what he called 'soul-winning'. Evangelism, he used to say, is one beggar telling another where to find bread. His church was a fine testimony to his own evangelistic efforts, for in the 1950s it was the largest Assemblies of God church in the United Kingdom. Every week dozens of people would find Christ through his powerful and passionate preaching.

I met with him on several occasions at his church and every time a red-hot coal from his own heart would become lodged in mine. His great passion was to win young people to Christ. This didn't mean he had no interest in winning older people to the Saviour, but as he used to put it, 'the older a person gets the more stubborn they get in their ways. Reach out as much as you can to the young; your spiritual investment will bring a much quicker and greater return.'

So I decided that the first wave of evangelism I would lead the South Kirkby church into would be focused on reaching children and young people for Jesus Christ. I duly planned a week of special children's meetings, and had an attractive leaflet produced which simply said, 'For children only. Adults not admitted.

Every night this week in Carmel, Assemblies of God Church, Mill Lane, South Kirkby, 6pm – 7:30 pm. Games! Prizes! Fun!'

The mission team visited local schools to hand out these leaflets as the children were going home. I would play some popular tunes on the accordion and, as they gathered round to listen, they were handed invitations and encouraged to come early to get a seat.

The result was that on the first night the hall was packed with excited youngsters. This was repeated every night throughout the week. I had got a carpenter to make a steam engine out of hardboard. Brightly painted, it was called The Gospel Express. A child was chosen to sit on the seat in the engine and blow the whistle. With my accordion, I taught the children a chorus:

Join the Gospel Express! Come along, answer 'Yes'
We're leaving for glory soon.
And the guard is so glad he is waving the flag;
Hallelujah, it won't be very long.
Toot, toot, toot goes the whistle;
Chuff, chuff, chuff goes the train;
Chug, chug, chug goes the engine;
And we're off on the glory train!

They loved it! We would sing the chorus at least a dozen times, each time with a different child sitting in the driver's seat and operating the whistle. Several children would be invited on to the platform, one to act as guard and the others as passengers.

The meetings were fast-moving, with quizzes and group activities. Somewhere in the programme I would give a ten-minute clear gospel presentation. The strategy behind these meetings was to encourage children to attend the regular Sunday school at Carmel. This certainly boosted the numbers who came to Sunday school, but some of them dropped off when they discovered that it was not as fast-moving and dramatic as the special meetings had been. The number of those who stayed, however, certainly justified the effort.

The success of that special week led me do something similar in some of the surrounding villages – a visit to the schools, a few nights of children's meetings and the establishing of a new branch Sunday school. Soon we were running several branch Sunday schools which served two main purposes: to tell children the truths of the gospel and to provide an avenue of Christian service for those 'unemployed' in the church who were gifted to work with children.

Once the branch Sunday schools were operating, my second wave of evangelism was directed at teenagers. Near my home was an industrial estate where hundreds of teenage girls were employed. One day I went along to talk to the managers of the factories and to ask them for permission to talk to the girls for a few minutes in the canteens during their lunch break. Only one of the five managers gave me permission, but it was the largest of the factories, with about 200 workers.

At that time there was a radio programme called *Workers' Playtime*, which was a half-hour sing-along with jokes and other things. The manager allowed me just 15 minutes, so I called my programme 'Workers' Playtime – Abbreviated'. On the first day the manager introduced me as a pastor from one of the local churches who had come to lead a sing-along.

I began by playing some popular tunes on my accordion and invited them to sing along with me. They did so enthusiastically. I had a simple formula for the meetings: seven or eight minutes' sing-along, a three-minute talk on something topical which I related to the gospel, and five minutes teaching them one of the choruses we sang in church.

The first chorus I taught them was 'Give me oil in my lamp, keep me burning'. Because of its fast catchy tune it soon caught on. I'm not sure the words meant much to them, but whenever I asked them in subsequent weeks what they would like to sing they invariably chose that one. Soon they knew enough choruses to allow me to abandon the popular worldly songs.

Several weeks after I began the factory visits the church arranged a few weeks of meetings with Norman Humphreys, an evangelist from Houghton-le-Spring, Durham. With him came a small team consisting of a brilliant young accordionist and an appealing gospel singer. I took the opportunity during their visit to arrange a daily lunch-time open-air meeting for the factory girls. This meant we could invite girls from the other factories to come and hear something of what we had been doing in my weekly visits to the canteen of the only factory which had given me permission. Then I invited them to come along to Mill Lane on the following Sunday.

I was delighted, and astonished, on the Sunday, when I saw a crowd of girls from the factories in the church. By the end of the service many of them had given their hearts and lives to Jesus Christ. That night there was not only great rejoicing in heaven over sinners repenting, but great rejoicing amongst the members of our church, too.

Night after night we continued the special evangelistic services and every night people found Christ. It was one of the most intense and powerful evangelistic efforts I had been involved in up to that moment. Once the mission was over the work of discipling had to begin. If ever I was grateful for my Bible college training it was then. It had prepared me to understand and handle the needs of new Christians, so week by week I taught them the basics of the Christian life, such as establishing a daily quiet time, drawing from God's Word, the

Bible, how to pray, sharing Christ with others, financial support of the church, water baptism, baptism of the Spirit. I have no hesitation in saying that discipling those who came to Christ while I was at South Kirkby were some of the happiest days of my life.

The attendance of so many young girls had a spin-off: many young men soon started coming to the church as well. While some were motivated to come for reasons other than spiritual, several experienced genuine conversions. For months I was caught up in an endless round of teaching, discipling, preparing the young Christians for water baptism, helping them discover their basic spiritual gifts and encouraging them to move into the roles that God had for them in His church.

I quickly learned that young people needed to have plenty of organised activity. So we arranged regular visits to the swimming baths, rambles and our own sports events. We even bought a bus for their use. On Sundays it picked up members living in outlying areas where there were no bus services that day.

The church deacons, Bert Hobson, Emlyn Williams and Harold Griffiths, were fully supportive of everything I wanted to do. Their encouragement and involvement meant a great deal to me, perhaps more than they will ever know. As the church was prospering and income was increasing, they suggested that I moved to a better part of the village. We quickly found a house that was everything Enid and I desired. As soon as we had settled in they suggested that the increased workload meant that I also needed a car. They gave me some money to help me buy one – the first I had owned.

It was in South Kirkby, too, that I conducted my first wedding. I remember thinking at the time it was strange that, having been in the ministry for close on five years, I had never before been asked to officiate at a wedding. With so many young men and women in the church becoming courting couples, I finished up conducting about ten weddings.

The influx of young people into the church meant that the meetings became more lively, the singing more enthusiastic. Because of this change of atmosphere, I felt it appropriate to invite a long-standing member of the church, Ron Lloyd, to bring his drums to church. The regular and excellent pianist for the church was his sister, Peggy Stocks, and they made a wonderful duo to accompany the new energy that was flowing through the congregation. I used to marvel sometimes as I watched Ron play, as I knew that if I had suggested six months previously that he bring his drums to church some of the church members would have walked out.

Not everything I did gained full acceptance with everyone in the congregation but generally speaking the older Christians demonstrated a willingness to adapt to the changing atmosphere of the church. When they did voice their concerns they were gentle, caring and loving. That deeply impressed me. One old lady spoke for several of the older folk when, with a smile, she said: 'I love to see so many young people in church, but they sing so fast that they have finished a song before I get to the middle lines!'

The whole period of my pastorate at South Kirkby is largely filled with happy and blessed memories. Longstanding members said they had never before experienced such blessing. At one of the church's anniversary services it was a special joy for me to welcome my old Bible college principal, John Wallace, as speaker. He was warm in his praise of the work that I had done in South Kirkby and let the people know that he was proud to have had, as he put it, 'a little hand in Selwyn's spiritual development as he prepared himself for the ministry'. He also told one or two stories about my pranks at Bible college, which came as a surprise to many as they could not imagine their staid and very respectable pastor getting up to such things.

Several other friends came to minister at the church. Derek Thomas, who shared with me the distinction of being expelled from Bonsall camp, was one. By this time Derek, too, had become an Assemblies of God minister, although he later left the movement and became a key figure in the Baptist churches. Then there was Clifford Rees, another AOG pastor, Griff George, a Welsh evangelist, Philip Jackson, a young preacher who went on to great fame in the USA and Eric Dando – all excellent preachers who through their ministry visits greatly contributed to the spiritual growth and development of the church.

In the middle of my time at South Kirkby several young families who were members decided to emigrate to Perth, Australia. It is always a sad moment when, for whatever reason, one family leaves a church, but even more so when several families who are active in the congregation leave together. Yet there was gladness for the new life opening up for them. When these families were settled in Australia and wrote back to their friends in the church telling how they were enjoying their new life, several more families followed suit. It was a particular joy to me 40 years later to meet them again when I visited Perth. By this time the families had grown in size, with children and even grandchildren.

Although I was now pastor of a sizeable congregation, I did not let up on my emphasis on evangelism. We constantly organised outreaches not only in our church, but also in the villages around. We showed evangelistic films, organised special suppers and children's activities.

Some people felt I was putting too much pressure on the congregation, but all their arguments would fall flat when someone got up to testify that had it not been for one of these evangelistic events they would have gone to a lost eternity.

South Kirkby was the place where my son, David, started school. The school was quite a distance from our home and I had to drive him there and back. But on the first day he was due to go there my car would not start, so I borrowed the church bus. I did that for several days until my car was repaired. David was the envy of his classmates when they saw him being delivered to the doors of the school in his own private bus! During the time my car was out of action I also used the bus to visit people, and the local newspaper got to hear of it. They took a picture of me and published it with a report of the pastor who visited his congregation in a bus. It made a good story and some free publicity for the church.

As an AOG minister I attended the regular meetings of the Yorkshire District Council of the Assemblies of God, where matters relating to all the churches in the South Yorkshire area were discussed. Everyone had heard what God had been doing at South Kirkby and I was often asked to address the group on evangelism. Because of my strong emphasis on this subject, I was given the task of directing new evangelistic outreaches in the area, which included looking at the possibility of starting new AOG churches.

After I had been at South Kirkby for four years I began to feel a little restless in my spirit. I felt I needed something bigger to go at. I shared a little bit of what I was feeling with fellow ministers of the Yorkshire District Council. In one of my talks on evangelism, I said, 'What if every one of us gave up our churches and went out and started another one? What sort of difference do you think that would make in our county?' After the meeting one of the ministers came up to me and said, 'I think what you said was very challenging, but it would have greater weight if you set the example, if you gave up your church and went out and started another one.'

I left the meeting feeling that the tables had been turned on me. I had set out to challenge the ministers, but now I had been challenged myself. I spent the next few days in prayer and fasting and came before the Lord with one question in my mind: Shall I give up my church and go out and start another one? And if so, where?

Little did I know that the decisions I would make in the next few weeks would lead me into one of the most traumatic times of my life.

CHAPTER 16

STORM OVER SHEFFIELD

My challenge to the ministers of the Yorkshire District Council of the Assemblies of God, to give up their churches and go out and start another one, reached the ears of a group of disgruntled young people in a small AOG church in the heart of the city of Sheffield.

Ken Harris, a representative from this group, and his wife, Joan, visited me at South Kirkby to tell me they were getting ready to move out of their church. They made it clear that if I was serious about giving up my church to open a new one and decided to come to Sheffield, they would give me their full support. There were about ten of them ready to do this, Ken said, emphasising that whether I came to Sheffield or not they would not be able to stay much longer in the church they attended. He listed many reasons why he and others felt that way.

Had I been wiser and more experienced, I would have seen the danger signals right there at the start. If someone came to me today and asked for my advice in a similar situation, I would tell them that to start a new church by dividing another one would require careful and prayerful thought; and unless there were clear and biblically justifiable circumstances it ought not to be done. But I was young – just coming up to 30 years of age, on the crest of a successful spiritual wave and, to put it bluntly, headstrong, arrogant, and over-confident.

Over the following few weeks Ken and I looked for a venue

to start the new church. We discovered that the Memorial Hall, attached to the Sheffield City Hall, and seating several hundred people, could be booked for regular Sunday meetings. We made a tentative booking for a period beginning several weeks ahead which meant it was pencilled in until confirmed by a deposit and at that point written in ink. At that stage we had not paid any money and we could cancel without incurring any financial penalty. I duly informed the deacons of my church in South Kirkby that I was planning at some point to move to Sheffield, and that in due course I would be offering my resignation.

News of my plans to go ahead and open up a new church in Sheffield reached the ears of the members of the Yorkshire District AOG Council, so at the next meeting I was questioned about my intentions. It was pointed out to me that two things concerned the council members. One was that I was intending to open up a new church within half-a-mile of an existing Assembly of God – in violation of the movement's official guidelines. The second problem was that I was planning to do this with the support of some of the existing church's present members.

At that time I was not fully committed to the idea of conducting evangelistic meetings in the Memorial Hall (there was still the issue of raising funds to pay for its use in advance), so when it came to answering questions I prevaricated until the chairman asked, 'Selwyn, you can dispel any doubt by simply answering "Yes" or "No" to this question: have you booked a hall in the centre of the city for this purpose?' I thought for a moment and, as I knew the booking to be a tentative one and there was still a little uncertainty whether I would go ahead, I answered in the negative.

That resolved matters for the moment. But before the next council meeting someone from the Copper Street Assembly of God telephoned the Memorial Hall to see if a booking had been made in my name. 'Yes,' was the reply, so this was quickly reported to the council, who summoned me to meet with them once again. I have never been able to ascertain if whoever answered that call to the Memorial Hall explained that it was a tentative booking and was still awaiting confirmation.

At the next council meeting it was put to me that I had not been open with the members. I was told that that the answer to the direct question put to me by the chairman about whether I had booked the hall or not should have been 'Yes', not 'No'. I explained that the reason I had said 'No' was because I knew it to be a tentative booking and not a confirmed one. I was still uncertain about going ahead with it and therefore I did not regard it as a definite booking.

I was then asked to leave the room so that the members of the council could discuss the situation without me being present. Later I was told I was suspended from attending all council meetings for three months because members felt that my statement had misled them. I felt very angry that my explanation had not been given the consideration it deserved and wrote along that line to a special Appeals Committee of the Fellowship set up to deal with complaints of this sort.

It usually took the Appeals Committee a month or two to arrange a date for such hearings, so I decided to go ahead with opening a new church in Sheffield, believing that my appeal would be upheld. I arranged to buy a newly-built house in the city and set a date for the beginning of regular Sunday meetings in the Memorial Hall.

The members of the South Kirkby church were all aware of my intentions to open up a new church in Sheffield well before I tendered my resignation. The District Council's suspension of me, however, created some confusion in the congregation. Some thought I was unwise to go against the wishes of the council, while others made it clear they fully supported me. The result of all this was that my farewell meeting at South Kirkby, though fairly pleasant, had a cloud of misunderstanding and confusion hanging over it. It was a sad ending to what had been a very happy and successful period of ministry.

We began regular meetings in the Sheffield Memorial Hall in May 1958. With me were the group of young people who by this time had left the church they had been attending. They threw themselves enthusiastically into distributing leaflets through the doors of hundreds of homes in the city centre. Ken Harris, a brilliant violinist, and Joan, his wife, an accomplished pianist, provided the music for the services, while I led the meetings and preached. Invaluable help came from Brenda Parsley, who handled the administration and, with her varied talents, kept things on track. People came to Christ almost every Sunday. During the week we met in various homes throughout the city and it was there, with the help of the team working with me, that the discipling was done.

Eventually, after a few months, the Appeals Committee of the Assemblies of God to whom I had referred the matter, wrote to tell me that they had upheld the decision of the Yorkshire AOG District Council. It was made clear to me that if I did not close down the Memorial Hall meetings within the next three months I would be dis-fellowshiped and my ministerial credentials taken away.

As the meetings were going so well and numbers increasing, albeit slowly, the thought of closing down what appeared to be a very successful venture was more than I could take. I felt the only solution was to resign from the Assemblies of God and continue my ministry independently of the movement.

After a few weeks of heart-searching I decided to offer my resignation, which the Executive Committee of the Assemblies of

God accepted. I continued ministering weekly in the Memorial Hall, but though God's blessing was evident in the conversion of people, there was one great difficulty: the cost of renting the Memorial Hall was so high that the weekly offerings left little over to pay for the upkeep of my family. Not long after we moved to Sheffield, Enid had given birth to our second son, John, and this meant that I had to take a job for three days of the week with the Refuge Assurance Company. This helped me financially, but it divided my attention and I worked under considerable mental and emotional strain.

The stress eventually led to a physical breakdown that took me almost to death's door. I was stricken with a strange illness, which, at first, my doctors were unable to diagnose, but which led to double pneumonia. The doctor kept coming to my house every day and, according to Enid, looked graver every time he left. Months later a medical friend of mine told me that he thought the stress I had been under had played havoc with my immune system, leaving me extremely vulnerable to all kinds of illness.

At one point my temperature began to soar. Drugs to combat double pneumonia were not available as they are today and the doctor, who was a very open and honest character, told Enid that if he couldn't get my temperature down in the next three days there was little hope that I would survive. Understandably, Enid panicked when she heard this and came into the bedroom with tears running down her face, saying that the doctor said I had only three days to live.

After hearing the news that I was at death's door, I tried to put my thoughts into some kind of order. What will happen to my wife and two children? Why should God permit me to depart this life when my ministry was just beginning? Must I resign myself to this situation and accept it as the will of God? I had always believed that people should die well. But how could I die well when so many of the things I planned to do for the Lord were unaccomplished?

In search of comfort, I reached for the Bible at my bedside. I tried to turn to John 14, that well-known chapter of comfort that pastors read to people in time of trouble, but for some reason the pages seemed stuck at chapter 10. Too weak to separate them, I began to read from the first verse of chapter 10. When I reached verse 10 something amazing happened. I read: 'The thief comes only to steal and kill and destroy; I have come that they may have life, and have it to the full.' As my eyes took in the words and registered in my brain, it felt as if an explosion took place in my mind. A wave of supernatural power spread from my head to the soles of my feet and I realised that I was being divinely healed.

I had not had much experience of healing until that time. I had always believed that God heals today, but my theology of the subject was somewhat vague and fuzzy. Yet here I was experiencing the miraculous healing power directly from God that I had read about and heard others testify to. It was as if thousands of volts of electricity were thundering through my body. I seemed to be flooded with divine power. The impact was staggering. In a blinding flash of divine revelation I saw that it was not my time to leave this earth and that though the devil would delight in robbing me, and God, of my service for Him in the future, the Lord had seen to it that this would not happen.

One thought that seemed to flash in my mind for a few minutes, like a neon sign going on and off, was that Satan was being outwitted and God, in His mercy, had come to my aid. From being too exhausted to hardly lift a cup to my lips, I felt new strength surging into my being. I shouted for my wife to come upstairs and when she saw the great change in me she said: 'What happened?' When I told her I had been miraculously healed she burst into tears. Then together we got down on our knees and thanked the Lord for what He had done.

Later we phoned our many friends who had been praying for us and within an hour or two a dozen or so friends crowded into our home to see with their own eyes the miracle God had done. For several hours we prayed, worshipped the Lord and sang hymns and choruses of praise. The joy that filled our home that night was something I had never quite known before, or for that matter since.

What I didn't know until then was that my younger son, John, was ill and receiving medical treatment also. Enid had not wanted to burden me with this situation, but when she did tell me we went into his room, laid hands on him and asked the Lord to heal him. Within an hour he had improved dramatically and needed no further medical treatment.

When the doctor came the next day for his usual 11am visit, he was amazed to see me dressed and sitting with Enid drinking a cup of tea. He seemed taken aback and asked, 'What has happened?' I said, 'Sit down with us, doctor, and I will explain. I don't know whether you believe in God and in God's intervention in human affairs, but last night I was the recipient of one of His miracles. I can't quite explain it because even though I have always believed and preached that God is able to work miracles today, I am not an expert on the subject. All I can say is that yesterday I was at death's door but today I feel my whole body throbbing with life.'

'This is quite staggering,' he said. 'I have seen many people go into remission with an illness, but nothing quite as dramatic as this. I am a God-fearing man, though I would not describe myself as a Christian, and all I can say is that I am very happy for you.' Then he gave me a thorough examination – blood pressure, body temperature, etc and declared: 'I can find nothing wrong with you.' But he couldn't help telling me to take it easy for a few days – 'just to avoid a relapse'.

He also examined John and pronounced him well, too. Enid watched him as he left the house and walked down the front garden path to his car shaking his head every step of the way.

The next week I was back leading the Sunday services in the Memorial Hall. I continued preaching there for a few months, until I came to the conclusion that in seeking to establish a new church in the centre of Sheffield I had been pursuing my own interests rather than God's. It was a very sobering time in my life but it was something I had to face. After talking things over with those who were close to me, we felt that the best thing to do was terminate the expensive contract with the Memorial Hall and encourage the people to join a church of their choice.

Surprisingly, no one seemed unduly upset by this decision. Although there was some sadness that we would not all continue to enjoy fellowship together, I took it as a sign of the Spirit's work in the people's hearts that the decision was the right one.

Now I had to face up to what I should be doing next. One option was to embark upon an itinerant ministry. I knew from the invitations I was receiving that there were a number of churches in the UK who would like me to hold crusades for them or preach at special services. Another option, and one that appealed to me enormously, was to take a secular job for a year or two and study counselling at the same time. Sheffield University ran such a course, so I went and talked to the tutor. I was in for a disappointment. 'Reverend Hughes,' he said, 'if you take this course it will be expected of you not to seek to impose your Christian beliefs on clients. The whole training will be geared to helping you help them come to their own conclusions about life rather than you telling them what to do. It is called non-directive counselling.'

I knew immediately that such a course was not for me. If

someone came to me for help and I knew they were violating one of God's commandments, then I would feel duty bound, at some point, to tell them so. I had known since the early days at South Kirkby, when I knelt and asked God to make me a counsellor, that there would come a time when I would come to grips with this issue, but it was clear this was neither the place nor the time.

After closing down the meetings at the Memorial Hall I spent several weeks prayerfully considering my future. I was aware that what I had gone through in the past year had changed me considerably. I was less arrogant, less self-willed and less self-centred. The circumstances had softened me a lot. As I prayed, I heard the Lord in a new way and His voice seemed to take the sword out of my hand. I didn't want to fight people any more. I would leave the fighting to Him. I think I was beginning to learn the lessons He had wanted to teach me, especially to be less self-reliant and more reliant on the Holy Spirit.

I think I shall always remember this difficult and black period with a kind of joy that I could not have believed possible. For during that time I learned invaluable things that have made me a better person. I knew there would be other lessons I would need to learn up ahead, but for now I had learned that life is all about letting go – letting go of those things that hinder the Spirit's work and laying hold of Christ's empowerment. I had learned how to let go of self-dependency, how to let go of children, how to let go of friends and neighbours, how to let go of the single life, how to let go of the work and efforts of one's hands, how to let go of churches.

And, some day, I would learn how to let go of life itself.

CHAPTER 17

A NEW FIELD OF SERVICE

fter closing down the new church in Sheffield, Enid and
I continued living in the city for a while and I became
an itinerant evangelist. Over the years I had received a
number of invitations from different churches, denominational
and otherwise, to speak at events such as anniversary services,
missions and youth rallies, but my pastoral responsibilities had
prevented me from accepting all but a few of them. I wrote to
these churches to let them know I was now free to respond to
such invitations and it was not long before my diary was filled
with engagements up to a year ahead.

As I went to different churches I testified, of course, about my
miraculous healing. If I was spending several days at a church I
was often asked to spend one evening on a biblical exposition of
healing and then to pray for the sick. This meant that I had to
study the subject of healing in depth.

I began to feel a compassion for sick people I had never known
before. I had always felt some sympathy for sick people, of course,
but not compassion in the true sense of the word. I found that the
word 'compassion' literally means to suffer with. It is not feeling
a detached pity, but a sharing of the pain. It is difficult to explain,
but I woke up in a new way to the silent thundering of pain
around me. I wanted to draw the sick and suffering into my own
heart and help them experience a real act of healing.

It almost became a compulsion to pray for anyone I saw who

was sick. I just wanted to be the vessel through whom the abundant life that had poured into my own sick body as I lay dying could come to them. It was not long before all my crusades turned into 'healing crusades' in the sense that every night I would pray for the sick. I witnessed some amazing things take place. Of course I struggled, as all healing evangelists do, over the question of why some are healed and others are not. But I came to realise that it was not my responsibility, although in later years I would always end a healing service with words of encouragement for those who had not been healed and give some reasons why, after prayer, healing might not be evident.

I told sufferers to always be open to the fact that God delights to heal and that it is part of His commission to the church (Mark 16:18); but at the same time to remember that when, for some unknown reason, healing does not come, God always gives sufficient grace to deal with everything we have to face.

I would never say to those who were not healed, 'You do not have enough faith.' That can be very discouraging, even damaging, to someone in the throes of some serious illness. Although there might be some truth in the statement, it is rarely appropriate to say it. My views of healing have not changed over the years, but there did come a time, which I will tell you about later, when I began to focus more on inner healing than physical healing, a switch which, surprisingly, resulted in more physical healings rather than fewer.

In 1959 I was at an evangelists' conference in Essex when I came across Vic Ramsey, whom I had met just briefly when I was a pastor in South Kirkby. He was a full-time evangelist with a group of churches in East Anglia functioning under the name Elim Pentecostal Churches. At that time they were a separate group from the well-known and larger Elim movement started by George Jeffreys, although in later years the two fellowships merged. Vic introduced me to the superintendent minister of the Elim Pentecostal Churches, George Stormont, who invited me to spend a few days with him in his home in Rayleigh, near Southend. The outcome was that he invited me to join the fellowship and put before me a very attractive proposition.

'We have a fine church in Colchester which needs a minister,' he said. 'If you were to take over the church and minister there on Sundays, we could arrange for you to use your evangelistic gifts by conducting crusades in our other churches in East Anglia.' That was a proposal that appealed to me immensely and, after Enid and I had discussed it, we felt led to accept. So in the summer of 1959 we moved from Sheffield to the manse belonging to the church in Colchester.

I loved Colchester immensely. I was fascinated with its long history, the cleanliness of its streets and friendliness of the people. Before my induction, which took place on a Saturday, I was told by George Stormont, the superintendent minister of the Elim Pentecostal Churches, that I would be expected to wear a clerical collar. He said it would make things easier for me in situations such as hospital visiting and school assemblies. Clerical collars were frowned upon in the Assemblies of God, although there were instances of some of the young ministers wearing them for special occasions such as marriages and funerals. I duly bought one and wore it for my induction service.

When I got back home I took the collar off and tossed it on the sofa. Upon getting up the following morning I found that the new puppy my mother had recently given our two children had played with it and it had teeth marks all over it. It was impossible to wear and so when I turned up at church the following day I felt it necessary to explain why I was not wearing my clerical collar. I told them the story of what had happened, whereupon the whole congregation burst into laughter for several minutes and I had great difficulty in bringing the meeting back on track again. After the service, as I shook hands at the door, the jokes came thick and fast. 'The dog probably thought that as it was a dog collar it had a right to try it on,' was one. 'I was under the impression ministers loved their dog collars so much they wore them to bed,' cracked someone else. 'You didn't look like a proper minister this morning,' quipped another. Within a few days I purchased another clerical collar and became a 'proper' minister again.

George Stormont's remark about the usefulness of a clerical collar was correct, not only when it came to visiting people in hospitals, but even in shops and offices. I was queuing in a bank when one of the managers walked over to me and said, 'Sir, if you would like to come to my desk I would be glad to deal with whatever business you have with us today.' Wearing a collar was, in a sense, a double-edged sword. As it revealed that I was a representative of Jesus Christ I needed to be on my best behaviour at all times – especially when driving!

Soon after moving to Colchester something happened that caused me a good deal of personal embarrassment. I had gone into the town centre on some errands and, being unfamiliar with the layout of the town, I parked the church minibus I was driving at the time near the bus station. There were no parking restriction signs so I felt comfortable in leaving the vehicle there to go and do what was needed. Later, as I made my way back to it, I saw that the traffic was at a standstill – something unusual because at that time traffic flowed freely through the streets of Colchester. I wondered what was the cause, but as I neared the bus station I noticed two policemen standing by my minibus.

As I approached one of them said, 'Is this your vehicle, Sir?' When I said it was, he told me, 'Well, you can see what has happened. Though your vehicle is not in a restricted zone, you have parked it in such a way that the buses have not been able to make the wide turn necessary for them to get into the bus station. If you had parked it a yard farther on there would have been no trouble. I can see you are a man of the cloth, but I am afraid I will have to report you for this, as it has caused great havoc in the town over the past 15 minutes.'

I apologised and explained that I was new to the town, but this did not prevent me from being called before magistrates a few weeks later and fined. One of the magistrates said, 'We are going to be lenient with you because you are new to the town, but we must give you a fine to reflect the seriousness of the situation. You brought the town to a standstill.' I was fined £30. Back in the late 1950s that was quite a lot of money. Fortunately, a kind member of the church paid it for me. After that I made sure that whenever I went into town I parked well away from the bus station!

Looking for a story, a newspaper reporter from the *Colchester Express* came to see me the day after my court case to try to get my view of how I had been dealt with at the magistrates' court. When he arrived he found a fire engine outside our house. It was a fairly cold day and I had decided to light a fire in the front room. As soon as I did so the chimney caught fire and soon flames and clouds of smoke were leaping up in the air. When it had been dealt with, and the reporter had got his story about my holding up the traffic in town, his comment was, 'One way and another you certainly have let everyone know of your arrival!' Both incidents were reported in the *Colchester Express*.

Some time later, the editor of the *Colchester Express* called me one day and invited me in to his office for a chat. After I had sat down he said, 'You have only been here a few weeks and your name is known all over town. I wondered if you would like to cash in on your notoriety and write something for our paper now and again?' I asked for time to reflect on this and later went back to him with the idea of the 'One-Minute Sermon'. He was extremely pleased about this and began to carry it each week. Although I did not get any money for it, the fact that every week I was obliged to sit down and write, in a clear and condensed way, something meaningful and arresting that could be read in just a minute, was good preparation for a writing project I would begin a few years later.

My ministry in the church at Colchester, although it was only for about 18 months, was a very productive and happy time. There were about 80 members of the church, but sometimes on a Sunday night, the traditional evangelistic service, numbers would rise to 120 and often more.

The deacons were rather like the ones in the church at South Kirkby – men who were cooperative, had a real heart for God and who were ready to support new ideas and initiatives in proclaiming the gospel. The church was close to the town centre but in wintertime the street was dark and dismal. So one of my first suggestions to improve the appearance of the church was to have it floodlit and a neon sign put on the front of it saying: 'Elim Church – Welcome' and 'Christ is the Answer'. It not only brightened the appearance of the church considerably, but also again attracted the attention of the editor of the *Colchester Express*, who ran a feature on it.

Gradually more and more people began to come to the church. There was already a fine group of committed young people, including nurses, students and professional young men and women, so on Sunday nights I started an after-church meeting, specifically for this age group, which ran through the winter months with great success. With the introduction in this special youth service of drums and a small orchestra (including my piano accordion), it attracted people who ordinarily would not darken the doors of a church.

An idea I had soon after I arrived in Colchester proved to be a most effective evangelistic project. Looking through a diary one day, I noticed something I had not given much attention to before – Hospital Sunday. Enquiries revealed that this was not celebrated in Colchester, so I discussed with some of the nurses who attended the church the idea of having a special service to celebrate the work done by the medical profession and the hospitals in our town. They liked the idea and agreed to discuss it with other Christian nurses in the hospitals where they worked and who attended other churches in the town.

Their colleagues were very enthusiastic, so I went to see the Mayor, knowing that gaining his support would help me draw others to it. He greeted me warmly and immediately wrote the date in his diary, saying he would be there and would be willing to say a few words of gratitude to all those involved in the care of the sick and suffering in Colchester.

Then I visited all the hospitals in the area and informed the matrons that, with the approval of the Mayor, a special service of thanksgiving would be held in the Elim Church on Hospital Sunday and we would like them to be represented. Put that way, they could hardly refuse. Once I had their agreement I sent invitations to others involved in medical care, such as doctors and the St John Ambulance Brigade. The result was that the church was packed with 300 to 400 people for this service, the largest congregation since its opening. The service was held on a Sunday evening and was fairly formal, with various speeches and prayers being read out, but my sermon had a strong evangelistic content. Towards the end of the message I paid my own tribute to all those present who worked in the medical field. 'As a Christian,' I said, 'I find it comforting to realise that when the weight of human wickedness was placed on the back of the world's Redeemer, there were those who took the time to be kind to Him. And I find it comforting, too, that we have people spread throughout our town, in hospitals, medical centres and so on, who are ready to give their lives to ministering to those who find themselves sick, infirm or in deep physical need. In Christ's name I thank you for that.'

It did not seem appropriate to make a strong evangelistic invitation that night as I normally did in evangelistic services, but I did encourage those who had never received Christ to open their lives to the Saviour and inivte Him into their hearts.

I then suggested to those who prayed that prayer with me that it would be helpful to tell someone they knew to be a Christian that they had done this. The expression, I pointed out, helps deepen the impression. Several of the nurses told me over the following weeks that a number of student nurses had told them that they had prayed that prayer on Hospital Sunday in the Elim Church and now regarded themselves as Christians. There is nothing in this world more satisfying than to know that one has contributed in some way to helping a person come to know Jesus Christ.

CHAPTER 18

BROADENING MY HORIZONS

During my time in Colchester, apart from the evangelistic efforts I conducted in the town, I led missions in other places in East Anglia and from time to time I joined my friend, Vic Ramsey, in his crusades, either sharing the preaching with him or leading the meetings. Vic and I lived and breathed evangelism, so whenever we got together we talked about what could we do to lead more people to Jesus Christ. I found myself growing closer to Vic every time we met and felt him to be a kindred spirit. Little did I know that in the future we would form an even closer partnership.

It was while I was a pastor in Colchester that I was asked by my sister, Pamela, and her fiancé, Carey Morse, to conduct their wedding in a little church in a small hamlet called Penybank, a few miles from Fochriw. My younger son, John, was a pageboy at the event and for the occasion I wore my clerical collar which caused considerable interest among members of the family who had not seen me dressed in that way before. It was somewhat strange conducting the wedding of my own sister but it was a happy and joyful occasion and went off well. Carey and Pamela went on to have two sons, Mark and Carl, and a few years after their wedding both they and my parents moved to the nearby small town of Pontlottyn to live in houses next to each other.

A group of young Christians drawn from different denominations in the Colchester area had banded together to conduct evangelistic services for young people. Their leader approached me one day and said the group wanted to take over a disused church and re-open it as a place where young people could meet for fellowship and evangelism. The church they referred to was once known as the Primitive Methodist Church where the great preacher, Charles Spurgeon, had been converted.

When the leader of the evangelistic group told me that it was their intention to open up the church in which Spurgeon had been converted and that they wanted me to preach on the opening night, I saw it as a wonderful occasion to preach on the same text that brought the young Spurgeon to Christ. So on the night I ascended the pulpit and preached from Isaiah 45:22: 'Look unto me, and be ye saved, all the ends of the earth: for I am God and there is none else' (KJV). There was just one conversion – a young man sitting under the plaque that marked the spot where Spurgeon was sitting when he looked by faith to Jesus Christ and lived!

Another special venture in which I was involved while at Colchester was the purchase of the Christian Literature Crusade bookshop. CLC was finding it difficult to keep the shop going because of the small profits it was making and they had decided to sell it. As it was the only evangelical bookshop in Colchester, I felt sad that it should become defunct and drew together a small group of men who formed a company that bought the shop and turned it into a going concern. Called 'The Family Bookshop', it functioned for several years before it had to close down when the town centre was re-modelled.

But perhaps one of the most significant events that affected me personally while I was in Colchester took place during the summer of 1960. An American evangelist, Jack Martz, telephoned me to see if I would like his daughter, Renee, to preach in my church. Renee made a name for herself in the

United Kingdom in the early 1950s when, at the age of 7or 8, she was introduced as 'the child preacher'. I met Jack briefly at the time, and apparently my name had come up, in conversation he had had with a group of ministers in London, as someone who might like to sponsor Renee in a series of evangelistic meetings. Renee was now in her late teens and had become an appealing gospel singer as well as a powerful preacher. But it was not possible to arrange for her to come just at that time, because we were in the middle of a children's campaign with an evangelist from Bethshan Tabernacle, Manchester.

Jack, however, invited me to meet him and Renee in London, where she was holding a series of meetings in a hall near Victoria Station called Dennison House. The next day I drove up to London to spend the day with Jack, his wife Esther, Renee, and Ruby James, who had spent years travelling with the team as Renee's tutor. In the taxi that took us from the hotel to the meeting place, Jack, quite out of the blue said, 'Why don't you come to the United States for a time of ministry? I can arrange it for you. You'll find it will broaden your outlook, enlarge your experience and, who knows, you might find, as many Britishers have done before you, that a church will snap you up as their pastor.' I discovered later that Jack had introduced several British preachers to the USA who had gone on to pastor large and successful churches.

I was rather taken aback by Jack's suggestion, but I said I would ponder it and let him know. Later I talked it over with my wife, Enid. She was always ready to support me in anything that I felt I needed to do. Although there were times when she would say a cautionary word if it was necessary, her response was always, 'If that is what you feel the Lord wants you to do then go ahead and do it. I will support you in every way I can.' I telephoned Jack before he left London to fly home and told him

I would be open to the idea of undertaking a ministry trip to the USA some time and would leave it to him to suggest a date.

I forgot all about it until several weeks later, when I received a letter from an American pastor, Harold Groves, from Reading, Pennsylvania. He invited me to come to his church to hold a series of evangelistic meetings in January of the following year. Jack Martz, whom he respected enormously, had recommended me to him. Harold said he had no doubt that I could go on from his church to many others.

The invitation presented me with a huge problem. Should I resign from the Colchester church before going to America? What if a church over there asked me to become its pastor? Would it be fair to ask for three months' leave of absence and then come back and resign? After prayerful thought and discussion with Enid, I came to the conclusion that the fairest thing to do was to resign from the church before I left for the USA so that I could be free to make whatever decisions would be necessary.

Later Jack wrote to me to say that following the Reading meetings he had arranged for me to preach in a number of churches in Atlanta, Georgia, which was his home base. I decided on that basis to go to the USA for three months. I duly resigned from the church, found a flat for my wife and family and scheduled my visit to the States for early January 1961.

I preached my last sermon at the Elim Church in Colchester on Christmas Day 1960. The church accepted my resignation 'with regret', but everyone saw how helpful a visit to the USA could be to a minister, especially in terms of broadening one's experience and understanding the culture of our American 'cousins'.

As the days drew near for me to fly to New York, I became more and more concerned about what lay ahead of me. After ten years in the ministry there was a sense deep inside me that I was moving towards a horizon that I was not seeing clearly, that there was a destiny ahead of me I had not yet come to grips with. Would America be my destiny? I didn't quite know, but I was ready and eager to find out.

It was midday on New Year's Day 1961 when I boarded a flight at London's Heathrow airport for New York. I had never been in an aircraft before, and during a seven-hour flight I could hardly take my eyes off the panorama outside my window. We arrived in New York at 1pm, and after checking in at the YMCA hotel in Manhattan, I spent the next eight hours or so wandering around the centre of the city.

Next morning I boarded the train for Reading. When I stepped off at my destination I found Harold Groves, his wife and two daughters waiting for me. As we drove to their home he told me that the church had been considering an evangelistic crusade for some time, so when Jack Martz had telephoned him to say that I was planning to visit the USA he felt, as he put it, 'an immediate witness' that I should be the one to take the church into the New Year with a strong evangelistic outreach.

I had been scheduled to preach at eight days of meetings, but they were so successful that we continued for three weeks. I had heard much about American generosity over the years, but I was hardly prepared for the moment when, one evening, while I was shaking hands with people at the door of the church, a woman thrust a $100 dollar note into my hand – a good deal of money at that time. I told Harold about it and the next day he obligingly arranged to change it to an International Money Order so that I could post it home to Enid.

Harold enjoyed my preaching so much that he telephoned a friend in Winnipeg, Canada, Dr Philip Barber, the pastor of Calvary Temple, one of the largest churches in that country. Dr

Barber immediately booked me to come to his church a few weeks later, promising me that the church would cover the costs of my air travel to Winnipeg from wherever I was in the United States.

I left Reading and made my way to Atlanta, Georgia, where Jack Martz lived. It took almost two days to travel close on 700 miles by Greyhound coach, but it gave me an opportunity to see the country in a way I would never have done by flying. What jarred with me, however, as we got closer to Atlanta, was to see the evidence of the colour bar in the Deep South at that time. 'Coloured people' had to sit at the back of buses and white people at the front. Something in my spirit rebelled strongly against that.

Jack and his family were at the Atlanta bus station to greet me and take me to their lovely home on the outskirts of the city. Atlanta is one of the great cities of America and a focal point for the Deep South. People in Reading had talked a lot to me about southern hospitality, but when I arrived I found that only the half had been told. Jack and his family treated me like a king, not only taking me to the best restaurants, but also paying for a new made-to-measure suit, which was ready in just three days. 'You look a little dowdy in your British clothes,' said Jack. 'You don't have to turn into an American, but we do want you to look your best.'

Jack had arranged for my first preaching appointment in Atlanta to be at the Sunday morning service in the church pastored by Dr Tolbert Moore. It was a large Southern Baptist community in one of the suburbs. As soon as I met Dr Moore I knew I was meeting a kindred spirit. He warmly welcomed me to his church and as we sat together in his church office he said, 'I hear you are a fiery Welsh preacher. Well, don't be surprised when you start preaching that the more fiery you are the more fiery will be the response. Our people like to shout "Amen!" and "Hallelujah!" if a preacher gets going. I hope that won't put you off.' I assured him that coming from Wales, the land of revivals, I was well used to that.

I preached that morning from John 3:16, linking it with Ephesians 3:18, which talks about the length and breadth and depth and height of the love of Christ. At the end of the message Tolbert Moore asked me to stand at the front. He then invited everyone to come down, shake my hand and give me what he called 'a love offering'. People responded immediately and one by one came and shook my hand, pressing dollar notes into my other hand. I was faced with two difficulties – stuffing the money into my pockets before accepting the next person's offering and overcoming my embarrassment. Nothing like this had happened to me before, although, to be honest, the money was very welcome. It amounted to close on $500 and the next day it, too, was quickly on its way home to Enid by International Money Order.

CHAPTER 19

AN AMAZING OFFER

Over the few weeks I was in Atlanta I preached nightly in a number of Baptist churches in and around the city. I was quite astonished at the way the people in the churches responded to my preaching. The more fiery I preached, the better they seemed to like it. One night I preached on Hebrews 13:8: 'Jesus Christ is the same yesterday and today and for ever.' During the sermon I happened to say about the Saviour: 'What He was He is, and what He is He was, and what He is and was He ever will be.' A rather large Southern lady sitting near the front got so carried away with this that she ran on to the platform, picked me up, swung me around and said, 'Say it again, brother! Say it again!' So I said it one more time – to the delight of the whole congregation.

I received so many invitations from churches over those first few weeks in Atlanta that it would have taken me a year to fulfil them. But my visa only permitted me to stay in the country for three months. When talking to a Baptist minister after one of my meetings, I was intrigued when he asked if I could come to his church and preach at 'our spring revival'. I marvelled at first at the man's faith, that he expected a revival in the spring, but later I was told that the way they used the word 'revival' in the South was something quite different from the way I understood it. A 'revival' to them was simply a series of evangelistic meetings.

In mid-February I left Atlanta for Winnipeg. I had to change planes at Windsor, Canada, but as I was waiting for my connection to Winnipeg a heavy fog descended on the airport. It was so dense that all flights were cancelled and I was forced to book into a hotel. I telephoned the church in Winnipeg to let them know my predicament and was told, 'That's OK. Don't worry. Get here whenever you can. If it is late at night you will find an envelope at the reception desk of the airline you are travelling with which will contain information about how to get to your hotel. These fogs don't last more than a couple of days and if you are not here for Sunday then we feel sure you will arrive in time for the beginning of the crusade on Monday.'

On the Saturday afternoon I walked through the cold and foggy streets of Windsor and came across a long line of Roman Catholic nuns waiting outside a cinema. I asked one of them what was the occasion and she said, 'We are waiting to see the new film, *Ben Hur*. It's a fictional story about a man who came in touch with Jesus Christ, and it's been highly recommended to us.' As I had nothing else to do I pondered whether I should join them. I felt a tinge of guilt even as I considered it, because the church in which I had been brought up frowned on cinema-going. I had not, in fact, been in a cinema since my conversion. But I reckoned that what was good enough for the nuns was good enough for me!

As I watched the film, however, I had a deeply moving spiritual experience. I never dreamed that a movie could be a window through which God could come to me. I could not stop weeping as I watched the portrayal of Christ's miracles, and particularly the crucifixion scene. Although it was only a film, it triggered something in my soul that has never left me. It was as if my soul was being drawn out in hot, adoring tears of love. I had always been grateful for my Saviour's sacrifice for me on Calvary, but in the cinema that day I came to realise more vividly than ever before how Christ's sufferings had brought me salvation. It was an epiphany of understanding. I left the cinema with a more vivid realisation than ever of what it meant for Christ to be my Saviour.

On Sunday evening the fog lifted and I flew into Winnipeg around midnight. I picked up the instruction packet awaiting me at the airline reception desk and took a taxi to my hotel. After catching up with my sleep I met the pastor, who took me to see his church, which was a converted cinema. The illuminated sign outside the church fascinated me. It read, 'Tonight and every night this week, featuring Selwyn Hughes in sermons you'll remember'. I couldn't help chuckling to myself as I thought of what some of the more conservative Christians back home would make of that. That was the first, and only, time I saw my name in lights!

The week I spent at Calvary Temple was a most wonderful spiritual experience. The only drawback was the temperature, which was about 20 degrees centigrade below zero. Even when going from the entrance of the hotel to the taxi it seemed as if my skin was being ripped from my face. However, the warmth of the people was wonderful and night after night people found Christ, lukewarm Christians were set on fire and there was a touch of true revival in the air. From Winnipeg I was invited to go to a church in Brandon, a few hours' travel away, for just one weekend of meetings. After that I had to return to Atlanta to fulfil more engagements there. As I had a few days to spare before I needed to be in Atlanta, I decided to go by coach to see more of the countryside.

I got as far as Minneapolis when I remembered that Robert Owen, my friend from Bedlinog in Wales, who worked with me in the mine was now a pastor in Green Bay, Wisconsin, which was in the next state. I stayed in Minneapolis that night and the following day I managed to get in touch with him, and as a result I was able to spend a few days with him and his wife Miriam. It was so good to reminisce, sing a few Welsh hymns together and enjoy one another's company.

I left Green Bay in time for my scheduled appointments in Atlanta the following weekend, and once again met up with Jack Martz and his family, as well as my new friend Tolbert Moore. I will never forget those last few weeks of my American trip, spent in the Atlanta area. It was like being in a whirlwind as I was whisked from one event to the other. During the day, as Tolbert took me to see some of the sights in the area and we travelled to the various venues for meetings, we had time to share deeply about the faith. I happened to mention that I had a growing desire to write Bible notes similar to those published by Scripture Union and other organisations. I thought nothing more of it until the following Sunday, when I was preaching again in Tolbert's church. The children's choir were singing a song called 'Every day with Jesus is sweeter than the day before' when Tolbert leaned over to me in the pulpit and said, 'If you ever write devotional notes that would be a good title for it – *Every Day with Jesus*.' I made a mental note of it, but couldn't help wondering whether the day would really come when I would be able to realise that ambition.

Just before I was due to leave Atlanta and return to Britain I met with Jack Martz, Tolbert Moore and a group of Christian businessmen for an evening of quiet relaxation. As we talked, Tolbert turned to me and said, 'These businessmen have a proposition to put to you.' Their spokesman said, 'We have been listening to you preach many sermons during your visit and we feel sure that your ministry would be a great asset in this area. We are prepared to sponsor your family to come to the USA, build you a new home and also a church. There are several millionaires in our group and we would see it as a spiritual investment in the work of the kingdom of God here in the Atlanta area.' He added that I didn't even have to go back to the UK. He and the others knew that I didn't have any long-term commitments there. 'You can just pick up the phone and ask your wife to arrange to transport any furniture you want to bring, and we will pay for everything. Your wife and family could be here in a week or two.'

It was an amazing offer but I felt I needed some time alone to consider their proposal. I went into another room to pray over the matter. As I did so I thought of all the financial restraints we had laboured under in the UK. I thought of the things my children had gone without while other children enjoyed them, simply because the ministry did not give me sufficient financial resources for those kind of things. Here was a chance to end all that. On the other side of the door sat the businessmen waiting to put into action plans for the building of a home, a church and all the financial help I needed. What should I do? Should I ask for more time to return home, talk to my wife and get back to them at some time in the future?

As I pondered these things I suddenly felt a divine impression at work in my soul. As I look back at it now, I wonder whether God spoke to me directly or whether it was a thought dropped into my mind around which I put my own words. Whatever happened, the distinct impression I got was that the Lord was saying to me, 'This is not the place for your ministry to be worked out. Your next sphere of labour will be in the city of London. Prepare yourself for what I have for you to do there.'

Now everything was clear. I walked back into the room, sat with the men who were awaiting my decision and said, 'I am grateful beyond words for your offer and your confidence in me, but God has spoken to my heart in the last few minutes and told me that His plans for me are to go back to the United Kingdom.'

They graciously received my answer and one of them said later, 'We knew as soon as you walked back into the room that you were not going to accept our offer. The expression on your face said "I'm going home".' Then we all stood up, joined hands and prayed that the Lord would be with us all as we went our separate ways.

It was the drizzly wet morning of 31 March 1961, when the plane bringing me from the USA touched down at Heathrow airport, London. The half-hour or so that it took to collect my luggage and get through customs seemed like an eternity. I had arranged to meet Enid and my children at Liverpool Street railway station and I could hardly wait for the moment when our little family would be reunited.

As I travelled on the coach into central London I wondered how I would react when I saw my loved ones again. My younger son, John, was just three years old when I left for America and I had a terrible fear that my three months away from home would cause him to forget me. My elder son, David, strongly introvert, was just beginning to grow very close to me before I left. Would my separation from him over these months, I asked myself, hinder our developing relationship? I worried that if it did it would take a long time to rebuild a bridge across David's natural shyness.

Since Enid and I married we had not been apart for more than a few days at a time until these past months. Although there had been regular letters crossing the Atlantic between us there were still lots of unanswered questions in my mind, such as how had she really coped in my absence? Had problems arisen about which she had not troubled me? Was it much lonelier than she had made out? These and other thoughts were spinning through my mind as we got closer and closer to being reunited.

I found my family in the place we agreed to meet, the waiting room at Liverpool Street station. It is impossible to describe the flow of emotion that went through me as we met again. I felt I wanted to throw my arms around them and hold them for hours and hours. Enid looked thinner – and strained. I remember thinking, 'What have I done in staying away so long?' The boys were excited at seeing me, but I knew what was going on in their minds: what has Dad brought back for us from the USA?

We all went off for refreshments and, as we talked, I opened one of my suitcases and gave the children a couple of the many presents I had brought back. Some of my American friends had showered so many gifts on me for Enid and the boys that I had had to buy an extra suitcase to carry them all. Soon we caught the train to Colchester and in our rented flat I unpacked everything, to the amazement of my wife and children. There were silk stockings and jewellery for Enid, toys and gizmos for the children and little games and puzzles that the American markets shower on juveniles. Nothing can be sweeter than a family reunited. For days we did nothing except go for walks in the woods, eat out at restaurants (a habit I picked up in the States which took me some time to break!) and just enjoy talking and being together.

The more I talked to Enid, however, the more I realised how big a strain things had been for her while I had been away. In her letters she had only shared some of the difficulties she had been through, but now I was hearing the full story – loneliness, difficulties with John, who couldn't understand why Dad was not around, lack of a regular income, problems that had arisen in relation to The Family Bookshop. It took a while for her to recover from all this and I regretted my decision to spend so long in the States. Had I known the effect my absence would have on her and John I would have cut my trip to a month or six weeks at the most.

After a few weeks of rebuilding our family relationships, I began to ponder the words that the Holy Spirit had spoken to me in Georgia about the work God had for me to do in London. But what could it be? I decided that the only thing to do was to go to London and try to discover what the Holy Spirit might be saying to me. One morning in May 1961 I took an early train from Colchester to London and made my way to Trafalgar Square. As I sat in the square, praying for some divine leading, I called a newspaper boy over and purchased one of his London newspapers.

Immediately my eye fell on a notice. It was in small type, but to me it seemed to stand out in big bold letters: 'Flat to rent in Surrey – just 40 minutes to Waterloo Station.' I felt right away that this was something to be followed up, so I went to the nearest telephone box, rang the number given in the advertisement and arranged to view it that afternoon.

The flat was everything I wanted. It was in a fairly large but pleasant block called Kingfisher Court, had a small open-air swimming pool, well-manicured gardens and was close to Hampton Court station. The rent seemed fairly reasonable, but as I discussed terms with the agent he said something that made my heart sink. 'We will of course require three months' rent in advance.' I had received quite a large sum of money for ministry when I was in the USA, but most of it had gone to pay back the short-term overdraft I had arranged with my bank while I was away. It would have been impossible for me to have written a cheque for the amount of advance rent required, so I said, 'I will need to think this over and get back to you another time.'

As I was about to leave, however, the thought came into my mind that I should tell the agent that the flat needed to be redecorated. I believe it was the Holy Spirit who put that thought into my mind, for as soon as I said this the agent looked rather nonplussed for a moment and then replied, 'Well, I suppose it ought to be decorated before you move in.' Then after a slight hesitation he added, 'I'll tell you what: do the decorations yourself and I will waive the first three months' rent.' My heart sang as I took a pen and signed the lease.

CHAPTER 20

MY TIME IN THE WILDERNESS

Within a few weeks of signing the lease on the property in East Molesey I had moved my family into the flat and begun to pray earnestly about what the Lord had for me to do in London. I had not committed myself to many preaching engagements during 1961 as I had not been sure whether my trip to the USA might mean us moving there as a family. My bank balance was getting low so I had to arrange an overdraft. But with little security it meant I could only rely on a moderate sum.

With no clear leading about ministry in London and only a few preaching engagements, there was just one thing to do – find a job. I saw an advertisement in the local papers for operators at the Hampton Telephone Exchange, so I took a six-week course and was taken on to work on the night shift, from 10pm to 6am. This enabled me to sleep in the mornings and look after John in the afternoons while Enid worked part-time in the local chemist. The money we earned kept us afloat financially.

After a couple of months of working at the Telephone Exchange and receiving no clear leading from God, I began to wonder whether I had missed my way spiritually. Many times I asked myself questions: have I got to this place through God's leading or just wishful thinking? Am I so spiritually insensitive that I can't tell the difference between what I want and what God wants for my life? What troubled me most was that I had begun to lose my desire for prayer and my appetite for the Scriptures. I still read my Bible, but it didn't seem to speak to me any more. I read a book by C.S. Lewis one morning in which he said that there was an occasion in his life when it seemed that, as he tried to approach God in prayer, the Almighty not only shut the door of heaven in his face but he could almost hear the bolts being put in place. I knew how he felt.

Week by week my spiritual resources seemed to be depleted. I wondered whether I should give up all thoughts of pursuing the ministry and go for a career in teaching. At times it felt like being in a spiritual wrestling match without knowing who was wrestling against me – God or the devil. I had several weekend preaching engagements to fulfil, wrote a few articles for magazines, and when I was not away preaching I took my family to a local church. But it was as if the fire was going out in my soul.

One day, while reading the account of Jesus in the wilderness in Matthew's Gospel, I wondered whether I, too, was going through a divinely arranged wilderness experience. It is much clearer to me now as I write than it was at the time, but I distinctly remember thinking that perhaps God was taking me through this experience because it was what I needed as further preparation for whatever work He had for me to do in the future. I felt somewhat comforted by that realisation.

I studied and read a lot about what Christians refer to as the 'wilderness experience', and the conclusion I came to was that it is a prolonged or deeply intense period of trial and testing in which a particular providential purpose is being worked out. It is something we are led into by the Lord. God either arranges it, or allows us to enter into it, not because He wants to punish us but because He wants to prune us. He does this because it is the only way He can bring his purposes to pass in our lives.

My time in the wilderness lasted almost a year and taught me what Bible college or pastoral life could never have taught me – that there is nothing safe about life. It was in the wilderness that I had to prove to myself that I could believe in a God who sometimes leads us in ways that are baffling, but always can be trusted to do what is good.

I can almost pinpoint the day, even the moment, when I came out of the 'wilderness'. It happened late in the summer of 1962. I had begun to wonder whether there would ever be an end to this spiritual impasse I found myself in, or whether I would find myself in this mood for the rest of my life. On the day it happened I opened my Bible at the Song of Solomon 2:12–13 and read, 'Flowers appear on the earth; the season of singing has come, the cooing of doves is heard in our land. The fig-tree forms its early fruit; the blossoming vines spread their fragrance. Arise …' That was all, but it was enough.

Suddenly my spirit revived. I felt my old spiritual self again. It was as if I had been asleep and a hand brushed across my cheek, a voice called my name, and my eyes opened to a new world. The conviction entered my soul, deposited there by the Spirit, I am sure, that from now on things would be different, that out of it would come the message of my life, or at least the beginnings of it. For a while, spiritual exercises had been dutiful; now they were delightful. Prayer and the reading of God's Word was a joy once again.

Bible College prepared me to use my gifts; the wilderness prepared me to live my life. How could I know the feelings of the desperate if I had not been desperate myself? How could I know the feelings of the poor if I had not been poor myself? How could I know the feelings of the confused if I had not been confused myself? The wilderness is a place of pain, isolation, humiliation, uncertainty, loneliness, depression and desperation. I was convinced all were necessary for me to experience if I were to move into a higher level of ministry.

From my time in the wilderness I learned at least two things. Firstly, I needed to be there, and secondly, my dependency on God was deepened. Is it possible to thank God for a wilderness experience? By His grace I can say that I do.

During the last few months of my time in that spiritual state I hardly wrote a decent paragraph, let alone a page. I could write a sentence, several sentences in fact, but when strung together they didn't seem to make much sense. Now, however, as I focused on writing my thoughts on to an empty page, the sentences began to flow more easily.

In my files lay ideas on something I had been working on at one time called *The Soul Winner's Pocket Guide*. It was a booklet designed to answer some the questions asked by non-Christians when confronted by someone over spiritual issues. Questions such as, 'If God is good why are there so many problems in the world?' or 'I live a good life surely this will be enough for God to let me into heaven?'

I took out the rough notes and within three or four days had completed the booklet. Rather than approach a publisher with the idea, which could sometimes mean months or even years before the manuscript is turned into a book, I decided to publish it myself. While it was being printed I advertised it in some of the Christian papers. The editor of the *Sunday Companion* (a weekly paper now defunct) saw the advert because it was due to appear in his publication and asked to see a copy of the guide. After looking through it he invited me to lunch with him in his London office, saying that he had a proposition to put to me.

When we met he said that he had been searching for some time for something to boost the paper's circulation. After seeing *The Soulwinner's Pocket Guide* he had hit upon the idea of including it in one edition of the *Sunday Companion* as a free gift.

His plan was to build up interest by telling readers several weeks in advance that this would happen on a certain date. He believed that the resultant increase in the paper's circulation would offset the cost of purchasing the booklets. I readily agreed to his proposition, a contract was subsequently signed and I came away with a greatly appreciated cheque. The scheme was a great success and even 40 years later I come across people who tell me the first thing they ever read of mine was *The Soulwinner's Pocket Guide*. Over the years that booklet has been amended and become a bestseller.[1]

I began to seek the Lord in earnest about London once again. While I was praying one day about what God would have me do in the city, I received a vision – something I had never known before or, for that matter, since. I was lying on my bed with my Bible open beside me after reading the story of the rich man and Lazarus in Luke 16 when I was taken by the Spirit into a series of spiritual sequences that affected me most deeply. I was not asleep, for I was aware of the usual sounds around me – the murmur of voices outside, a dog barking somewhere in the distance, traffic moving down the street.

Suddenly I saw London as if it was laid out beneath me: church spires, towers, theatres, shops, offices. All these stretched to the farthest horizon. Arched over the city, stretching from east to west, was an enormous highway resting on massive pillars, with smaller lanes rising from different parts of London leading on to the main highway. I saw thousands of people walking up the ramps and on to the highway, and then moving towards the west. I found myself walking with the crowds, and as I did so I knew I was in the company of the ungodly, for curses, oaths and swear words filled the air. On the face of every person was a look of dull unconcern, now and again broken by a forced laugh or some kind of simulated gaiety.

Then, for some reason, the crowd slowed down, as if there was some obstacle on the road ahead. I felt myself becoming as impatient as those around me. Then I was lifted above the mass of people and shown the cause of the slow-down. Up ahead was a man holding a red lantern in his hand and pleading with the people to go back. No one seemed to take any notice. I could see the pain on his face as people pushed past him on either side and tears flowed down his cheeks as his pleas were ignored.

Then I saw why he was holding them back. In the distance the road ended abruptly in a sheer drop. The Spirit took me to the end of the road and for a few moments it was as if I was looking down into the pit of hell. As the crowds pushed forward unaware that the road came to a sudden end, the crush of those behind caused those who were in the front to fall over the edge of the precipice. As they fell they let out the most horrible and the most piercing of screams. I realised as I watched that I was hearing the cries of the lost – cries that have haunted me from that day to this. Whatever evangelistic zeal I possessed before was multiplied a hundredfold after that sobering and salutary experience.

Nowadays it is not fashionable to believe in hell, but that, according to Jesus, is where the finally impenitent will finish up. Personally, I wish the subject of hell were not in the Bible. It would make the task of evangelism a lot more 'user friendly', I believe, if we could tell people that if they died without Christ they would experience utter oblivion, but if they received Him as their Saviour and Lord then they would experience life that goes on for ever and ever. I would feel much happier as an evangelist preaching that kind of gospel, but it would, of course, be 'another gospel'. I dislike the whole idea of hell. It does not sit easily with me, but I preach it because Jesus taught it and warned the people of His day of its danger. As someone has put it, 'Hell may be out of modern-day pulpits but it is not out of the Bible.'

Not long after this experience I was praying about London when the thought came to me – once more Spirit-inspired, I believe – to go and look again at Dennison House, the auditorium in Vauxhall Bridge Road, near Victoria Station, in which I had heard Renee Martz speak. In my previous search for possible venues to establish a church I had not remembered this place, but now I found that it was possible to book it on a regular weekly basis. I was told that anyone booking it on a long-term contract would have precedence over everyone else, with the exception of a few groups who used it for annual meetings.

Everything I was doing now – so different from a year ago – seemed to be meeting with success, but the big question was, how would I begin? What would be the initial steps I needed to take to open up a new church in London? I continued to pray much about this and in the autumn of 1962 I felt led to contact an American evangelist, A.C. Valdez. I knew him from my days in the Assemblies of God when he came to the UK and held a series of very successful crusades in a number of cities. In fact, I had taken a coach-load of people from my church in Pontardulais to hear him in a concert hall in Newport, and the things we witnessed there were quite remarkable. A.C. Valdez was a healing evangelist with a warm and winsome personality. What I liked about him was the clear emphasis he gave to the fact that the greatest miracle that can happen in a person's life is a moral one. 'You can get to heaven with a sick body,' he used to say, 'but you can't get to heaven with a sick soul.'

Through my enquiries I found out that he had a church in Wisconsin, so I rang him to ask if he would consider coming to London to help me establish a new church. I made it clear that there were no funds to underwrite this, so he would have to pay his own fare to Britain. We would rely entirely on the offerings taken at the meeting to pay all expenses and at the end of it I would ask the people to give him a 'love offering'.

He seemed quite intrigued with my proposition, promised to pray about it and said he would get back to me in due course. A week later he telephoned me to say that he felt the Lord was leading him to agree to my proposal and that he would share the financial risk with me, expecting nothing in return. Then he said, 'If the expenses at the end of the crusade are not met then I will put any "love offering" given to me into the crusade budget.' I remember thinking to myself, 'This is a man I can work with!'

Within a few days I had arranged with the secretary of the Metropolitan Tabernacle (sometimes referred to as Spurgeon's Tabernacle) to rent their auditorium for a one-week crusade in January 1963. At the same time I negotiated a series of bookings with the management of Dennison House to follow the crusade, in the hope that there would be enough new converts to start a church.

Over the Christmas period I placed adverts in the Christian press announcing the one-week Metropolitan Tabernacle Crusade with A.C. Valdez, and almost immediately I was flooded with enquiries. One man who seemed quite excited about the evangelist's visit, having read about him in an American magazine he received regularly, telephoned me to ask if he could do anything to help. His name was Gordon White, and when he gave me his address I found out that he lived just around the corner from me! As soon as I met him I knew he was a kindred spirit with a passionate love for the Lord, a desire to win souls to Christ and a longing to see those who were sick and suffering find healing.

A.C.Valdez arrived a few days before the start of the crusade, accompanied by his teenage daughter, Sandra. Just before we opened, London was hit by one of the worst snowstorms for years, but it made little difference to the attendance. Right from the opening night people made their way from all over London through the snow-filled streets to the meetings. There were a number of things that worked in our favour. Firstly, A.C. Valdez was widely known and highly respected by the Assemblies of God. A second factor was that the charismatic movement was just beginning to get going in the United Kingdom and anything to do with the work and ministry of the Holy Spirit was capturing the attention of the various denominations. Several Anglican vicars had experienced an encounter with the Holy Spirit which some called 'the baptism in the Spirit' and others 'the fullness of the Spirit', so a crusade such as this one, where the Holy Spirit's power and presence was seen in action, attracted the interest of many Anglicans and other denominations who were hungry to learn and experience more of the Holy Spirit's power.

What would come out of that crusade was far greater than anything I could have imagined.

Notes

1. It is now available from CWR as *The Pocket Guide for People Helpers*.

CHAPTER 21

'THINK BIG'

The crusade at the Metropolitan Tabernacle, London, was a tremendous spiritual success. Night after night A.C. Valdez presented a simple but clear gospel message, then invited those who wished to receive Christ to come to the front of the church to give public testimony to this fact. After the new converts had been instructed, A.C. (as we often referred to him) prayed for those who were sick. Some of the people who were dramatically healed in that crusade are known to be healed to this very day and claim that their disability or illness has never returned.

Back home in the USA, A.C. Valdez was very closely involved with a new Christian men's movement, the Full Gospel Business Men's Fellowship International. Started by a wealthy dairy farmer in California, Demos Shakarian, it was growing at a tremendous rate. A.C. suggested that at the end of the crusade we organised a dinner for Christian businessmen with the aim of beginning a London chapter of the FGBFI. In a telephone conversation with Demos Shakarian before the meeting, A.C. got his approval to appoint me as the first president of the new organisation and to make that announcement at the dinner. The more I thought this over, the unhappier I felt about the appointment. I could not see myself leading businessmen into the deeper things of the Spirit as the world of business was neither my calling nor inclination.

But we went ahead with the dinner and, although there was nothing officially announced, this was probably the first occasion in which the work of the Full Gospel Businessmen's Fellowship International was introduced to the UK. Many well-known London business personalities were invited to this dinner and listened to A.C. telling how the organisation was growing in the USA. Then he prayed for many of those present that felt they needed a greater sense of God's power in their lives. One of London's foremost Christian businessmen was Lindsey Glegg, a magistrate and the owner of a large printing business, and though he was unable to get to the meeting he sent me a note saying, 'Selwyn, whatever you do in London – *think big.*'

After the Valdez crusade was over we started regular meetings in Dennison House almost at once. I had compiled a fairly large mailing list by asking everyone who attended the crusade to fill in a visitor's card, so it was a simple matter to write to everyone and let them know we were starting regular meetings in central London. The opening night was filled with converts from the Valdez crusade and those interested in knowing and experiencing more of the Holy Spirit's power. When I made it clear that we would be holding weekly meetings in Dennison House, with a strong emphasis on Holy Spirit revival, there was a spontaneous round of applause. I also said that we saw ourselves as a centre where people of all denominations who shared a desire to know more of God could come and be part of the move of the Holy Spirit that was beginning to invade London. For that reason I announced our meetings and activities would be under the banner of the London Revival Crusade rather than a narrower church title.

The Valdez crusade had a particularly deep impact on a policeman from East Finchley. His name was Peter Douglas, a Baptist deacon and a lay preacher. He received the baptism in the

Holy Spirit when A.C. laid his hands on him, an experience, he said, that transformed his life. In one of the early meetings at Dennison House, I got him to talk about this experience. He also said that he felt God had called him to join me in the work that God had called me to do in the city. Peter's testimony that night inspired others to commit themselves to the work of the London Revival Crusade. I am so grateful that the Lord led both Peter Douglas and Gordon White to support me. They were the 'Aaron and Hur' who upheld me and stood by me in the founding of the London Revival Crusade.

Meetings in those opening weeks at Dennison House were only held on Saturday evenings, but soon we added a Sunday afternoon meeting (Sunday evenings were unavailable) and later Thursday and Friday meetings. I spent a good deal of time during those weeks defining exactly what is meant by revival because many people then, as now, were confused as to what it was all about. The word is often misapplied, as in the case of a London pastor who told me, 'Revival broke out in our church last Sunday night.' When I asked him exactly what he meant, I found out that he was referring to the conversions of six people. My concern about using the word 'revival' in that way is that we will easily settle for something less than God wants to give us.

Revival is not just people getting converted, or a spate of exceptionally God-blessed meetings. Revival is an awesome and extraordinary flood of God's Spirit that sweeps everything before it. Its impact is felt not only in the church, but in the community outside it. Anything less, in my view, does not deserve the description of 'revival'.

The weekly meetings in Dennison House captured the attention of people not just in London, but in other parts of the country as well. It was nothing unusual on Saturday nights to find people from Brighton, Birmingham, Manchester,

Nottingham, Southampton and even Wales sitting in the congregation. Many of them would come just once, but their lives were touched in ways that transformed them. The power that flowed through the Saturday night meetings was something that I had never witnessed before. Over the years, as I have travelled up and down the country, I have often met people who have told me, 'I was converted at Dennison House,' or 'It was there I was healed,' or 'God filled me with the Spirit the first time I attended,' and so on.

In the months that followed the opening of Dennison House many were saying, 'If you want to see the new thing that God is doing, then pay a visit to Dennison House. There is nothing in all London like it.' It was not unusual, either, to see well-known denominational leaders there on Saturday evenings. Having heard about the meetings, they came to see what was going on. Geoffrey King, a well-known Baptist minister at the time, was among them. So was the minister of the Anglican church in Portman Square, where monthly nights of prayer for revival were held.

Another place where the need for revival was being emphasised was a weekly lunchtime prayer meeting in Fleet Street. It was at one of these prayer meetings in the spring of 1963 that I met Roy Jackman, a fellow Welshman, who was to play a major role in the development of the London Revival Crusade. Roy was an artist with offices in Oxford Street, rather prestigious, I remember thinking.

He happened to mention to me one day that if I needed a small office for the London Revival Crusade, one of his rooms was available at a small rent. I jumped at the opportunity and the Oxford Street office was quickly set up as the London Revival Crusade's centre of operations. Now that we had an office in the city and the work at Dennison House was going so well, it became obvious that I needed to sit down and prayerfully work out a five-year plan. I set aside a week of prayer and fasting to seek divine guidance on how to proceed in the future. Lindsey Glegg's words also kept hammering in my mind: 'Whatever you do in London, *think big*.' But I realised that as well as thinking big one also needs to think in harmony with the purposes of God. And that can only be done through prolonged times of prayer.

Far more than any other influence, more than home, more than my church life, more than Bible college, my dreams and goals have been shaped in times of prayer. I have found that the more time I have spent talking with God in prayer the more successful and on target have been the projects I have launched. When I have done something just because it seemed like a good idea and failed to pray it through, then almost inevitably it has ended in failure.

I emerged from this special time of prayer with three clear objectives. One was to continue and develop a vigorous and active evangelism programme in the city, especially in Soho. The second was the need to pray and believe God for a Holy Spirit revival. The third was the purchase of an auditorium and offices for the work of the London Revival Crusade. I also felt a strong urge to arrange another central London evangelistic and healing crusade, this time much bigger and more widely advertised than the meetings held by A.C. Valdez at the Metropolitan Tabernacle. A name that kept coming to my mind was that of an evangelist based on the West coast of America, Morris Cerullo. I first read about him in *Voice of Healing*, an American magazine I was receiving at that time, which carried reports of the many evangelists who were shaking some American cities and Third World countries with great crusades drawing thousands and thousands of people. Names such as Oral Roberts, William Branham, T.L. Osborne, A.A. Allen – and Morris Cerullo.

I noted that the *Voice of Healing* magazine listed Morris Cerullo's office as being in San Diego. After thinking it over for a few days, I phoned this office to invite him to conduct a crusade in London. His secretary told me told that at the moment he was conducting a crusade in Belo Horizonte, Brazil. She gave me the number of the hotel he was staying at and when I called I was instantly put through to his room.

I said, 'Mr Cerullo, you won't know me, but I pastor an evangelistic centre in the heart of London. During a recent prayer time I felt impressed to telephone you and invite you to hold a crusade in this city.' 'That's quite amazing,' he replied. 'I have just been praying recently about London. I have never been into the city, but I stayed overnight in a hotel at Heathrow airport and sensed, as I was praying in my room, that one day I would be called to the city.' We then talked briefly about a possible date and he promised to send his crusade manager, Clair Hutchins, to London to talk with me about the details.

Clair arrived a few weeks later and we sat down together to go over all the arrangements. Once again, as I did with A.C. Valdez, I made it clear that no financial guarantees could be given. It would be expected that the nightly offerings would cover the local expenses, then if there was anything left over it would be given to Morris Cerullo to help defray the costs of his and Clair's travel to the UK. Clair said that from Morris's point of view there were just two requirements. One was that an attempt be made to recruit the support of other churches beside my own, with the promise that converts from the Crusade be given a list of these churches so that they could decide which one they might want to attend. The second requirement was for a banquet to be held at the end of the crusade, at which Morris would present the challenge of world evangelism and invite people to give towards that work.

I raised no objection to either of these proposals and the discussion then focused on a possible venue. Clair suggested that, if it were possible, the crusade should be held in a tent. It was thought that non-Christians would be more easily drawn to a tent meeting than to a large church such as the Metropolitan Tabernacle or Westminster Central Hall. We set the date for July 1963, and as soon as Clair returned to the USA I began to contact a number of London churches likely to be sympathetic to the kind of crusade envisaged. About 15 churches responded at once and a committee was formed to oversee the details.

The next challenge was to find a site in central London on which to pitch a large tent. My first thought was to try to negotiate with the organisers of the Chelsea Flower Show to use their large tent following the end of their activities, but initial discussions with the secretary of that organisation failed to bring a positive response. As I drove around the city I found an old bomb site near the Elephant and Castle. I went to the local authority responsible for the site and succeeded in gaining permission to erect a tent on it for two weeks. There was no charge for the site, but I was expected to ensure that the rubble was cleared and the ground made safe for the public to walk on.

So my next task was to hire a group of contractors to clear the site. Bomb clearance experts made sure there were no unexploded bombs on the property. The Second World War had been over for nearly two decades, but unexploded bombs were still occasionally being unearthed in the city. Work proceeded slowly, but a few days before the tent was due to go up I found myself (with the contractor's permission!) helping to drive a steam roller over the site in a last-minute effort to ensure that the ground was perfectly flat. We opened right on time, and from the opening moments the huge marquee was packed night after night.

Morris Cerullo has since become a rather controversial figure in the UK and several TV companies have featured him in a somewhat negative light, but at the tent crusade at the Elephant and Castle he was deeply impressive. Night after night hundreds of people came to know Christ. I also witnessed some of the most remarkable healings I have ever seen. One man, well known to me, who had had a neuromuscular disorder for years and couldn't stop his arm from shaking was instantly healed. Dozens of unmistakeable healings took place that I know have stood the test of time. Morris's faith for miracles was quite staggering.

After the crusade, Morris Cerullo held a banquet in the Piccadilly Hotel, Piccadilly Circus. Several hundred people attended, and after Morris had shared his vision for world evangelism he received a pledged offering amounting to well over £10,000. The crusade resulted in many more new people coming to Dennison House, including Harry and Olive Curle, who were to play major roles in our work. Olive became my secretary in the Oxford Street office and Harry, who was a printer, helped with our publicity needs.

A month after the tent crusade the celebrated evangelist, Oral Roberts, paid a visit to Newport in South Wales. Many of the people who attended the Dennison House meetings said they would like to attend the final Saturday event, which was to be held in a stadium. My first reaction was to book several coaches, but it soon became clear that there were so many people wanting to go that it would be better to try to organise a special train for the occasion. Once this became known, the bookings came thick and fast. On Saturday 8 August, 500 people boarded what we called *The Oral Roberts Special*, which left Paddington at 9am and arrived in Newport just after midday, in plenty of time for the mid-afternoon meeting.

This was Oral Roberts' first visit to the UK and because he

was probably the most well known healing evangelist in the world at the time, people came from all over the country to see and hear him. His style was to pray and lay his hands on everyone who sought healing. I estimated that he prayed for over 2,000 people, which took him well over two hours. Attendants walked with him down the line providing him with coffee to help him complete the mammoth task. His willingness to give himself to people in that way greatly impressed me. It revealed something of the heart of compassion this man had for the sick and suffering.

I said earlier that the more time I have spent talking with God in prayer the more successful and on target have been the projects I have launched. But when I have done something just because it seemed like a good idea and failed to soak it in prayer it has almost inevitably been a flop. Something I did soon after the Elephant and Castle crusade with Morris Cerullo is a striking example of this.

CHAPTER 22

'THE MIDNIGHT EXPRESS'

S ometime early in 1964 I received a letter from A.C. Valdez saying that a friend of his was coming to London – a former Mr Universe by the name of Richard Du Bois – and asking if I could arrange some meetings for him. Richard had a wonderful testimony to the power of Jesus Christ to change his life and when I agreed to this request I immediately began to think where the meetings could be held. I reckoned that Dennison House, which seated around 400 people, would be too small for such an event, so I decided to book the Royal Albert Hall. Advertisements were placed in the Christian and secular press announcing that Richard would be giving his testimony on a Saturday night in October.

The Royal Albert Hall rally was preceded by a special lunch at the Piccadilly Hotel for all those who wanted to meet Richard, including London Revival Crusade team members, friends and press representatives. Later in the afternoon we moved on to the Albert Hall to prepare for the evening event. The building seats just over 5,000 people, but when the day of the event arrived only 500 tickets had been sold. I hoped that another 500 people might buy tickets at the door, but minutes before the meeting was due to start I peeped out from behind the curtains and saw only just over 500 people.

That would have been a sizeable congregation in many places, but in the Royal Albert Hall it looked so sparse that I felt sick to the pit of my stomach. I wanted to run away and hide! The thought also hit me that we needed to sell at least 2,000 tickets to cover the budget for the meeting, and I wondered how the deficit would be made up. As I stepped on to the platform, accompanied by Richard, to welcome people and announce the opening hymn, I wished, as the old cliché puts it, that the earth would open up and swallow me. Many in the congregation that evening sensed my disappointment and, as one told me after the service, 'The people in our row sang twice as loud as we would normally to encourage you.'

Richard gave a marvellous testimony to the power of Jesus Christ in his life and several people came forward to surrender their hearts to Christ that night. I found it difficult to talk to people at the end of the service. I just wanted to get back home, fall asleep and wake up to find that it had all been a bad dream. In later years we would fill the Royal Albert Hall twice in one day, but if someone had asked me just after the Richard Du Bois meeting if I would ever book the venue for another event I would have said an emphatic 'No!'

A few days later, however, someone who was at that meeting sent me a cheque that more than covered the deficit. I felt deeply humbled by that experience, but in the humbling I still felt the presence of God close to my heart. I am constantly amazed at the fact that, although God may humble us in His mercy and grace, He does not abandon us. I came away from that experience having learned that it is one thing to think big; it is another thing to think wisely.

On occasions when Dennison House was not available to us because of a previous longstanding booking by another group, we held meetings in places such as Caxton Hall, Orange Street Congregational Church (close to Trafalgar Square), and Westminster Central Hall. For several weeks we booked the

Prince Charles Theatre just off Leicester Square for a series of evangelistic meetings on Sunday evenings. One very fruitful evangelistic outreach was the meetings we held in Trafalgar Square itself. Permission to use the square had to be obtained from the local authority, but our requests to hold monthly meetings there were always dealt with speedily, efficiently and positively. A young man who assisted me in the early days of London Revival Crusade was David Rushton. After a comparatively short time he departed for the United States, where he set up his own evangelistic ministry.

Another of the men who became linked to us in Dennison House was a photographer, Ron Howe. Ron was a brilliant personal worker with a passion to reach people for Christ and formed what he called The Mobile Evangelistic Crusade. He and his small team would park his comfortable and well-equipped van in some area of London and give out leaflets to people informing them that, if they wanted to chat with him over any spiritual matter, they could come into his van to do so.

One evening Ron's van was parked near Trafalgar Square. There was a knock on the door and Ron opened it to find a rather despondent and dispirited individual there, asking to talk. He said his name was Terry Dene. He had been a pop idol in the late 1950s and his rise to fame and riches was rapid. Originally named Terry Williams, he was spotted by BBC television producer Jack Good and signed up for *Six Five Special*, the top-rated music show of its day. Later he was signed for Decca records.

Terry's descent from stardom was as rapid as his ascent. After experiencing some psychiatric problems and being beaten up by a gang of thugs, he left the music scene altogether. After hearing the gospel from Ron Howe, Terry found Christ in Ron's van near Trafalgar Square that evening and later became a street evangelist himself.

On occasions we would hold evangelistic meetings on the streets of Soho, which often prompted the strip club owners to telephone the police, claiming that our singing and preaching were discouraging people from entering their premises. We formed the Crusade Trio with singers Esther, Marion and Eustace, who not only sang in Dennison House, but also came with us on most of our evangelistic forays into the heart of the city.

A significant event took place in Dennison House towards the end of 1964 which was to have a great impact on the life of my colleague, Gordon White. Gordon had faithfully supported me through the opening months of founding the Crusade and we had grown very close. At that time he was working for the Inland Revenue and I had a growing sense that one day, like Matthew the disciple, he would leave the job of tax gathering and work for the Lord full time. I had never shared this feeling with him, but one weekend in November this was wonderfully confirmed when Dick Carter, whom I first met in Colchester and again in the USA, paid us a visit at Dennison House.

Dick had a wonderful prophetic ministry. During a time of personal ministry to people towards the end of a service, he prophesied over Gordon that the Lord would call him to full-time Christian service and he would have a prophetic ministry himself in the body of Christ. That was very moving for Gordon, and also for me, as I sensed that our being drawn together was part of God's purposes for us both. I saw a great change in Gordon after that evening. It was as if he was marching to the beat of a distant drummer.

Early in 1965, I organised an evangelists' conference in Dennison House, the main speaker being Gordon Lindsey, editor of the *Voice of Healing* magazine and later the founder of Christ for the Nations College in Dallas, USA. A good number of young

British evangelists were beginning to appear on the scene, and I felt it would be helpful for them to hear from someone who was closely involved with the well-known evangelists who were ministering with great power in the USA. Don Double, today one of Britain's better-known evangelists and founder of Good News Crusade, was at that conference and preached one evening. Vic Ramsey was there. He and his wife, Jan, were living in South London at the time and regularly came to the meetings at Dennison House. Among many others taking part in the conference were Donald Bergagard (well-known as an evangelist and gospel singer in his native Sweden), and many others. Many of the evangelists spoke of how wonderful it was to meet with others who were like-minded and some approached me saying they felt it would be helpful while so many evangelists were present to form an Evangelists' Fellowship for those whose ministries encompassed not only the preaching of the gospel but also praying for the sick. That was not something I felt led to organise and excused myself from the discussions.

The Saturday night services at Dennison House were still a great draw for people from all denominations. And more and more were coming to the Sunday afternoon meeting, a time I set aside for Bible teaching. Because it was an afternoon meeting and did not conflict with other church services, it drew many who were not directly linked with the London Revival Crusade. Cars full of people would travel in from Croydon, East London, Wimbledon and other parts of the city to be with us. I did not receive a regular salary from the London Revival Crusade, but on Sunday afternoons a 'love offering' was collected and this provided the financial support for my family and me.

My sons David and John were extremely happy in their schools in the East Molesey area and joined Enid and me on Sundays in the London Revival Crusade meetings in Dennison

House. Often on the way into London in the car they would question me as to what the London Revival Crusade was all about. Having previously spent their lives in a church setting they couldn't understand why we were meeting in a rented hall rather than a church. It took some explaining before they understood the difference between what their father had been doing previously and what he was doing now. I cannot be sure that they understood it until they were much older but they did enjoy their weekly trips into the heart of the city.

One Saturday evening in March 1964 I preached a sermon on the Second Coming of Christ. I based my talk on 1 John 3:3:

> But we know that when he appears, we shall be like him, for we shall see him as he is. Everyone who has this hope in him purifies himself, just as he is pure.

The results were astonishing. More people than usual responded to the appeal to be converted. Many of the Christians present gained a fresh realisation that the hope they carried in their hearts of meeting Christ at His coming ought to motivate them to rid their lives of all wrongdoing (as the text makes clear), so they responded by dedicating themselves to being the best they could be for God. It was a very moving and deeply spiritual time. Many told me afterwards that they had never before heard a message on the Second Coming of Christ. Some who said that had been believers for 10 or 20 years.

I became greatly exercised at that time over the fact that the return of Jesus Christ did not seem to figure in modern evangelism in the way it once did. I prayed a lot about this and came up with a somewhat radical idea. I went to see Derek Sangster, a Christian and an experienced newspaper editor based in Brighton. Over lunch I said, 'Imagine you are the editor of a newspaper the day after Jesus Christ has returned. How do you think you would fill the pages? Come up with some ideas and perhaps we can use it as an evangelistic and teaching tool to alert people to the fact that Christ is one day going to return to this world.'

Derek responded by coming back to me with a mock-up of a newspaper which he called *The Midnight Express*. There are, of course, several theories about the return of Christ to this world. The view Derek presented, with my approval, is known as the Rapture Theory – that Christians who are alive at the time of Christ's return will be caught up to be with Him in the air. It is based on 1 Thessalonians 4:16-17:

> For the Lord himself will come down from heaven, with a loud command, with the voice of the archangel and with the trumpet call of God, and the dead in Christ will rise first. After that, we who are still alive and are left will be caught up together with them in the clouds to meet the Lord in the air. And so we will be with the Lord for ever.

The Midnight Express was extremely well put together and I placed a print order for a million copies! I planned to launch it in London through teams handing them out at all the major railway and underground stations during the morning rush hour, shouting, 'Dramatic news! Read all about it!' I soon had a large group of volunteers. A director of operations was appointed to make sure that on the day of this evangelistic initiative a fleet of vans would be ready to pick up the copies from the warehouse where they were stored and deliver them to the station entrances.

Several weeks before the event I sent copies to all the newspapers in Fleet Street, and to the Christian press, to alert them to what I was planning, with a strict embargo not to publish any articles in advance.

Maurice Rowlandson, who headed up the Billy Graham Evangelistic Association in the UK at that time, was sent a copy. On instructions from his colleagues in the United States, he expressed their concern about the inclusion of an article in the paper by Billy Graham on the Second Advent of Christ. Derek Sangster had included it because he felt that when the Second Coming took place, and millions of people were missing from the earth, one of the first things an editor would do would be to see what Billy Graham had to say on the subject and to include an article by him in the paper.

Maurice expressed their concern that permission had not been obtained for the article (which, of course, it should have been), and perhaps also had a deeper concern that Billy Graham should be identified with a particular theory of the Second Coming such as the one that was being presented in *The Midnight Express*. He wanted the article by Billy Graham removed, but as the newspaper had already been printed this could not be done. When this fact was made known to the solicitors acting for the Billy Graham organisation, they announced that they would have no option but to issue an injunction, preventing *The Midnight Express* from being distributed. My solicitor made the point to them that if an injunction was issued all the Fleet Street newspapers would hear about it, and this would bring unacceptable publicity to all concerned. People might not understand how two Christian organisations could be in conflict over an issue like this. The threat of an injunction was withdrawn, the solicitors asking for an assurance that if the paper were ever reprinted the article by Billy Graham would not appear in it. I agreed to this.

A number of prayer meetings were held all over London before the day of distribution, in which we sought the Lord's blessing on the project. It went off as planned, with the teams in place and copies of the paper delivered on time. The first commuters emerged from their trains to be met with the cries about dramatic news and having copies of the paper containing it thrust into their hands. Hundreds of thousands of copies were given out between 6am and 9am. *The Midnight Express* carried special phone numbers and I had people standing by at these telephones to answer enquirers.

By the time people reached their offices and other places of work many had read the paper on the underground or bus. Hundreds telephoned to ask, 'Has this actually happened?' The reply they got was along the lines of 'No, it hasn't happened yet, but according to the Bible it will happen one day, perhaps sooner than we may think, and we thought this would help you be prepared for the event.' Whoever answered the telephone would then offer to send the enquirer a free Bible and a Bible correspondence course that would help them understand much more clearly. A large number of people accepted this offer and from the mailing list that resulted we were able to direct people to churches in the areas where they lived.

The *Evening Standard* that day reported the giving out of the newspapers, but even though a reporter came to see me the next day to do a follow-up article, nothing more appeared. This was due, we were told, to the news 'being displaced by more hot political news'. Some of us who met later to review the project concluded that although the impact had been brief, there were souls who had stepped into the kingdom of God because of it and thousands had been alerted to the truth of Christ's return to this world.

I was deeply saddened that our thoughtlessness had caused a rift between the Billy Graham organisation and myself, but happily I had an opportunity some years later to apologise personally to Maurice Rowlandson over the matter when he attended a seminar I conducted in the city of Liverpool. He was very gracious about it and told me recently that the seminar he attended at that time proved to be a defining moment in his life. How good it is when problems between Christians are dealt with in a way that brings glory to the Lord Jesus Christ.

CHAPTER 23

PENETRATING THE LONDON DRUG SCENE

T he success of the printed word through the one-off publication of *The Midnight Express* gave me a taste for launching a monthly paper carrying news of what God was doing in many of the denominational churches. Well-known Christians were making it known that their lives had been overturned by the Holy Spirit and were speaking in tongues. One of them was Michael Harper, then a curate at All Souls, Langham Place. Publicly declaring that he had been baptised in the Spirit and was speaking in tongues, he began encouraging others to seek the same experience.

One very memorable meeting, organised by Michael, to which I was invited, was held in the Langham Hotel, London, when he invited David Du Plessis from South Africa to be the speaker. David was known as 'Mr Pentecost' because of his strong emphasis on the work of the Holy Spirit. At that meeting, packed largely with Anglicans, many were prayed for by him and came away speaking in tongues. Michael later began meetings in London and other cities in the UK under the banner of the Fountain Trust, a ministry that reached not only Anglicans, but also blessed the lives of thousands in other denominations.

I decided to call my monthly paper *Revival* as my concern, then, as now, was to encourage people to thank God for His present blessings (one of which was renewal), but not to settle for less than the best God is able to give us – revival. The paper carried reports of the many wonderful things God was doing in some of the denominational churches, but my concern has always been to underscore the fact that God has much more to give us than renewal. As the editor of *Revival* I had the opportunity to talk to, and report on, the many Christian leaders who were coming into what was then known as 'the things of the Spirit', men like Arthur Wallis, Mike Pusey, Tom Smail and Geoffrey King. The magazine *Revival* has continued in one form or another to the present day. The most recent editor was John Peters who also wrote my biography.

During the summer of 1964 Morris Cerullo returned to London, once again under the auspices of the London Revival Crusade and other supporting churches. His meetings were held this time in Wimbledon Town Hall, where he ministered to packed congregations. During the crusade, Morris, Clair Hutchins and myself visited the Prime Minister of the day, Harold Wilson, in his office in the Houses of Parliament, to pray with him and present him with a special copy of the Scriptures inscribed with his name, which Morris had brought with him from the United States. Harold Wilson appeared to be intrigued with the idea of having his name inscribed on a Bible and told us that, although he did not read the Scriptures often, he firmly believed that they contained God's instructions for an effective life here on earth.

A highlight of Morris Cerullo's visit to the Wimbledon Town Hall for many of the ministers and leaders was when he invited them to his hotel, ministered Communion to them, laid his hands on them and prayed over every one asking God to empower their ministries in a greater way than ever before. Don Double, who was there, said he went out from that meeting to speak at an event in Wellingborough, where he preached far better and more powerfully he had ever preached before.

After the Wimbledon crusade Morris invited me to join him and Clair in a series of meetings in what was then the largest church in the world – the Assemblies of God church in Belo Horizonte, Brazil, which had around 250,000 members. Since then that distinction has been overtaken by a church in Korea and one in Nigeria – the Nigerian one boasting a membership of half a million! It was a thrill to be invited with Clair to speak to the Sunday morning congregation, certainly the largest I had talked to face to face at that time. The Wimbledon meetings were the last we sponsored for Morris Cerullo as he opened his own office in London to look after future ministry in Britain.

That summer I had the pleasure of conducting the wedding service of my colleague, Gordon White, and his fiancée, Barbara. This was the first of several weddings that came out of the relationships formed through the Dennison House meetings.

Gordon eventually took over the leadership of the Friday night meeting at Dennison House. It was basically a prayer meeting called The Faith Pool. From this small beginning Gordon has gone on to develop a ministry that now takes him and Barbara from their home in the United States to many parts of the world. Peter Douglas, also a close colleague with me in Dennison House, later went on to become a minister who is still active in the field of teaching and evangelism.

It was also in 1964 that two other gifted men joined the London Revival Crusade team and went on to play a major part in our evangelistic outreaches. One was Tony Holloway, who lived in South London and was involved in the National Young Life witness team. Having heard what was going on in Dennison House, he decided to pay us a visit. First he started attending the Sunday afternoon Bible teaching sessions, then the Saturday evenings. Soon he became involved in the regular Wednesday evening evangelistic forays into Soho. We would preach on the street corners with loud-speaking equipment, visit the pubs and clubs with literature printed in all kinds of languages and use every means we could to bring Christ to the people who frequented those places.

The other man was Eric Bowtell. He lived in Reading, heard how God was blessing the work of the London Revival Crusade and came with his wife, Grace, to see what was going on. A gospel singer and an accomplished accordionist, it was not long before Eric moved to London and became actively involved in the meetings. He also joined in the evangelistic work being done in Soho.

Our Soho evangelistic outreaches brought us in touch with a number of drug addicts. The drug problem had begun in London in the early 1960s and a number of us were thinking through how we could tackle it. My attention was drawn to *The Cross and Switchblade*, the book that told the story of how David Wilkerson, a young Assemblies of God preacher, had built up a successful ministry among the drug addicts of New York. In the autumn of 1964 I decided to visit New York to seek David's help and guidance on how best to minister to Soho's drug addicts. I met both him and his brother, Gary, and spent a week studying their rehabilitation programme, as well as joining the teams on their evangelistic outreaches into the dark alleyways and disused buildings where the drug addicts hung out. I came away with a good deal of helpful information.

Back in London I talked and prayed things over with Vic Ramsey who, with his wife, Jan, was at that time running a guest house for students in South London. Vic, I knew, carried a great burden for those who were caught up in the drug scene. We decided together to rent the basement of the Orange Street Congregational Church, which was close to Leicester Square, for a regular Sunday night outreach meeting to the addicts. We prepared leaflets, which explained in 'streetwise' language that a special meeting would be held every Sunday night at 8pm, and that free coffee, tea and refreshments would be available, together with some lively music. These leaflets were given out one Wednesday in the late autumn. The first Sunday meeting was packed. Loving hands had prepared refreshments, The London Revival Crusade Trio sang, young men and women who had been set free from drug addiction through the power of Jesus Christ gave testimonies. In the weeks that followed, Vic and I used to take it in turns to give a brief evangelistic talk.

It became clear that a great need was being met through these meetings and the news of what was happening spread far and wide. Reports appeared in the Christian press, and others involved in this type of evangelism travelled from far and near in their desire to see first-hand what was going on. One very well-known Christian personality, Colonel Orde Dobbie, made it a rule to be there every Sunday night. It moved many of us to watch Orde and his wife, Flo, serving sandwiches to the young addicts whose backgrounds were so different to theirs. One reporter who witnessed this described it as 'love with a stoop in it'.

Addicts were converted at almost every meeting and were followed up during the week, encouraged to break the drug habit, return home (if that was appropriate), find a job and begin to put into practice the basic principles of the Christian life. Those who work in this type of evangelism will know from experience that it is one thing for someone to make a commitment to Christ, but another thing to keep it. Recidivism is an enormous problem in the drug addiction scene and soon it became obvious that we needed to do something else to help rehabilitate those who made a profession of faith in Christ. The solution was to get them away from London to a place where more time could be given to helping them stay off drugs and begin to take the first steps in Christian living. But where? That was the question to which, in late 1964, we had to give urgent and most prayerful attention.

Providentially, a lady who attended the meetings at Dennison House heard of our concern and told us that she owned a large guesthouse in Herne Bay that was closed for the winter months. She offered to rent it to us at a token rate for a few months as a place away from the London drug scene where we could bring converted addicts and help them take their first steps in the Christian life.

Eric Bowtell and his wife, Grace, were invited to oversee this experiment. Although we all understood the theory of drug addiction rehabilitation, none of us had any previous experience in the field, so we were working very much in the dark. We decided to name the Herne Bay project the New Life Centre.

As we crossed from 1964 into 1965, little did I know I was moving into what was to be a watershed year. Some months previously at Dennison House I had been asked how I did my personal study of the Bible. I explained that my preferred approach was to take a biblical theme and trace it through the pages of Scripture. At that time, for example, I was studying the theme of the Bloodline in the Bible. I was fascinated with how the river of blood, which starts in Genesis, widens as it goes through Scripture. In Genesis, blood was shed to cover the sins of an individual, then a family, and in later books the blood covered the sins of a nation. When we come to the New Testament, we read that the blood shed by Christ covers the sins not just of an individual, a family or even a nation, but the sins of the whole world (John 1:29).

The enquirer seemed enthralled by this and asked if I could

write the Scripture verses I was looking at on a postcard so that he could study them as well. I sent him the list and he immediately responded by asking if I would do that for him every week so that he could study whatever theme I had decided to pursue. After a few weeks several others who had heard what was happening came to me with the same request, so I found myself writing between 12 and 15 postcards weekly, which I called *Theme of the Week*.

As the requests continued to come in, it became impossible to hand-write so many cards, so early in 1965 we began printing hundreds of them. A few months later, one recipient wrote to me, saying, 'It's wonderful following these Scriptures with you and so many other people, but what would be more wonderful would be if you could comment on each of the texts. I know this means much more work for you, but think of the help it would be for those to whom you are ministering day by day.'

I gave a lot of thought to that request and, as it was such an important matter, I had a time of fasting and praying to find the Lord's mind on it. As I prayed I realised that I was on the threshhold of an important stage in my life; I was coming to grips with the desire that had been on my heart for many years – the writing of daily devotional notes. I had a feeling that I was about to go through a door that had been marked 'destiny' from the time I was born, and that all that I had learned and had gone through in previous years had been preparing me for this time in my life.

I realized, however, that the challenge of writing daily notes on a regular basis would mean a radical re-ordering of my priorities. I spent a few days experimenting with the idea by writing on the theme that has always dominated my thinking – revival. Soon I had come up with a whole month's daily readings on the subject. But I knew that once I launched a theme of the month with daily notes it would need to be continued, so I decided to think over it for a few months and see how things worked out.

The meetings at Dennison House, especially the regular Saturday night meeting, continued to draw people from all parts of London and the Home Counties. The numbers involved in the regular Wednesday night outreach into Soho increased dramatically when a large group of young people from Croydon, led by a very active youth worker, Lyn Turner, joined forces with us. Lyn, a young married lady who had been closely involved with the National Young Life Campaign, had been attending Dennison House for some time and felt a clear call to give herself to the work amongst the Soho drug addicts.

The Sunday night meeting in Orange Street not only continued to attract the attention of Christians who were keen on this kind of evangelism, but several London social workers and medical students as well. The latter were keen to discover if we had an answer for the growing problem of drug addiction. During the week following each Sunday night meeting in Orange Street our team followed up those who had made decisions for Christ, helping them to find jobs, make contact with their families, and in those cases where they had to appear in court because of a previous misdemeanor, speak there on their behalf.

The Herne Bay experimental rehabilitation programme under Eric and Grace Bowtell's direction saw some success, but not as much as they or ourselves had hoped. Inexperienced as they were, the problems they encountered in getting the young men to turn their backs on their old lifestyle and follow in the steps of the Saviour were enormous. Supporting this project also stretched our financial resources to the maximum. Finally, Eric and Grace came to the conclusion that it was not the sort of work they were really suited for, so the experiment ended after four months.

After Eric and Grace returned to London the rehabilitated drug addicts lived for a while with Vic and Jan Ramsey at their Guest House in South London. A few weeks later the Bowtells received an invitation to become part of a missionary team working in Portugal, a country that had been on Eric's heart for a number of years. So with the blessing of the London Revival Crusade, Eric and Grace left for Portugal in the late spring of 1965. They had left the rehabilitation of drug addicts' ministry behind, but Vic, on the other hand, knew God had called him to this work. In fact it was not long after the closure of the New life Centre in Herne Bay that a businessman in Bromley offered him some premises in which he could establish a rehabilitation programme.

Within a few months Vic and Jan moved there from Upper Norwood to Bromley to lay down the foundation of what became a widely acclaimed ministry to drug addicts. At this point the work came under the banner of New Life Foundation and ceased to be part of London Revival Crusade. The story of its tremendous growth can be read elsewhere, but the work Vic and Jan did in the 1960s, 70s and 80s in helping to set Britain's addicts free is deserving of the highest praise.

CHAPTER 24

A WATERSHED YEAR

It was in the summer of 1965 that Tony Holloway, who had worked with us in different ways in the London Revival Crusade, and particularly in the work being done in Soho, joined our ministry team at Dennison House as full-time Director of Evangelism.

In a preliminary interview I had with Tony, I made it clear that I expected him to give up every other Christian activity he was involved in so that he could be single-minded in the task I was asking him to do. It says much about his character that he did not flinch at this request and from the start threw himself wholeheartedly into his new role.

One of the Tony's first tasks was to organise special meetings to pray for evangelism in various London boroughs. Evangelism, like every other aspect of Christian work, rises and falls in relation to prayer. God's Spirit is constantly at work in us, prodding us and entreating us to avail ourselves of the power that is available to us only through prayer. Someone has said that His power is like an inverted triangle and flows through into human hearts at the point of prayer. A little prayer and a little is accomplished, a lot of prayer and a lot is accomplished.

About the same time that Tony became a full-time worker with the London Revival Crusade he began courting Beryl Field, a fine young Christian girl from the Croydon area. Beryl was an excellent pianist and it was not long before she began to play for us in Dennison House, taking over at times from Roy Jackman, who had filled that role almost from London Revival Crusade's inception. Beryl was also an effective street preacher – fiery, articulate and dynamic. She was a great asset to the Soho outreach team and the combination of her and Tony's talents was a tremendous contribution to London Revival Crusade's ministry.

During July, one decision pressed heavily on me: should I go ahead and replace the Theme of the Week with a Theme of the Month – daily readings covering a whole month with Scriptures and about 300 words of comment on each page? I talked it over with several people and the consensus of opinion was: 'Go for it.' One of my colleagues said, 'You are surrounded by plenty of workers. Take the time to write and leave some of the running of London Revival Crusade to us.' After a talk with my wife I decided to launch the first *Theme of the Month* in September, and placed a print order for around 500 copies.

Having thought I would call the notes *Theme of the Month*, the words of my friend, Tolbert Moore, four years earlier in Atlanta, kept coming back to me: 'If you ever write devotional notes, that would be a good title for it – *'Every Day with Jesus'*. Thus I settled for those words as the title and something that had been a dream for many years was now about to be born. Little did I know at the time that I would continue writing under that title for close on 40 years (so far!) and that the time would come when it would be read in its various forms by nearly a million people every day.

Every Day with Jesus, like the *Theme of the Week*, was given free of charge to those who requested it, but on one condition: they were asked to promise to pray daily for Holy Spirit revival in our land. Recipients were also asked to send a gift, whenever they were able to, to help with the production costs. The new publication was warmly received and from the very first edition testimonies flowed in about how God was using it to deepen readers' spiritual convictions and whet their appetites to dip daily into God's Word.

The thought occurred to me at the time that, as the ministry of the written word was beginning to spread beyond London to other parts of the country and even overseas, it would be more appropriate if this part of the work functioned under another name – a name that would not limit it to one city. So I met with my legal adviser, Graham Ross Cornes, who suggested that a charity be formed and asked me what name I would like to give it. My response was to say that I was a crusader at heart (in the sense of being a vigorous campaigner for what I believe in), and I wanted to use my voice in calling the church to pray for and believe God for a flood of His Holy Spirit to flow through the worldwide church. The only word I could think of to describe that was revival. Thus the name of the charity should be Crusade for World Revival. And so in late 1965 the charity Crusade for World Revival was born, the first trustees being Enid, John Wyndham Hughes (my father), Cary Morse (my brother-in-law), David Cecil Jones and myself.

To make the demarcation clear between the London Revival Crusade and Crusade for World Revival, we took over a house in Selsdon Road, Croydon, which was owned by Lyn Turner, to run the new organisation. Lyn herself worked for some time as secretary. Roy Jackman's lease on 25 Oxford Street expired around this time, and the London Revival Crusade moved its offices to 52 Victoria Street, opposite what then was known as Scotland Yard.

The autumn of 1965 saw an invasion of London by the American chapters of the Full Gospel Business Men's Fellowship International under the leadership of Demos Shakarian and his family. They took over the Hilton Hotel in Hyde Park and for a week held meetings every night in Westminster Chapel. At the weekend a team joined us in Dennison House and with them was the celebrated ex-drug addict, Nicky Cruz, who featured in *The Cross and Switchblade*. During the ten days the team was with us, Nicki came down to the Orange Street basement one night and spoke to the drug addicts. As we had previously given out many copies of *The Cross and Switchblade* to them, many were aware of his celebrity status and reputation. Nicky was a little difficult to understand because of his thick Puerto Rican accent, but one could have heard a pin drop as he gave his testimony to Jesus Christ. There were many lasting conversions that night.

My old friend, Jack Martz, came to London at the same time as the FGMFI party and was excited when he saw what was going on among the drug addicts. Being an amateur film-maker, as well as a good preacher, he offered to make a film for promotion purposes. With his wife and Ruby James, he shot various scenes – the Wednesday night outreach in Soho, interviews with ex-drug addicts, and so on.

We showed the film, first in a private session to those who attended Dennison House, and then later premiered it in the New Gallery, Regent Street. When thinking of a title for the film, someone suggested we called it *Heaven and Hell* – the same name as one of the notorious cafes in the heart of Soho. The film opened with a dark screen and a strong voice asking the question, 'Where are you going tonight? Heaven … or hell?' Then there burst on to the screen the different sights and sounds of London leading eventually to the Orange Street Congregational Church basement where every Sunday night the drug addicts congregated to partake of the free refreshments and listen to the evangelistic programme we presented. Jack Martz had secretly and controversially filmed a drug addict shooting heroin into his veins in a toilet in Soho. At that time this was something few people had seen and it had a very dramatic effect on those watching the film. After its London premiere we took it to several major cities in the UK.

Towards the end of the year, Eric Bowtell returned from Portugal and began working with us once more for both the London Revival Crusade and CWR. He and Grace were living near the latter's offices in Croydon.

I regard 1965 as a watershed year because two things happened that would take my life in a new direction – the launch of *Every Day with Jesus* and the founding of Crusade for World Revival. A new ministry had begun to open for me that before I had only dreamt about. But the year was not without its problems. The decision to draw a clear demarcation between the London Revival Crusade and Crusade for World Revival did not sit well with some who were part of the congregation at Dennison House. There were quite a number who struggled with the fact that *Theme of the Week*, which started off as a peculiarly London Revival Crusade project, had now been replaced by *Every Day with Jesus*, which was being distributed under the banner of Crusade for World Revival. They could not understand why another organisation needed to be created – and said so, some very forcibly. Even those who were closest to me would sometimes ask, albeit facetiously, 'Who are you working for this week – London Revival Crusade or Crusade for World Revival?' Beneath the banter I sensed a serious concern.

There was no doubt that my new commitment to Crusade for World Revival, including the writing of *Every Day with Jesus* and the planning and setting up of meetings in other parts of the country, prevented me from working on new London Revival Crusade projects. There was also something happening in the congregation that I did not understand at the time. Research done in later years on newly-founded churches has shown that often after three years a new church goes through a process known as 'settlement'. During those early years there is sense of newness, of being part of a pioneering project, which produces a special kind of excitement, but later the excitement dies down and people begin to settle into more predictable patterns.

In addition to this, the work of the Fountain Trust under the leadership of Michael Harper, with regular meetings in London, was providing an alternative option for those who were interested in experiencing what was then being called the charismatic renewal. On the surface, things appeared to be fine – the meetings still vibrated with spiritual energy, people were being converted, Christians were being blessed and the evangelistic outreaches in Soho were as powerful and effective as ever. But there were rumblings beneath the surface.

One thing that began to trouble some members of the congregation was that there was no evidence of a church structure being considered. Things were very much in my own hands. London Revival Crusade was a business name for which I was solely responsible. I would talk with my co-workers, pray with them and share my vision and thoughts with them, but the final decisions rested entirely with me.

When my co-workers asked if I was considering the appointment of deacons or elders, my answer was that it was early days for that, and I was waiting to see if the right people to hold those positions would begin to emerge. Honesty compels me to admit that my style of leadership at that time was fiercely autocratic – something I now regret. I knew there was concern that I was not accountable to anyone, but I reasoned to myself that, as I was the one who had taken all the financial risks in founding the organisation, the choice of when to establish a church structure should be mine and mine alone. Christ may well have lived in me, but I am afraid arrogance was still very much alive.

As the circulation of *Every Day with Jesus* began to increase, I found myself receiving invitations from churches in different parts of the country to hold crusades or speak at their special functions. On several occasions during 1966, in company with Eric Bowtell, I held crusades in Birmingham, Belfast, and several other smaller towns and cities. At each event I would introduce *Every Day with Jesus* to those who had not yet heard of it and slowly the circulation was extended from the first print run of 1,000 copies to 25,000. Later it was to peak at 100,000 copies, all of them still being given free on confirmation that the recipients would pray for revival and send whatever gift they could afford for its production.

As Crusade for World Revival, unlike the London Revival Crusade, was a charitable trust, I was not allowed to receive any money for myself. So I continued to exist on the love offering that was taken for me every Sunday afternoon in the teaching service at Dennison House. Wherever I preached outside London during the week, I made sure I was back for the Sunday afternoon teaching service in Dennison House!

Midway through the year I conducted the wedding service of Tony Holloway and Beryl. That same summer Gordon White felt led to start developing his own itinerant ministry, which he called Living Waters Revival Ministry. Later, he and his wife, Barbara, settled in the United States from where, as I said earlier, they have operated a successful international ministry.

Vic Ramsey, who by this time had settled in Bromley, and was not so involved in the London Revival Crusade because of his work with the New Life Foundation, still came to Dennison House on Sunday afternoons to lead part of the meeting and supervise the love offering for me. But the loss of three active workers, albeit for good reasons, left some people feeling a bit insecure. An old and wise lady whom I deeply respected asked me at the time, 'Is the Lord stirring up our nest so that some might learn to fly? Or is He drawing our attention to the fact that, beneath the surface, things are not the way they should be?' I found that question very challenging and one that I was unable to answer. My reaction in the past when faced with such a question would have been to ask the Lord, 'Is there something wrong with me? Am I the one in need of a repentant heart?' But, much to my shame I say it, I managed to avoid such introspection.

Late in 1966 we were given the opportunity to open an office in Dennison House itself. In addition to the auditorium on the ground floor, there were offices on the upper floors. One became vacant, so we moved from Victoria Street. Olive Curle ran this office, taking over much of the work that Tony Holloway had been doing in looking after the administration and coordinating events. The programme at Dennison House continued with evangelistic outreaches in different parts of London, meetings in Trafalgar Square and the regular Saturday night meetings. From time to time we welcomed visiting preachers and evangelists such as David Greenow, an Irishman, my friend Tolbert Moore, Don Double, Dick Carter, Clair Hutchins and many others.

As we entered 1967 I began to experience some feelings I knew I needed to confront. At first I pushed them away, but they became so dominant that I could not ignore them any longer. As I sat down to think them through I began to wonder whether, really deep down, I had a pastor's heart. I had been a pastor for over 16 years and I think that I mainly did the work well. But the thought of looking after one congregation for the rest of my life, even a growing one, began to pall on me. I was, I knew, an acceptable preacher and teacher (during my first preaching tour in the USA in 1961 a ministers' fraternal in Atlanta voted me

'Preacher of the Year'), but was I really a pastor?

These were the thoughts uppermost in my mind as I led the London Revival Crusade into the new year. I continued in a pastoral role with people, helping them with their spiritual problems, visiting the sick and all the other duties that befall a pastor. But though we were involved in an almost endless round of spiritual activities there was not quite the same 'buzz' in the meetings, and the more I became involved in meetings outside London the less were my appearances in Dennison House.

Activities under the banner of Crusade for World Revival were now beginning to mean more to me than what I was doing with the London Revival Crusade. I made several visits to the United States that year to speak at conferences and a trip to Jamaica to speak in several churches on the island. My writing was going well, the circulation of *Every Day with Jesus* was increasing and making my name known around Britain. I knew, however, that compared to how things were in the first three years of the London Revival Crusade, there was a marked deterioration in spiritual excitement. At times it felt as if I was pushing a vehicle uphill and afraid to stop in case it fell back on me.

CHAPTER 25

KOREAN JOY – AND A PARTING

In April 1967 an event occurred that figures high on the list of the most remarkable things that have happened to me. I was relaxing at home in East Molesey one Friday evening when the telephone rang. An operator with a foreign accent asked if I was Selwyn Hughes and on confirmation of that said, 'I have a person-to -person call to you from a Mr Sam Park. Please hold the line.' As I waited I wondered who Sam Park was. A few seconds later another voice came down the line: 'You don't know me. My name is Sam Park. I am from Korea and I shall be arriving at London Heathrow tomorrow on a Swissair flight' (then he gave me the time and flight number) 'and I would like you to please meet me as I have something very important to talk to you about.' Then he put down the phone.

I stared at my phone in disbelief. Was I being set up for a joke? My curiosity got the better of me, however, and the next day I went to Heathrow to meet the flight. In the arrival hall I held up a card with Sam Park's name on it and soon a little Korean man came up to me, bowed in the Oriental way and said, 'Thank you for meeting me. Can we go to your home, please?' I drove him to my home and during the half-hour journey he hardly spoke a word, keeping a handkerchief to his mouth. When we arrived he removed it and a thin stream of blood poured from his mouth. Excusing himself, he went to the bathroom to clean up and when he returned he told Enid and me a remarkable story.

He said, 'I am the Principal of a high school in Pusan, Korea and also the Korean representative for an organisation called The Voice of China and Asia. I have been in Finland and Switzerland on deputation work, seeking to raise funds for the organisation, but while I was in Zurich a few days ago I took a drink of water in my hotel room and instantly began to cough up blood. I became alarmed because my first thought was that I had tuberculosis of the lungs – an illness that is endemic to my country. I was afraid to go to a doctor in case I would be isolated for treatment and not get back home. I had been given a copy of *Every Day with Jesus* in Switzerland and had read of your testimony of how God had healed you, and I felt that if I came to you God would heal me through you. I contacted an English-speaking minister who helped me find your phone number and so here I am. Please lay your hands on me and I know God will heal me.'

I was stunned! I had prayed for many people since my own miraculous healing, but confronted with this need I felt I wanted to go away to pray and build up my faith for this occasion. I suggested that perhaps we could talk and I would pray later, but he kept on saying, 'No, please, pray for me now. Now, please. Now!' Seeing my reluctance, he took my hands and put them on his head and I prayed a brief prayer, which went something like: 'Lord, heal my brother now. In Jesus' name.' It was probably the most faithless prayer I have ever prayed, but as I did so he began to breathe heavily and after a while his hands shot up and he shouted at the top of his voice, 'Praise the Lord! God has healed me. I can breathe all the way down to the bottom of my lungs. Now I feel so hungry. I have not eaten for days.' 'What would you like to eat?' Enid asked him. 'Bacon and eggs, please,' he replied. 'We do not eat these often in the East but since I have been in the West I have taken to them very much.' Enid set about preparing him a meal of bacon and eggs which he tucked into with relish.

I had witnessed a number of remarkable healings in my life, but nothing as sensational as this. Sam Park stayed in our home over the weekend and I took him with me to Dennison House for the Saturday night meeting, where he told the people what had happened to him. When he finished people broke out in spontaneous applause – something not done in Christian meetings in those days.

The following Monday I took him to Heathrow for his flight back to Korea, but before leaving my home he asked me to lay my hands on him once again, this time that he might be baptised in the Holy Spirit. We studied the Book of Acts together for about half an hour and then I prayed for him. As I did so I thought to myself that I had never seen anyone so hungry to be filled with God's Spirit. No sooner had I begun to pray than God's Spirit came upon him. His experience was similar to that of the disciples in the upper room on the Day of Pentecost: the disciples there were accused of being drunk, and that was the impression Sam gave as we drove to Heathrow airport. As he made his way through customs he looked back to say goodbye. With his hat slightly askew he looked for all the world as if he was slightly tipsy.

I thought that may be the last I had heard of Sam Park, but a week later he phoned me to say that he had met with the ministers of the churches in Pusan and told them what had happened to him in London. They wanted me to come and conduct a crusade for them as quickly as possible, before the winter months set in. A decision, he said, was needed right away because the grounds where the crusade would be held needed to be booked the following day! I promptly got out my diary and agreed to the dates he had given me for three weeks in July.

When I put the phone down I realised that I was in something of a dilemma. How was I going to finance a trip to Korea? I did not, and could not, expect the Koreans to pay my fare, as I knew from what Sam Park had told me that their economy at that time was very poor. I knew, too, that there was not sufficient money in the Crusade for World Revival funds to finance such a trip. As I shared the matter with Enid we knelt together and prayed, 'Lord, if this is to happen then you must provide.'

A few days later an *Every Day with Jesus* reader in Germany telephoned the CWR office in Croydon to say that she had felt led by the Lord to put a cheque drawn from her London bank in the post and wanted me to know it was on the way. The eagerly-awaited cheque arrived three days later. It was the exact amount needed to cover the return air fare from London to Pusan!

The journey from the UK to Korea in 1967 was a long and tedious one. It took twice as long as it would today. I got as far as Rome when the aircraft developed a fault, which meant an unscheduled overnight stay there while we waited for a spare part to be flown in from London. From there we flew to Hong Kong where I met up with Ruby James, a member of Jack Martz's team who had agreed to accompany me to Korea and be my pianist and gospel singer. Ruby had arranged for me to speak at a Christian school in Hong Kong before we flew on to Tokyo for another overnight stay. Then we headed for Seoul and after another change of aircraft we finally arrived in Pusan.

We were met by a delegation of the ministers from the city and taken immediately to a banquet in our honour, which was attended by some of Pusan's dignitaries. After welcoming speeches lasting several hours, we were taken to our hotel and told that the crusade began the next day with a 5am prayer meeting, where I was expected to speak. At 10am I was scheduled to address a devotional service for ministers and leaders, while the main event, the evangelistic service, would start in the large grounds at 6pm.

After managing to get a few hours' sleep, we were collected from our hotel at 4:30am so that we could arrive at the prayer meeting just before 5am. I already knew that early-morning prayer meetings were a way of life with Christians in South Korea and on the way I asked how many would be there. I was told the hall would probably be full, so I assumed the meeting would be in a church holding several hundred people. But our destination wasn't a church – it was a large auditorium seating about 5,000 people. I entered to find the place packed, with people sitting cross-legged on the floor. I had to remove my shoes (an Oriental custom) at the entrance and it took me some time to make my way to the front so that I could give my address. I spoke for about 20 minutes with the aid of an interpreter and the rest of the time was taken up with prayer for the nightly crusade meetings. In Korea people pray in concert – everyone cries out loudly to God, all at the same time. The sound was deafening as 5,000 people stormed the gates of heaven with a fervency I had never experienced before.

It was in one of those morning prayer meetings, a few days later, that I came the closest I have ever been in my life to what I consider is true revival. I had just finished commenting on the story of the Holy Spirit descending on the people gathered in the house of Cornelius (recorded in Acts 10) when suddenly something similar happened in that large auditorium. The Spirit fell upon the people in such a way that it felt as if the building was being shaken. People stood up with their hands in the air and began praising God not only in their own language, but in other ones as well. One of the ministers standing beside me told me through my interpreter: 'Some of these people are praying in languages I have never heard before.' I felt shivers go up and down my spine as I listened to an old Korean lady standing just a few yards in front of me praising God in Welsh. She was saying over and over again, *'Diolch i ti Arglwydd'* – 'Thank you, Lord. Thank you.'

The 10am meetings, when I preached to the ministers, again through an interpreter, were equally enthralling. Each time I made an interesting point, or said something they had not heard before, they stood up and spent a few minutes praising and worshipping the Lord. It really blesses a preacher's heart when a congregation receives the word with such eagerness and responds with spontaneous praise and worship. It is not the kind of thing we see very often in our very proper and dignified Western Christian communities, but perhaps when revival comes it may well be common practice.

The nightly crusade meetings were held on a large area of open ground, which could take up to 30,000 people. The ministers estimated that on the first night there were around 20,000 present – certainly the largest congregation I had preached to. Sam Park was my interpreter for those meetings, and before I began to preach he told the people what had happened to him in my home. I could tell by the response as he spoke that this was a man who was held in high esteem in the community. Ruby James, the daughter of missionaries to Hong Kong, knew a little Korean and sang songs that contained at least one verse in the language, which won the hearts of the listeners.

After I had preached my evangelistic message, hundreds of people flocked into the special tent set up behind the platform for those who wanted to give their hearts and lives to Jesus Christ. One of those who did so on the first night was a Buddhist priest. I was introduced to him after counsellors had ministered to him. He told me through an interpreter that he would dispense with his priestly robes and thenceforth be a follower of the Lord Jesus Christ. A report and picture of him appeared in a Pusan newspaper the following day and on the second night of the crusade the crowd swelled to around 30,000.

Day after day and night after night during those three never-to-be-forgotten weeks God did some amazing things in Pusan. Out of all the crusades I have conducted around the world, this was the most inspiring and rewarding. It took place, of course, in the days before Dr Yonggi Cho and Billy Graham made such an impact on Korea. Our crusade numbered tens of thousands, but theirs have numbered hundreds of thousands.

The blessings that came out of that crusade were not just the thousands of people who found Christ, or the many ministers who were revived and their lives set on fire, but also the spiritual impact on my own heart and life. I returned to Britain a changed man. My appetite for this kind of work was whetted to such a degree that I knew it would not be long before I would withdraw from London Revival Crusade and embark upon a worldwide ministry.

Just after I returned from Korea we moved our home from East Molesey to the same large house in Croydon which contained the Crusade for World Revival offices. My elder son, David, was now 16 and soon to leave school. He showed some prowess at tennis and one of his teachers told me that he had the potential for becoming a professional player. David had made a decision for Christ when much younger and he told me that his great desire in life was to help me. The best way he felt he could do that was by learning how to be a printer. He sensed and saw even in his teens that printing and publishing would play a large part in my life. I was deeply moved by his attitude.

Although we needed to use professional printers for *Every Day with Jesus* and other publications, we bought a small printing press for producing such things as our regular newsletters and the *Revival* paper. After a short period of training, David took over the printing of much of CWR's material – a task to which he committed himself with great enthusiasm. David's other love was cars and at 16 we were able to help him buy a three-wheeled Robin Reliant, which at that time could be driven by 16-year-olds. Later his interest in cars took him into drag racing – something Enid and I worried greatly about because of the risks to his physical well-being.

I now decided that it was time to hand over the work at Dennison House to a group of men who had visited from time to time under the banner of International Gospel Outreach. These men had impressed me with their spiritual zeal and dedication. I met with them, and after much discussion and prayer they said they were ready to take over the work whenever I chose to leave.

There were many different emotions as you can imagine when I broke the news that I was leaving. Many in the congregation had come to know Christ during my time in the city and I was the only pastor they had known. While they were glad for me that I was moving towards what I felt was God's purpose for my life, they were sad that we would soon be parting company. I tried to make the changeover as harmonious as possible and stayed on for several weeks, but the final break had to come. It was hard leaving a work that I had pioneered, but I assured the people that I would not be leaving the country and that we would meet up from time to time whenever I held a meeting in London.

I felt a great difference in my spirit after my last meeting at Dennison House. I realised I was now free to pursue the work that I felt I was best fitted for – leading evangelistic crusades, preaching and writing. The words of John Wesley came often into my thoughts: 'The world is my parish and all who perish are in my parish.' The fact that I could give more time to writing *Every Day with Jesus* also filled with me great joy. I knew that when done under pressure, much of my writing was often superficial. Now I had the time to really concentrate and put more into its pages than I had ever done before.

I had the feeling that a new day was dawning and I was slowly getting closer to the true purpose that God had for my life.

CHAPTER 26

GETTING MY PRIORITIES RIGHT

If someone had told me ten years earlier that there would come a time when I would leave the pastoral ministry and never return, I think I would have responded with disbelief. But now I felt I was not just moving away from something, but moving towards something that had been beckoning to me for almost two decades.

My experience with London Revival Crusade was a learning curve I would not change for anything. But the transition from 18 years of pastoral life into a more itinerant ministry was one that brought me deep and unending joy. In travelling round as a full-time crusading evangelist, I found a lightness in my step that had never quite been there before. I felt I had the freedom to do things that were more suited to my personality – evangelistic crusading, teaching and writing.

As soon as my friend, Donald Bergagard, the Swedish singer and evangelist, knew I was free to travel, he immediately arranged for me to tour some of the new Swedish, Danish, Norwegian and Dutch charismatic churches that were opening up under the name 'Maranatha' – a Greek word meaning 'Christ is coming'. I spend several months during the autumn and early winter of 1968 preaching in these churches. I would return home after two or three weeks to write the next edition of *Every Day with Jesus*, then after a short break I would be off again to Stockholm, Malmö, Jönköping and Utrecht, and a number of the

Maranatha churches in Copenhagen, Denmark and Norway also. Donald Bergagard accompanied me on these tours as song leader and interpreter.

Returning home from one of these trips to be met at Heathrow airport by Enid and our two sons, we happened to take a wrong turning driving back to Croydon and found ourselves in Walton-on-Thames. Enid noticed a newly built block of flats with a 'Flats to rent' sign. 'Now you are travelling so much, wouldn't it be better if we lived nearer to Heathrow airport?' she said. 'Why don't we take a look at one of these flats? There's no harm in looking.'

We found the caretaker, who told us that only 10 of the 36 flats had been taken, so we had a wide choice of position. We found one on the seventh floor that had a clear view of the River Thames and in the distance, about five miles away, we could see the planes landing at Heathrow. We all fell in love with it instantly and within a few weeks had made the move from Croydon. This made it so much easier for my trips abroad and we were to enjoy living in that flat for 16 years, although, sadly, it was there in 1986 that Enid died of cancer. That story, of course, will be told later.

Just before Christmas I was coming back from a preaching trip to Oslo when the Lord spoke to me about the condition of my marriage. Above the English Channel, as the plane was making its approach to Heathrow, the Holy Spirit whispered in my heart that I was not treating my wife the way I should. I knew exactly what the Lord was drawing my attention to, as I had often pondered in the past few months how my long absences from home were affecting her. In the half-hour it took the plane to complete its approach and land, I came to some decisions that completely transformed my relationship with my wife and, in consequence, my children.

Prior to these moments on the plane my prayer had always been, 'Lord, I will take care of the business of your church; you take care of my wife.' It came home to me forcefully that I had been praying the wrong kind of prayer. I had been putting the church before Enid. A phrase came into my mind (either put there by the Spirit or through being reminded of something I had read) that went like this: 'A man must first be a priest in his own home before he is fitted to take on a priestly role in the church.'

I could not believe how utterly foolish I had been to put church matters before my wife and family, when Scripture is so clear about this issue: 'Husbands,' says the apostle Paul, 'love your wives, just as Christ loved the church and gave himself up for her' (Eph. 5:25). I knew without a shadow of doubt that I would be ready to give my life for my wife, but was I willing to give my life to my wife? Was I more concerned about the health of the Church than the health of my wife and family? Should I reduce my preaching schedule to spend more time with my loved ones? These were the questions hammering in my brain as the wheels of the aircraft touched down on the runway. Enid was at the airport to meet me and during the 20-minute drive home I desperately wanted to tell her some of the thoughts that were going on in my mind. I knew, however, that it would probably involve several hours of discussion, so I decided to leave things until later.

That evening, after David and John had gone to bed, I sat down with Enid and shared some of the thoughts that had been going through my mind near the end of my flight. As soon as I began to speak I could see by her expression that I was touching on something that was very real to her. Not once had she complained about the number of trips that I took overseas, but as I began to apologise for my insensitivity to her needs and my preoccupation with matters relating to the church, tears of relief began to flow down her cheeks. The tears turned into sobbing. As I took her in my arms, the realisation of my inattentiveness to her physical, spiritual and psychological needs overwhelmed me to the point where I found myself sobbing, too.

Over the next few days I rearranged my speaking schedule so that I had more time to spend with my family. I worked out a plan that cut my engagements down by 50 per cent of what they had been previously. I believe this decision to put my wife first, before the needs of the church, was the biggest single step I have taken to building a good and godly marriage. When my wife realised that, next to the Lord, she was first in my life it produced such a release in her spirit that she seemed a different woman. She told me on one occasion that it had felt at times as if I was having an affair – not with another woman, but with the church.

Before this time I never used to consult Enid when I received a speaking invitation. But from then onwards I never once accepted an invitation without discussing it with her. Soon what had been a reasonable marriage became a great marriage. It also made it possible, in the years that followed, to contribute to the enrichment of other's people's marriages through the seminars I have given and the books I have written on the subject. My marriage wasn't perfect. Sometimes there were tensions. But it was good.

Though many of my bookings for 1969 were re-scheduled and some cancelled, there was one that Enid and I felt I simply must keep – to conduct a crusade in Madras, South India. *Every Day with Jesus* had been distributed in India for some time by Mrs Barnard, an Anglo-Indian lady who lived in Bangalore. She was a great enthusiast for the publication and had been supplying copies to a church in Madras, pastored by Henry Joseph. He enjoyed *EDWJ* so much that he wanted to meet me. After consulting with several other churches he invited me to conduct a crusade for the churches of Madras during March. Once again I invited Eric Bowtell to join me, and early in that month we travelled to Bangalore to meet Mrs Barnard before going on to Madras.

The crusade was held on open ground, supported by about 20 of the city's churches. I fell in love with the people of Madras as soon as I met them – a love affair that has gone on for over 35 years, during which time I have been back seven times to lead crusades there. Night after night for two weeks, I preached to a large crowd and at every meeting people surrendered their lives to Jesus Christ. On some nights there were a dozen or so conversions and on other nights people came forward in scores. They rapturously received Eric Bowtell's singing and accordion accompaniment.

There was one never-to-be-forgotten night when Eric, his energy level sapped by a heavy attack of dysentery, decided that he would only be able to sing one song. I have seen Eric minister powerfully through song many times in different parts of the world, but I have never witnessed anything like what happened that night before or since. The Spirit of the Lord came upon him so powerfully as he sang that he stepped down from the platform and danced among the crowd. In an open-air crusade of that nature in India, people usually sit on the ground. To my amazement, and everyone else's, Eric danced through the crowd for several minutes without touching or stepping on the toes of anyone.

It brought to mind the occasion, recorded in 2 Samuel 6:14, when King David – leading the procession of men returning the ark of the covenant to its rightful place in the temple in Jerusalem – 'danced before the Lord with all his might'. Often when I return to Madras, people who were at that first crusade say to me, 'We have never forgotten when brother Bowtell danced through the crowd.'

During the mornings of the crusade I held meetings for the ministers, when I shared about some of the ways the Lord had worked in my life. I was told by one member of the crusade organising committee that several of those ministers were deeply discouraged and on the verge of leaving the ministry. I spoke to them one morning on King David's conflict with the Amalekites and how David's enemies had destroyed Ziklag, his and his men's home at that time. David was terribly upset when he discovered this, but in 1 Samuel 30: 6 we read: 'But David found strength in the Lord his God.' My theme was 'How to defeat discouragement' and during my message I said, 'The problems ahead of us are never as great as the power behind us.' Suddenly the place erupted as the Spirit took my statement and used it to touch the hearts of the small group of discouraged ministers.

They rose to their feet as one man and began to shout and sing praises to the Lord. They told me afterwards that it was not just the words I had uttered, but also the Spirit flowing through them that seemed to banish all their discouragements in a single moment and lift them to a new place in God. I never cease to marvel at how the Holy Spirit takes an ordinary word, a phrase or a sentence and charges it with such spiritual energy that it not only changes people's perspectives, but also transforms the whole of their life.

It was in that meeting that I also happened to say, 'I would rather be a preacher of the gospel than the King of England.' A young man, a worker in one of the churches, was so affected by that simple statement that he decided right there and then to become a preacher. He trained for the ministry and today is one of India's finest ministers. He has a great teaching ministry and has influenced many for Jesus Christ.

Returning from India, the rest of the summer was taken up with meetings in the UK. Although I had decided to cut down my speaking schedule somewhat, there were some engagements I had to fulfil, simply because it would have caused problems to those churches where the events had already been advertised. Enid and I agreed that I should accept one more overseas invitation that year – from East Africa. It had come from several pastors in Kenya who had been reading *Every Day with Jesus* and were keen for me to visit their nation. Coincidentally, Jack Martz wrote to me to say he was planning a trip to East Africa with his wife and Ruby James to film some of the wildlife. When I gave him the dates I was due to be in Kenya, he arranged his visit to be there at the same time.

We met up in Nairobi during October. Jack and his team helped me in the crusade, which was held on open ground near the city's central bus station. Although it was well supported, it soon became obvious that it was not a good idea to hold it near the bus station, as people were more interested in catching their buses home after a hard day's work than to stand and listen to the preaching of the gospel. So we moved into a large church and night after night had a much more successful series of meetings. As soon as the crusade was over, a number of pastors came to me asking if I would return the following year and speak in their churches. One of them was a tall African pastor by the name of Silas Owittit. He pastored a group of churches in Kisumu, about 100 miles from Nairobi. I was drawn immediately to this man, with his dignified bearing and gracious demeanour, and I promised that if I returned I would try to visit his church. I didn't know it then, but Silas was to become a good friend in the years ahead.

The first Board of CWR Limited, 1986. Left to right standing: Gill Morgan, Maurice Paine, Geoff Winson, Michael Nightingale, John Hoskins. Seated: Trevor Partridge, me, Enid, David Rivett

Caring seminars in Central Hall, Westminster, 1986
(Mick Rock)

Lord Tonypandy opens Waverley Abbey House, 29 August 1987.
Left to right: David Rivett, Lady Anson (Mayor of Waverley),
Lord Tonypandy, myself and Trevor Partridge

Planning in the Woodlands near Waverley Abbey House
with David and Trevor, 1989

Caring seminars in Auckland,
New Zealand, 1992

Colin Nelson, for many years CWR's
International Ministry Coordinator

John Muys, at one time CWR's
International Consultant and CEO

School of Counselling, Melbourne, Australia, 1994

In Kampala, Uganda with Pastor Gary Skinner, October 2002

In Lagos, Nigeria with Remi Ayida.

In Uganda with Olivia Kyambadde, 1996

Evening rally in Lagos, 1993

Marriage God's Way seminar in
Colombo, Sri Lanka, 2003

In Sri Lanka with Ruki and
Neville Mendez, who introduced
EDWJ into Sri Lanka.

Samson Gandhi,
CWR's distributor
and coordinator
in India

Hilary Fernando, CWR's
distributor and ministry
supporter in Sri Lanka

National Pastors' Conference, Hyderabad, India, 2002

Jeannette Barwick and Philip Greenslade with me at the National Pastors' Conference, Langkawi, Malaysia, 2000

In Kuala Lumpur, Malaysia with Rev Lawrence Yap

In Miri, East Malaysia with Bishop Anthony Lee, 2000

Jeannette Barwick (far right) and myself, guests of the British High Commissioner and his family in Brunei, 2000

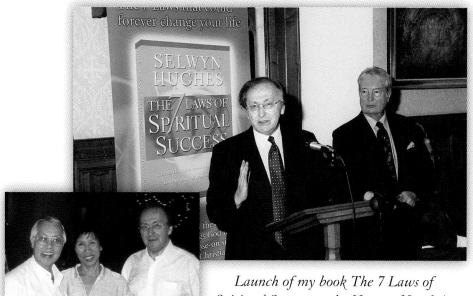

*Launch of my book The 7 Laws of
Spiritual Success at the House of Lords in
2002 with Lord Archer of Sandwell*

*In Singapore with Canon James
Wong and his wife Esther*

*Christ Empowered Living seminar at The City Harvest Church,
Singapore, 2002*

With the CWR staff team at Waverley Abbey House, 2004

Mick Brooks,
Chief Executive

Sean Gubb,
former Head of
Training

Matthew Taylor,
Creative Services
Manager

Paul Bexon,
Company
Secretary

With my nephew Mark and my mother Lily, grandchildren Suzanne, Leighton and
Sheryl, daughter-in-law Sue and great-grandchildren Jazmine and Kian in 2002

CHAPTER 27

AN UNEXPECTED NEW VENTURE

Before leaving Nairobi I had one last speaking engagement – a businessmen's lunch meeting in the Hilton Hotel, Nairobi. I was talking with a group of American missionaries who sat at my table when one of them asked me what airline I had travelled with from London to Nairobi. I told him that I had come on a charter flight for a third of the fare charged by the scheduled airlines. Around the late 1960s, there was a great deal of concern among regular travellers that the scheduled airlines were acting as a kind of a cartel – keeping prices much higher than they need be. A group of businessmen had discovered it was possible for groups to charter aircraft from one destination to another at a fraction of the cost: this led to the charter flight revolution around the world.

When the missionaries knew what I had paid for my return trip from London, they became so interested that they stayed on talking with me for several hours after the meeting was over. One of them said, 'Do you realise what travelling at reduced rates could do for missions? It would mean our travelling budgets could be reduced and the money saved put to better use.' Another said, 'It would also mean that we would be able to return on furlough more often and the whole thing, if it worked, could revolutionise the work of missions.' They virtually pleaded with me, 'Please help us take advantage of this kind of travel. You would be doing a tremendous service for the kingdom of God.' I promised them I would do what I could.

Just after I returned home from Nairobi I was inundated with requests from a number of missionary organisations in Kenya, such as the African Inland Mission, who had heard from some of their missionaries of the low fare I paid from London to Nairobi, asking if I could help them set up low-cost travel for their missionaries to and from the field. I decided to visit the London office of the charter operator through whom I arranged my own low-cost travel. I put it to him that over the following year it was possible that I could put hundreds, if not thousands of passengers his way, mainly missionaries and Christian workers for whom the high fare structures of scheduled airlines were financially draining.

He recognised at once that this represented a considerable amount of business and immediately offered a commission based on every ten passengers booked with him. As he was an Asian I knew he would enjoy a little bartering (as indeed do I), and after about 15 minutes together we agreed a much better rate of commission. My intention was to handle the business through the Crusade for World Revival office in Croydon, but as I was leaving he said, 'If you expect a large number of passengers, why don't you set up an office in this building and start your own agency? You could buy the seats from us and sell them to your own people. There's an office upstairs waiting for someone to take it over. Come and see.'

The second floor office had three rooms and the rent was comparatively low. As soon as I saw it I sensed that a Christian travel company could operate from there. But a lot of thinking had to be done about how much of my time it would take to establish the business, interview and appoint staff, research the whole subject of low-cost travel on a worldwide basis and, more particularly, how it would affect my speaking schedule. I talked things over with Enid, the CWR trustees and my solicitor, Graham Ross Cornes. They all thought that pioneering low-cost air travel for missionaries and Christian workers was a service to the kingdom of God that would more than justify the time it would take to establish. Graham Ross Cornes said, 'It looks like a challenge has been thrown at your feet and one that you are going to have to pick up.' Several weeks of prayer and further thought followed, and early in 1971 I took over the office at 111 Oxford Street in the name of Crusade Travel, a department of Crusade for World Revival.

Advertisements in the Christian press attracted a number of people for interviews, and within a few weeks I had employed a small staff who were soon booking people on charter flights to different parts of the world. We quickly built up a list of charter operators who ran return flights from London to almost every country, but Board of Trade regulations stipulated that anyone going on a charter flight must be a member of the organisation chartering the aircraft. I took out associate membership with all the charter companies in the name of Crusade Travel, so that everyone who booked with and registered as a member was automatically regarded as member of the various charter groups.

My son, David, moved his printing press into one of the rooms so that letter headings, booking forms, vouchers, advertising leaflets and so on were available to us within hours of needing them. Letters to the many missionary organisations in the UK brought a swift response, as they saw a way of reducing their missionary travel costs, sometimes by more than a half. This information came to the attention of Steve Stevens, a former director of Mission Aviation Fellowship, and he came to talk to me about it. This resulted in him helping me to research and develop a worldwide programme of conveying missionaries from one part of the world to another at the lowest possible cost.

Steve's experience in aviation, as well as his dogged determination to help find an alternative to high scheduled airline fares for missionaries, was a tremendous help. He threw himself enthusiastically into the work. He told me recently that, in his opinion, Crusade Travel, along with the charter operators of that time, did much to shake up the scheduled airlines and get them to reconsider their high fare structures. Steve worked with me for just under a year before leaving to give his support to a new spiritual movement begun in London in 1971 that emphasised the need to take morality more seriously – the Festival of Light.

Inevitably, the work of Crusade Travel cut into my speaking engagements and the time available for evangelistic crusades during 1970, but the conviction grew deeper every day that the work I was doing was still a matter of tremendous consequence to the kingdom of God. I knew that it would take at least a year to establish the travel department, so I was determined to make the most of every opportunity to turn it into a going concern.

Because of my connections in the travel industry, Enid and I were given free seats over Easter 1970 to travel to Israel. At the Garden Tomb in Jerusalem, after the service on Easter Sunday morning, we discussed the possibility of organising Holy Land tours under the auspices of Crusade Travel. When we returned it was a simple matter to put an advert in *Every Day with Jesus* for an autumn visit, and within a few weeks over 100 people had applied. As accommodation had only been booked for 50 people we ended up taking two tours, in September and October, led by Eric Bowtell and myself.

Throughout the autumn and winter of 1970–71 I devoted almost all my energies to dealing with issues relating to low-cost travel. I still preached in various places at weekends and spent a day each week writing *Every Day with Jesus*, but my main preoccupation was ensuring that missionary organisations knew of our work and could take advantage of the savings that the charter flights offered.

In March 1971 Eric Bowtell and I made our way once more to India, this time to the city of Trivandrum, 300 miles south of Madras. Henry Joseph had been distributing *Every Day with Jesus* in the churches there for some time, so my name was fairly well known. Henry acquainted the ministers who had wanted the crusade with how it should be set up and he was with us for throughout the week it lasted.

On the opening night a man who was mentally ill (some thought he was demon possessed) came into the grounds armed with an axe and declared that he was going to 'split the skull of the preacher'. He came up to the platform as I was preaching but several strong men stopped him going up the steps, disarmed him and sat with him until the end of the service. The incident caused the ministers to meet together in prayer early every morning; they were convinced that there was a satanic ploy at work to disrupt the crusade. Certainly their prayers brought a tremendous sense of God's presence into the meetings. Although it was only a short crusade and smaller than the one we held in Madras, we saw many people won to Christ.

On my return from India I found the travel business had increased considerably. More and more missionaries and missionary organisations were beginning to hear about low-cost travel and we were receiving requests for information from all parts of the world. It was in connection with travel during the summer of 1971 that I first met Trevor Partridge. He came to see me at the Crusade Travel office about a low-cost flight to the United States and to chat about his future. Trevor was studying at a Bible college in Seattle and still had two years of his course left. His father was an avid *Every Day with Jesus* reader and

Trevor talked about what he hoped to do when he returned to the UK at the end of his studies. We agreed it would be worthwhile meeting up again at that time to see if there was a way in which we could work together. Little did I know then that this brief encounter would result in his becoming a close colleague and working with me for nearly 25 years.

A six-week postal strike in the autumn of that year caused many businesses to grind to a halt. Crusade Travel managed to keep going on telephone bookings, and our staff met the missionaries at the airport to give them their tickets. During those six weeks I wondered how we could make good use of our time. I have always been struck by the fact that Jesus, whenever He was blocked in one direction, would break out in another. If He was unable to minister in one village He would move to the next. I am a great believer in the fact that blocks can become blessings – if we stay alert.

My attention was drawn to a new film produced by the Billy Graham organisation. Entitled *His Land*, it featured Cliff Richard and Cliff Barrows (Billy Graham's song leader), who went through the Holy Land following in the footsteps of Jesus Christ. Cliff Richard sang several songs in the film which, as well as being a documentary, also had a powerful evangelistic thrust. It had not been long since Cliff had announced his personal commitment to Jesus Christ and, as he was a highly popular performer, I guessed the film would have a big appeal, especially to young people. I talked to Steve Stevens about this and we decided to use the weeks of the postal strike to travel the country with the film. I figured that our tour would fulfil three purposes: bring people under the sound of the gospel; make good use of our time; and acquaint people with our Holy Land tours.

We placed adverts in the local papers of major cities including Birmingham, Bristol, Manchester, Sheffield, Leeds and

Nottingham, letting people know they could book by telephone and collect their tickets at the venue on the night of the showing. We were deluged with requests and every venue was packed to capacity. After the film was shown I made an evangelistic appeal and we saw hundreds of people surrender to Christ in those weeks of the postal strike.

The number of people who made enquiries about visiting Israel after we had shown *His Land* was beyond our expectations and we planned another two tours for 1972. These focused not only on visiting the sacred sites such as the Shepherd's fields in Bethlehem, and Nazareth, Galilee and Jerusalem, but at each site we read the Scriptures and I spent about 15 minutes commenting on some aspect of what we had read. It became clear to me that the Holy Land Tours were to become a regular feature of CWR's ministry in the future. In fact they continued well into the 1990s.

Towards the end of 1971 Eric and I went back to East Africa and this time not only held open-air crusades, but meetings in various churches throughout Kenya. In Nairobi we ministered in the Elim church, and from there went to a large church in Mombasa established by Bud Sickler, a Canadian missionary. We travelled to Kisumu on the equator to the church pastored by Silas Owitti. There I was required to use two interpreters, one translating from English to Kikyu, the other from Kikyu to Swahili. Silas took it upon himself to interpret from English to Swahili and a colleague of his from Swahili to Kikyu. A problem arose when Silas, a strong extrovert who was always ready to let his feelings be known, would listen to something I said and be so taken with it that he would raise his hands in the air, do a little dance and forget his role as interpreter for a few minutes. This caused the second interpreter to get frustrated at times, but the sight of Silas' evident enjoyment of what he was hearing more than made up for the unevenness of the services.

While we were in East Africa one veteran missionary placed his hand on my shoulder and said: 'Selwyn, we are grateful for the work you are doing in missions to help us get the most for our money, but don't leave it too long before you return to the full-time preaching ministry again. Never forget you are first and foremost a preacher and a writer; get others to look after our travel needs and, if you want my opinion, the sooner the better.' His words left a deep impression on me and I came away determined that as soon as Crusade Travel was established I would withdraw from an active role in it and let others take over.

CHAPTER 28

'I CAN DO THAT'

lthough I have never kept a journal (much to my regret) New Year's Day 1972 is a date etched in my memory. It should have been a day to relax, but after spending the morning with the family I went into my study to finish writing the next edition of *Every Day with Jesus*. I was behind on that particular edition and I was feeling a little anxious. But as I bowed my head in prayer, as I always do when beginning to write, a much greater concern than meeting an editorial deadline gripped me: how I could withdraw from running the low-cost travel business? Crusade Travel was meeting the needs of many missionaries, but now that it was established it needed to be taken over by someone else. I prayed a good deal about this and an amazing peace settled on my soul and with it came the assurance that before the year ended my prayer would be answered.

The Crusade for World Revival office in Croydon having been closed down, Enid did quite a lot of the work at home and some was done in the Crusade Travel office in London. As *Every Day with Jesus* continued to grow, the demands for copies stretched the small group of volunteers who met once a month in a rented hall to pack and dispatch parcels all over the world. Enid suggested that we should open an office close to our home in Walton-on-Thames. After poring over the local newspapers, we found accommodation in what used to be the old Post Office building in Weybridge. The place was quite run down, paint peeling off the walls, water seeping through a leaking roof, but it was in a good position near the railway station. So, in January 1972, we signed the lease and it became our new CWR headquarters.

Enid took over the office management and we soon had a small staff from the local area. Later I made a key appointment when Lorna Paine joined the team as my personal secretary. During her interview she told me that while on holiday in Cyprus with her husband, Maurice, she was sitting on a beach reading *Every Day with Jesus* and other CWR literature when she came across an announcement that I was looking for a secretary to serve me in the new office in Weybridge. She applied as soon as she returned home and got the position. Loyal and efficient, she served me faithfully for nearly nine years.

After the opening of the office in Weybridge I rearranged my priorities so that, when I was not ministering overseas or elsewhere in the UK, I spent two days in the Crusade Travel office in Oxford Street, one day writing and two days at Weybridge. One evening in February, Irene Mitcheson, who did some freelance artwork for CWR, brought her brother to see me at the Weybridge office. He lived in America and he told me about an amazing spiritual development there: thousands of young people had been attending a week-long seminar based entirely on the Bible. The seminar was called 'The Institute in Basic Youth Conflicts', and was being presented in cities all over America by Bill Gothard, its founder, to crowds upwards of 5,000. I found myself so intrigued and excited about young people listening to nothing but biblical concepts from Monday evening to Saturday, that I immediately decided to go and see this spiritual phenomenon for myself.

The following day I telephoned the office in Michigan and found out that the next seminar would be held in Atlanta,

Georgia in a few weeks' time. My schedules meant that I could only attend for the first three days, but I considered that was long enough to understand what it was that caused so many young people to be fascinated by someone talking only about the Bible. When I arrived at the venue to register, I was told that all 7,000 seats had been taken. After explaining that I had come all the way from the UK, I was moved to the top of the standby list. A few minutes before the seminar began I was told that someone had not turned up and I could have their seat.

I found myself high up in the second balcony of the auditorium and right on the scheduled start time Bill Gothard walked on to the platform, switched on an overhead projector and with visuals projected on to a huge screen began to talk about the power and importance of the Scriptures. 'Successful living,' he said, 'depends on how close we keep to the principles of Scripture. Obey them and we get results; violate them and we get consequences.'

I was enthralled by his use of an overhead projector. These are now seen everywhere in churches, of course, but at that time I had never seen one in use. Looking around at the large audience, I could see that the truths and texts being shown on a large screen were making a powerful impact on people. Sometimes Bill would use prepared visuals and other times he would draw freehand on the transparent projector roll. This particularly fascinated me. Everyone was given a large red binder that contained copious and clear notes. Some pages were left blank so that participants could fill them in from the words or drawings appearing on the screen. I had never seen this style of teaching before and, to the best of my knowledge, no one in Britain was doing it – certainly not in the churches I knew. I was deeply impressed.

Halfway through the first evening I thought to myself, *'I can do that!*' I imagined myself in Westminster Central Hall with an overhead projector and a large screen presenting the truths of God's word in this new and dynamic way. When the evening finished I couldn't wait for the next night. I watched and listened over the next two evenings and more and more ideas flashed through my mind about how this new medium could be used. I saw that not only could it illuminate truth from the Scriptures even more powerfully, but it could also be used to present the gospel to those who were not Christians. My appetite was so whetted that I decided to book in for the next seminar, in Chicago, and go through the rest of the course. Those who attended one seminar could attend the following one free of charge. So a few weeks later I flew again to Chicago for the Thursday, Friday and Saturday of the seminar.

When I returned home after completing the course one of the first things I did was to purchase an overhead projector with rollers and begin to practise using it in the way I had seen Bill Gothard do. It took me just a few days to learn how to draw stick figures and other illustrations, and in just over a week I had written a course similar to Bill Gothard's but with a British slant. I also included concepts that I felt were missing in his course, particularly on the work and ministry of the Holy Spirit.

I called the course 'Life in a New Dimension' and wrote to a group of *Every Day with Jesus* readers in the London area inviting them to be my 'guinea pigs' at my first presentation over a weekend at the Wycliffe conference centre in High Wycombe. The impact on those who attended was astonishing. Everyone said they had never experienced anything like it before. My use of the overhead projector intrigued people so much that after every session they would crowd around trying to figure out how it all worked.

The course consisted of eight intensive sessions, each session lasting an hour and 20 minutes. People told me that before the course started they had wondered how they be able to sit for that length of time listening to someone talking about biblical principles, but use of the overhead projector, along with the printed notes (which required their interaction), made it so interesting and intriguing that an hour and 20 minutes seemed like just half-an-hour.

It was a weekend that proved to be a turning point in the history of CWR, for in the years that followed, the teaching seminars have become a major part of our ministry.

A few days after the first presentation of Life in a New Dimension I had an appointment with my solicitor, Graham Ross-Cornes. He was concerned that the travel department was fast becoming a thriving commercial business and unless there were changes it was likely that we would fall foul of the Charity Commissioners. I pointed out that the profits from the travel department were being used for charitable purposes – overseas crusades and subsidies for *Every Day with Jesus* (which was still being given away free). While agreeing with that, he thought it best to separate the travel department from CWR and turn it into a limited company. He referred me to a Christian accountant, Glyn Macauley, who gave me similar advice. Glyn agreed to his firm becoming CWR's accountants, and they remain so to this day.

A few weeks later I happened to be talking in my office to a young Christian businesswoman, Christine Wheeler, who was also involved in low-cost travel. I told her that I was planning to separate the travel department from CWR and asked if she would be interested in joining me in this venture. She asked for some time to think about it and we decided to meet up a week later. The firm appointed David Rivett to look after the CWR account. David later became a Director of CWR and has played a key role in the development of the ministry. In the meantime I also shared my thinking on forming a new company with a young Australian Christian, Peter Clouston, who had connections with the travel industry and often came into our office to discuss low-cost travel. Peter ran a small organisation called Courier Travel.

As we chatted over a cup of tea his eyes lit up at the idea of the travel department becoming a limited company and after further discussion made it clear that he would like to become involved in the formation of it. I quickly set up a meeting with Christine and Peter, at which we agreed to establish a new company called Christian Travel International. I made it clear that my only involvement could be as a consultant. I would not be involved in the day-to-day running of the business.

All this was a great relief to me, as it meant that I could still maintain an interest in something I had started, and draw a small salary for my role as consultant. Just five months after I had prayed, the whole matter had been resolved in a way I could never have foreseen. I never cease to marvel at the ways God answers prayer. I stayed in the consultancy role for about a year and then withdrew completely when the work of CWR became even more demanding.

In the summer of 1972, in answer to an advertisement we had put out for a journalist, a young man by the name of Alan Richardson came to see me. He struck me as being extremely gifted, and I had no hesitation in employing him. When Alan studied the Life in a New Dimension Seminar material he was tremendously impressed, and showed a keen interest to present some of the sessions himself. I was a little reluctant at first, as Alan had not been a Christian all that long, but his enthusiasm for the teaching, the sharpness of his intellect and his ability to communicate led me to invest some time in training him to work alongside me in presenting the seminar.

Encouraged by the spiritual impact that had been made on those attending the weekend course, I decided to launch it in Westminster Central Hall. It was advertised in *Every Day with Jesus* as a one-week seminar, beginning on a Monday evening, continuing every evening to Friday and then the whole of Saturday from 10am until 10pm. I wondered how many would be willing to commit themselves to a whole week of seminar teaching – something quite new to the UK Christians at that time – but over 300 people enrolled, some coming from as far away as Cornwall, Northern Ireland and Scotland.

The Westminster Central Hall has facilities for all kinds of numbers, and we had booked a hall seating around 350, so it looked comfortably full. The impact of the teaching was quite staggering. On the Wednesday evening, after I had lectured on the importance of maintaining a clear conscience, Alan Richardson and I walked outside to find dozens of people queuing outside the telephone booths. When we asked what was happening, we were told that the people couldn't wait to contact relatives and friends they had hurt or wronged in order to apologise and clear their consciences as quickly as possible.

It was evident from the success of the Westminster Central Hall seminar that this was something we must present across the country, so right away we started scheduling seminars in various places. In addition to his work in writing copy, this also became Alan's responsibility, and I left him to set it up while I flew to Helsinki with Eric Bowtell to conduct an evangelistic crusade in one of the large halls in the centre of the Finnish capital. This crusade came about after one of the pastors of a very large church in Helsinki had heard me speak in Stockholm and he, together with other churches, sponsored the event which was a great spiritual success. Many people made commitments to become followers of the Lord Jesus Christ. Finnish singing reminded me very much of Wales, because they sang so many songs in the minor key. Sometimes I would close my eyes and would be back in the valleys once again. It was a wonderfully moving experience.

Late in the autumn of 1972, I flew to the USA to speak at a series of meetings in Atlanta and from there to Jamaica for the purpose of meeting up with some of the converts from the crusade I had held there earlier. When they met me at Kingston airport they begged me to stay for a few days and hold a three-night crusade in the King George V Memorial Park, where I had held the previous one in 1968. It was not possible to build a platform at such short notice, but they hit on the idea of driving a large truck with loudspeakers into the park and having me preach from the back of it. Once again many people committed their lives to Jesus Christ as I preached.

On the last night, one of the concrete lamp posts in the park gave way through the crush of people around its base and toppled towards me as I preached. There were screams and I looked up to see it coming down on me, but I managed to step back in the nick of time and the post hit the back of the truck – missing me by inches. When people realised I was unharmed there were great shouts of praise and gratitude to God. Unfortunately the falling lamp post had struck a lady and she was taken to hospital with a shoulder injury. I finished my message and gave an appeal for people to come to Christ. I don't know whether it was due to the drama that had taken place, but it seemed more people came to Christ that night than the other two nights put together. Later, I went to the hospital to visit the injured lady and found that she was someone whom I knew from my days in Dennison House and was now on holiday in Jamaica.

There was a very interesting sequel to that incident. Some

weeks later I received a letter from a woman who said she had been awakened one night with a heavy burden to pray for me. She gave the date and the time and when I checked it I found it was while I was in Jamaica. There was just one problem: she said it happened around 3am. I couldn't make sense of it until I realised that 3am in the UK was 9pm the night before in Jamaica, because of the time difference. That was when the lamp post fell towards me.

In my hotel room in Jamaica I gave a great deal of thought to the fact that the Life in a New Dimension seminars were destined to interest many in the contemporary Christian church, but what would follow them? I had been around long enough to know that when Christians have been exposed to something new, what they often go on to ask is, what's next? Most Christians, when they have their spiritual appetites whetted with teaching, are keen to be taken further. I hit on the idea of organising what I called an Advanced Seminar for those who had participated in the Life in a New Dimension experience. I booked a hotel in Newquay, Cornwall, and invited some of those who had attended an LND seminar to a one-week Advanced Seminar. It quickly filled up and so successful was the week that once again I came away gripped with the conviction that the launching of the Life in a New Dimension seminar was like an expanding telescope and the Advanced Seminar would not be the only thing that would come out of it.

CHAPTER 29

PARTNERSHIP WITH TREVOR

I did not see it quite clearly at the time, but development of the Life in a New Dimension seminars introduced an entirely new emphasis into Crusade for World Revival. Before this the emphasis had been on evangelism and revival, but now there was a strong thrust towards teaching and the equipping of Christians to handle life's problems and difficulties through the application of biblical principles. Ever since I had left Bible college my emphasis had been on the 'what' of Christianity – what to believe. Now I was adding the 'how' – how to deal with wrong thoughts, how to do battle with the devil, how to accept yourself, how to discover your basic gift. I thought of the young man who said to me after a Bible study in Colchester: 'I know what I should do as a Christian, but I wish somebody would tell me how.' Now I was taking up that challenge.

Early in 1973, Alan Richardson and I embarked on a tour of the country presenting Life in a New Dimension seminars. We criss-crossed the UK and almost every weekend we were in one place or another, beginning on a Friday night and continuing all day Saturday. Many who attended the seminars became life-long friends and some even came to work with us. Two couples who attended the seminar in Millmead Baptist Church, Guildford, went on to play a major role in the development of CWR's ministry.

One was David Boulnois and his wife Gill, the other Sidney

and Janice Barrington. David was a businessman and former wartime RAF Coastal Command pilot, while Sidney was the vicar of Cobham, Surrey. Both couples were deeply impressed with the Life in a New Dimension presentation. Sydney said it was the kind of teaching he had been looking for all his life. Later Sidney and Janice became part of CWR's teaching team, while continuing in the Anglican ministry at Cobham. David Boulnois took on an important role in CWR's administration and management as an adviser and, more particularly, shared with me a burden to see revival come to our land. David was one of the greatest intercessors I have known and contributed greatly to CWR's ministry right up to his death in the late 1990s.

Another person whose attendance at a Life in a New Dimension seminar led to him working alongside us, albeit in a freelance capacity, was David Poyser, from Newbury. During a break at the Reading seminar, David introduced himself, explaining that he was a graphics artist and offering to help in any way he could. Within a week we met in my office in Weybridge and began a business relationship that was to last for over 20 years until, sadly, he died from cancer in the year 2000, at the age of 54. Those who regularly received CWR's literature often praised David's skill. 'Whoever is your artist?' they used to say. 'His work is absolutely superb.' David's contribution to CWR was monumental and I regard him as one of the key players in the rise and development of the ministry.

By this time my son, David, had moved his printing equipment from Oxford Street to a workshop near Weybridge and was kept busy producing the seminar notes and other materials. Every binder had about 40 pages and this was an almost perpetual printing task, along with other things. He and David Poyser fast became friends and built a strong working relationship together.

In the middle of that year Alan and I visited Nairobi, where some friends of mine in the university there, having heard and read about the Life in a New Dimension seminar, wanted to experience it for themselves. We took the overhead projector with us. No one in Kenya had one at that time. On the first night of the presentation, Silas Owitti, my pastor friend from Kisumu, arrived late. Never having seen an overhead projector before, he was quite startled to see words of Scripture and figures appearing on a large screen. 'What miracle is Selwyn performing now?' he thought.

He told us afterward that shivers kept going up and down his spine as he wondered whether he was witnessing something similar to what happened in Belshazzar's feast when supernatural writing appeared on the wall spelling out the doom of the godless individual (Daniel, chapter 5). That university seminar in Nairobi, attended by some of the keenest students I have met, is one I shall never forget. They sat on the edge of their seats, not wanting to miss a single word. They were enthralled not only by the presentation with the overhead projector, but also by the biblical concepts which most had heard before but were now coming across in a fresh way.

Following the success of the Advanced Seminar in Newquay the previous year, a second one was held in October 1973 at the Ashburnam Conference Centre at Battle in Sussex. Sidney and Janice Barrington were there, and as we walked together in the grounds during one of the afternoon breaks Sidney told me how deeply the teaching of both Life in a New Dimension and the Advanced Seminar was affecting his life. 'My goal,' he said, 'is to be able to present these concepts myself, but I think I need to come to several more seminars before I will be able to do that.' A year or two later Sidney and Janice were closely involved, first acting as facilitators in group work and then having a hand in teaching the material. Introducing herself to one group, Janice said: 'I think Selwyn was so fed up at seeing us in the different seminars and listening to the material he was teaching that he thought we might as well be up front and teach it!'

That autumn I met up with Trevor Partridge again. He had finished his studies in America and returned to England, and was now praying about what he should do in the future. I invited him to attend the Life in a New Dimension seminar in Leicester. During the presentation Trevor felt a deep impression that he would become closely involved with CWR and would one day be presenting Life in a New Dimension himself. Later we had a meeting in my office at Weybridge and after prayerful discussion I felt it right to invite Trevor to join the CWR team. We talked about the role he would play when he started work with us in the New Year. Before that, however, Alan Richardson left to work full time in his local church. As the situation was no longer the way I had described it to Trevor, I felt I had a responsibility to tell him this and wrote suggesting that he should not come at this time. But after talking it over with his pastor, Trevor telephoned me and said, 'Look, I worked my way through Bible college in the USA, and I am confident I can deal with the unexpected. Why don't I come down as planned and see how things work out?' His confident manner impressed me and I agreed that we would keep to our earlier decision for him to join us in January 1974.

A new chapter began in the story of CWR when Trevor linked up with me. From the earliest days of our partnership, which was to last almost 25 years, it became clear that we were at one in our view of Scripture, our spiritual ideals, and our strong commitment, not only to Christ and the Bible but also to excellence. We both felt that whatever was done for the Lord should be done well and to the highest standards. Looking back over the years in which we worked together, it is clear that we were able to accomplish more together than we could ever have done apart.

Trevor was born in Baseford, Nottingham. Brought up in Loughborough, he was converted to Christ as a young boy, but did not make a serious commitment until his late teens. Later he spent four years studying theology at Seattle Bible College in the USA. The course was more broadly based than any available in British Bible colleges at that time, and it enabled him to study biblical psychology as part of his theology degree. He supported himself during his time in the States, graduating with a degree in theology in 1972.

Trevor's first duty when he joined me was to pick up one of Alan Richardson's tasks – coordinating the Life in a New Dimension seminars. These were arousing great interest in the Christian community in Britain.

From the start Trevor threw himself wholeheartedly into co-ordinating CWR's ministry programme in the UK and overseas. Apart from the seminars, there was the annual New Year rally and Communion service at Westminster Central Hall, evangelistic rallies, Holy Land tours, and weekend conferences. After the New Year rally Trevor organised a new one day Advanced Seminar in the same auditorium in early spring. However, it became clear after the first presentation in the Central Hall that the material did not lend itself to this kind of condensed format. The seminar contained so many concepts relating to counselling that it needed to be revamped and re-launched as a counselling course.

The seminar programme we conducted in our first year of working together was an even heavier and more punishing one than the previous year with Alan Richardson. Almost every Friday and Saturday saw us in some part of the country presenting Life in a New Dimension. Usually Trevor and I travelled together in one car, with two staff members using the CWR van that carried the seminar notes, overhead projector and screen. John Nash, a newcomer to our team, was responsible for setting up the projector and screen and distributing the notes. Only 17 at the time, John's life had been deeply affected through the first LND seminar at Westminster Central Hall the previous year. So were the lives of his parents, Spencer and Grace. They have all remained great friends of CWR.

During the many hours of travelling up and down the motorways, Trevor and I shared our ideas, hopes and desires for the work of God's kingdom. While one of us drove the other would make notes about our discussions. We would think aloud and bounce ideas off each other as we went along. I have never found anyone whose thoughts and ideas sharpened my own thinking as Trevor's did.

Often the pressure to present and attend so many seminars with such a small staff meant that we had to arrive early at a venue and collate the printed notes in time for the opening session. On some occasions a collating machine would have done the work in minutes, but such an investment would have pushed us beyond our slender budget. To keep accommodation costs down we would go to a hotel after the Friday evening seminar, at around 11pm, and ask if there were any rooms available. If there were we would bargain for a reduction with the hotel manager or manageress. We argued that it would be unlikely they would let rooms that time of night and rather than get nothing for them it would be better to let us have them cheaply. The strategy worked. Trevor and I were committed to getting the best deals we could in everything, without being unfair to the seller, to make our money go as far as possible.

Often people would ask us, 'What keeps you going up and

down the motorways most weekends conducting these seminars?' Our answer was the sheer joy we experienced as we saw the truths of God's Word piercing like a rapier into people's lives and bringing them into a deeper relationship with God. Out of all the eight sessions, the one on gaining a clear conscience was the most powerful. In almost every seminar we saw evidence of people's consciences being touched and cleansed as they yielded to God in the most amazing ways.

In Glasgow we conducted the LND seminar in a hall next to the Bible Training Institute and a number of the students attended. One was a former jockey who was so affected by the session on maintaining a clear conscience that he knew he had to put an important matter right. While riding for a stable at Newmarket he had been involved in several burglaries but without being caught. When he spoke to us about this we advised him to see the BTI principal who urged him to go back to Newmarket and confess to the police. In court he explained what had happened to him and how, through the Life in a New Dimension seminar, he had felt he must own up to the offences so that he could have a clear conscience. The magistrate fined him but was so impressed with his honesty and willingness to make restitution that he paid the fine himself!

A factory worker who attended a LND seminar went to his boss afterwards and confessed that had been fiddling the accounts. His boss was so impressed with his honesty that he immediately promoted him to look after his account books, explaining, 'If you have a conscience that works like that then I am ready to put some more responsibility your way.' He gave his new accountant a wage rise and also said, 'By the way, when is the next seminar? I would like to send all the staff to it.'

Those most challenged about clearing their consciences were young people who were sexually active outside of marriage.

Many times we would see young people talking with each another after the session on the biblical standards of courtship. We received many letters from young people confessing that they had violated biblical standards in their relationships and saying that they were now committed to no sex before marriage. This sort of thing made every mile of the many journeys we made up and down Britain's motorways worthwhile.

The more seminars we presented, the more fulfilled I felt. My evangelistic heart was satisfied because the seminar made clear the need for conversion and, invariably, an invitation would be given to receive Christ, which was often accepted. My teaching heart was being fulfilled because the whole seminar was built on Scripture. I was aware that I was moving closer and closer to the ultimate purpose God had for my life, but I knew also I had not quite reached it. There were still other things I had to do. But what?

CHAPTER 30

A SIGNIFICANT ANNIVERSARY

───────────

The year 1975 was a most joyous year for Enid and myself as it marked CWR's tenth anniversary. I had read a report around that time that if an organisation can survive the first ten years it is likely a foundation will have been established that will take it on into the future.

When I shared this with Enid she opened her Bible and read me this verse: 'Then Samuel took a stone and set it up between Mizpah and Shen. He named it Ebenezer, saying, "Thus far has the Lord helped us"' (1 Sam. 7:12). 'Let's give thanks to God for what He has done and for what He will do in the future,' said Enid. And we both then knelt in prayer and raised our own 'Ebenezer', thanking God for both the difficulties and the joys.

The year began with a move of offices. The Old Post House in Weybridge had become too small to handle the rapid growth of the organisation, so we took over a suite of larger offices in Hersham, on the outskirts of Walton-on-Thames. At first we occupied about half of the top floor then took over the remaining space when the occupiers moved out later that year. We took on one or two more staff to help us cope with the increased workload brought about through seminars, Holy Land tours and other activities.

During the winter of 1974 we had started regular monthly prayer meetings in the Salvation Army Conference Centre in Sunbury-on-Thames. These monthly prayer meetings were crowded with people wanting to know and experience more of the Spirit in their lives. At every meeting people were given opportunities to be prayed for personally, either to receive more of the Spirit or physical healing. Incredible things happened in those meetings and I still meet people today who tell me how their lives were radically changed or affected by them. We held several small conferences there at Sunbury Court, one with Henry Joseph from India and another with Jean Darnell.

The prayer meetings were an excellent 'fishing pool' for recruiting new staff. One such recruit was Roy Swan, a production manager at the Hawker Siddeley aircraft works at Kingston-on-Thames. Roy had a powerful encounter with the Holy Spirit at one of the meetings, and soon afterwards became our office manager. He was an efficient administrator who brought in new office systems, modernised our procedures and paved the way for the installation of computers. It was Roy who persuaded me to change over from writing *Every Day with Jesus* on a typewriter to using a word processor. I strongly resisted this at first, but when he showed me that it would cut down my time by a third I was won over. Roy stayed with us until his time of retirement in 1984.

Roy had the ability to mobilise our staff to respond to the new ideas that Trevor and I came up with while driving back from seminars. We would come into the office on a Monday morning and tell Roy about a new seminar we had thought up, an additional Holy Land tour or some other project we had planned. Roy would then call the staff together and say, 'Selwyn and Trevor have had this great idea which we need to respond to quickly. We need to drop what we are doing at the moment for a little while to get this information out to our mailing list. Let's pray together about it and then we can get going.' Roy was the right man in the right place at that time. Trevor and I will always be grateful to him for the years of loyalty and support he gave us.

We added to our staff almost month by month. My son, John, had left college and joined us for a while before deciding where his future lay. There were also two young ladies who joined us straight from school; one was Mary Hambleton, who eventually married my son John, and the other was Debbie Hartland, who became Trevor's wife some years later. And in April that year my other son, David, was married to Sue Hedges in a ceremony I conducted in Walton-on-Thames Baptist Church.

John and Mary went on to have two children, Colin and Suzanne. David and Sue also had two children, Leighton and Sheryl. Sadly, John's marriage broke up after a few years and he became increasingly dependent on drink. The strain of their break-up meant Enid and I did not see Colin and Suzanne and it was only many years later that I was able to make contact with them again. Nowadays all four are close to me and make me a very proud grandfather indeed – and also a great-grandfather!

An anniversary year can be useful for remembering the past, and also for checking the changes needed to face the challenges of the future. A major change that took place that year was in relation to *Every Day with Jesus*. The publication had been distributed to people free of charge on condition that they prayed regularly for revival and sent contributions towards production costs whenever they could. Although distribution had climbed to nearly 100,000 each edition, gifts had not kept pace with the increased costs and we were beginning to get heavily into debt.

Don Heston, a friend at the Christian Sailing Centre on the Isle of Wight, where we had held a Life in a New Dimension seminar, pointed out that many *Every Day with Jesus* readers did not share the burden for revival in the way I did and yet to obtain it they had to agree to pray for it. He suggested that we should charge for *EDWJ* and start a separate Prayer Chain for those who wanted to pray for revival. After some thought we realised that was the right way to go.

For some time I had been thinking about making *EDWJ* a bi-monthly publication, as I felt one month was not sufficient to deal with a theme in depth. I often felt, when writing on a theme over 30 or 31 days, that I had to stop before I had finished. Thus the tenth anniversary edition of *EDWJ* (September 1975) became not only the first edition to carry a cover price, but also the first bi-monthly edition. The announcement that people would have to pay a cover price caused the circulation to plummet from around 100,000 to 8,000. It confirmed what someone had told us, that when people are asked to pay for something they believe can help them, that is when their belief is put to the test.

We tried to get Christian bookshops to sell it, but few were interested; Scripture Union had cornered the daily Bible notes market. We knew, however, that many people were open to a different approach to daily Bible study, but it would take a great deal of time and energy to break into the market. The main difference between *EDWJ* and the SU notes at the time was that our publication dealt with a biblical theme and Scripture Union focused on the exposition of a book. This later changed and for many years now I have rung the changes in *EDWJ* by one month dealing with a topic and another a book of the Bible or a particular biblical passage.

We suggested to our readers that they try to order *EDWJ* through their local bookshop, rather than receive it directly from us. Some bookshops responded to this, but it was slow going until Trevor later hit on the idea of inserting free copies in Christian magazines, such as *Crusade*, *The Life of Faith*, *Family* magazine, *Renewal* and *Buzz*. Trevor also had the relevant magazines' names on the front of *EDWJ*, which tied it in closely to the readers of those magazines.

We gave away about 250,000 copies in this way. Results were a bit slow at first, but within six months there was an increase of 50,000 copies, most of them being sold through Christian bookshops. Since then *EDWJ* has continued to be sold through Christian bookshops, as well as by subscription, and one Christian magazine found through a survey that it had become the most popular daily Bible devotional in Britain.

A contribution that has greatly enhanced *EDWJ* for many people is the poem composed by Susan Lenzkes on the inside cover of every edition. I first came across a poem by Susan many years ago in one of Billy Graham's magazines and was immediately impressed with her devotional style. After contacting her, she agreed to let me use some of her previously published poems, but in more recent years she has written a new poem to fit in with the theme of each particular edition. Susan lives in San Diego, California and, although a great distance separates us, we are regularly in touch through email. She is a good friend of the CWR ministry and has visited the UK several times, having spoken at two of the Women's Weekends at Waverley Abbey House. I regularly receive letters from *EDWJ* readers saying how Susan's poems impact their lives.

Another decision we made was to close down the annual New Year rally in Westminster Central Hall after the 1976 event. We had held these events on the first Saturday of the new year, or as near as possible to it, since CWR's inception in 1965. At the end of the evening we would invite people to re-dedicate themselves to the Lord's service and seal it with Communion. The rallies had grown to packed attendances in the 2,500-seat Great Hall and serving Communion was difficult.

That summer we held our first Leadership Seminar, which lasted for a week at London Bible College (now known as the London School of Theology). I wanted to bring what I considered were the biblical principles of leadership to the attention of some of Britain's Christian leaders. Much was being said about leadership in the Christian church at that time, but a good deal of it was based more on secular ideas than scriptural ones. It was a remarkably successful conference, not only because it was attended by many key people, but because of the tremendous spiritual atmosphere that developed throughout the week.

Jenny Trust and Lorna Espenhahn were at that conference – two women who played major roles in CWR's ministry in later years. Lorna became my secretary after Lorna Paine's retirement, while Jenny was the first to enrol in CWR's partnership programme and later she became course tutor in our one-year counsellor training programme.

We held the CWR tenth anniversary celebration service at Westminster Central Hall in September – the same month as CWR had been founded. The service was in the evening, and in the afternoon we had a private tea party for a group of specially invited individuals. Lindsey Glegg was there, and so was Maurice Rowlandson of the Billy Graham organisation. Another was John Fear, a journalist and broadcaster, who deserves special mention because he introduced Trevor and myself to Trans World Radio, for which we did a series of programmes called *Insight*.

John was a great friend to CWR and helped us a lot with advice on broadcasting and public relations. It was he who arranged for Lindsey Glegg, then well in his 90s, to be with us for the anniversary. Lindsey was an avid *EDWJ* reader and that evening gave a wonderful testimony to how the notes had blessed his life. 'Read them as soon as you can in the morning,' he said, 'and you will find your heart leaping to prayer.'

Now that Crusade for World Revival was ten years old and

beginning to establish itself as a creditable parachurch organisation, I began to focus more intently on its future. The CWR story had been flowing with ease, and although I wasn't entirely sure where it was going, it was pleasant just to float downstream under the direction of the Spirit, without giving too much thought to what lay ahead. The tenth anniversary, however, was like a river turning a bend and revealing a vista of unending opportunity.

I began to see that the name I had given the organisation was not, as one critic of my use of the phrase World Revival had suggested, 'a pretentious attempt to aim beyond one's reach'. I had been stung by this criticism and by the comment someone had made in the Christian press in the mid-1950s: 'The title of this new organisation, Crusade for World Revival, is either prophetic or pathetic.' Now we had a small army of people who were praying daily for a worldwide outpouring of the Holy Spirit and we were developing resources and materials that were changing people's lives in several other countries. So I began to feel that the name was truly prophetic. I felt we were poised at a point where we could look beyond the UK and consider, albeit gradually, taking our teaching into different parts of the world.

Trevor and I began to talk about what might happen in the next decade rather than the next year. We dreamed about the possibility of establishing a Christian university similar to those in the United States, where young people could be trained in various disciplines within a Christian ethos. David Lloyd George, Britain's Prime Minister from 1916 to 1922, said, 'Education without God makes clever devils.' We longed to give young people the kind of education that would not just focus on the intellect but also on character. We both shared the view that although cleverness may get people to the top, only character can keep them there.

The more we looked into this idea of a Christian university and talked to Christian educators in this country, such as John Aston and John Dubbey, the more hurdles we saw that had to be overcome. Whether we would succeed in establishing a Christian university or not, we were both convinced that CWR needed premises where we could begin to provide courses that would one day lead to accreditation by the education authorities. That became a dominant theme in our minds, although we knew its realisation lay some way down the road.

We continued throughout 1976 with a range of activities and seminars, including Life in a New Dimension, Holy Land tours and evangelistic rallies, as well as regular counselling courses. Then someone told Trevor that Life in a New Dimension was too similar to Bill Gothard's seminar, which made us decide to sit down and re-design it from start to finish. Whereas before it had dealt with biblical concepts in no particular order, we now arranged it in such a way that each of the eight concepts of the course was seen as a step towards the following one, eventually leading to a door that one pushed open through an act of total commitment, which would result in a completely new way of living. This added greatly to its effectiveness and moved it away from Bill Gothard's presentation. Then an evangelistic book called *Life in a New Dimension* appeared in the UK, so we also changed the name of the seminar to Dynamic Christian Living. It took us several presentations of the course in 1976 before we were satisfied with the changes we had made, but by 1977 the revised course was proving more effective and life-changing than ever.

As a result of the Dynamic Christian Living course more and more people were enrolling on to the counselling courses. These were held in different parts of the country, and many were over-subscribed. Trevor and I realised that if we were to become leaders in the field of Christian counselling then we needed to go more deeply into the subject ourselves. I enrolled in a counselling course at the Rosemead Graduate School of Psychology near Los Angeles, under the direction of Dr Clyde Narramore. This was an intensive course for ministers and missionaries who felt they needed some in-depth training in the subject of counselling. Ever since the experience in South Kirby when the man I failed to help committed suicide, I had longed for the day when I could get down to a formal study of Christian counselling and the course at Rosemead seemed to be an opportunity that I ought not to miss.

Before I started the course, Trevor and I had been invited to present the Dynamic Christian Living seminar in the church of Sonny Argunzoni, of *The Cross and the Switchblade* fame. Sonny was one of those converted along with Nikki Cruz when David Wilkerson went into New York in the late 1950s and was now the pastor of a thriving church in a Los Angeles suburb, mainly comprised of converted drug addicts. The week Trevor and I spent there, sharing the truths and concepts of the Dynamic Living Seminar, is one we will never forget. We were deeply moved to hear the ex-addicts stand up one after another and tell how Jesus Christ had delivered them from drug addiction and crime.

I don't think I have ever been so reluctant to leave a church than that one. I believe Trevor felt the same. As soon as our involvement with Sonny's church came to an end, I duly made my way to the Rosemead campus for the course on counselling while Trevor returned to the UK.

CHAPTER 31

A NEW LEVEL OF PERSONAL DISCOVERY

A sign over the gates at Rosemead Graduate School of Psychology reads: 'Every person is worth understanding.' That motto has stayed with me and comes to mind time and again when I have felt like giving up on people whose lives seem too complex to sort out.

There were 50 of us from 30 nations on the month-long course, including people from Australia, New Zealand, South Africa, Hong Kong and European countries. As the course got under way I realised that this was what I should have been exposed to 20 years previously. My approach to counselling up until that time had been largely behavioural: I would seek to identify wrong behaviour, exhort change (usually with a variety of Scripture texts) and encourage the person to do what God says in His Word, whether they felt like it or not.

Men and women, we were told on the course, are not just volitional beings who can choose, but there are other parts of their personality that have to be considered, too, such as the thinking, the feelings and so on. A special stress was placed on the fact that physiological factors can sometimes influence behaviour – something a lot of Christian counsellors tend to ignore.

Clyde Narramore was the founder of the Narramore Foundation, a literature and radio ministry that also operated from the campus. He is regarded in the USA as the father of

Christian counselling. He was one of the first during the mid-1950s to emphasise the fact that there is a definite Christian approach to helping people with their problems. His thesis was simple, but very effective. People have problems because of three reasons: physical, psychological and spiritual. I had some difficulty in differentiating between the psychological and the spiritual, but apart from that I drank in every word that he and the other lecturers brought to us day after day.

We were not far into the course before we were instructed to break into small groups. The groups had two facilitators who were interns continuing their studies in psychology on the campus. They told us that they were there not to lead, but simply to observe and make any comments they thought appropriate. There was silence for about five minutes in my group, as we realised we were in a leaderless group. What should we do? How should we proceed? I couldn't bear the silence any longer and was the first to speak. 'Look, I come from a country where we don't sit around wondering what to do. That's not the way we won the Second World War! We get on and organise things. It's obvious the facilitators are not going to help us, so I think we should take it in turns to give our testimonies and get things moving.'

I noticed the facilitators look at each other and smile as I said this. I learned afterwards that when the announcement is made that there is no leader and silence descends, the first one to speak is usually the most insecure, and indeed, the 50 hours or so that I spent in that group brought home to me – in a way I could never have known by sitting listening to lectures – just how insecure a person I really was. I kept my insecurities at bay by *doing* things. I could not stand inactivity. Eventually, through the gentle but sometimes piercing observations of the facilitators, I came to see myself as I really was – someone whose security was rooted not so much in God, but in achievement and activity.

That revelation changed my life. At first I wept as I realised that although I made a great show of being secure in God, deep down I needed to be always stretching myself, pushing through barriers and overcoming obstacles in order to feel good about myself. One of the facilitators, Joyce Hulgus, said to me after the group experience was over, 'Selwyn, you are obviously a leader and you have an adventurous spirit. There is nothing wrong with that and God wants to use it. But you must always remember that your worth to God is not in what you do, but in who you are.'

I was not the only one to explore new levels of personal discovery in the group. The more we learned about ourselves, the deeper became our sharing, and when our time in the leaderless groups came to an end everyone claimed to have been transformed by it.

Several things from that experience have stayed with me and I have used them when teaching others about counselling. One is that the more a counsellor can share himself or herself deeply with another person (this is best done in training), the easier it will be for others to share with that counsellor. Another thing was that it is only to the degree that we come to know ourselves that we can know others. And thirdly, you can never take a person any farther than you have gone yourself. I have no hesitation in saying that, apart from my conversion, the infilling of the Holy Spirit and my marriage, that group experience did more for me than any other thing I have ever known. It opened me up from being a somewhat closed and tight personality to being more open, more ready to share myself, and more willing to be vulnerable.

Another great benefit of the course was the battery of psychological tests we were put through. One of them showed me to be mildly obsessive/compulsive. Obsessions are repetitive, persistent ideas, thoughts, images or impulses that are not experienced as subject to the will, but intrude unwanted into the consciousness. Compulsions are repetitive behaviours that also have no origin in the will. An interview I had with one of the psychologists who interpreted the psychological tests I had taken probed me: 'How do these obsessive/compulsive traits work out in your life? What do you get obsessed about?' My first reply was 'Jesus.' He smiled and said, 'Come off it now, Selwyn. Let's be real. Obsession is a psychological dynamic, not a spiritual one. You love Jesus, but what things do you find yourself obsessing about?' I thought for a few moments and said, 'Revival.'

As I said it, I felt rather upset by the thought that my preoccupation with revival might come from my obsessive nature rather than from the Holy Spirit. But the psychologist said, 'God knows the fabric of our personalities and He often uses it to His advantage. From my own reading of revivals in history, I can see that most of those who led them I would consider to be mildly obsessive/compulsive personalities. I would not be surprised if God dropped the burden for revival in your heart because He saw that your temperament, plus the Holy Spirit, would not allow the idea to become dimmed in your soul.' I found his words wonderfully consoling. Later I would read that Martyn Lloyd-Jones, whose burden for revival and whose talks on that subject inspired so many, was said by one psychiatrist to be also of the obsessive/compulsive type.

It is possible, I believe, to be obsessed about something, not from a psychological need to have a focus that pushes other worrying concerns to the margin of one's life, but because it is something God has laid upon one's heart. I have examined my soul many times since then. The more I have done so the more I have come to the conclusion that the thought of revival, which is there just below the level of consciousness all the time and emerges into consciousness from time to time, is a burden that God has put within me, not something that has simply become a focus for my obsessive/compulsive nature.

I greatly valued my time at the Rosemead Graduate School of Psychology and when I returned I shared what I had learned with Trevor. Together we re-designed the counselling course to include the new insights I had received. The integration of these considerably strengthened the courses.

When I returned to the UK in the autumn of that year I found that the pressures in the CWR office at Hersham were building up. Increasing subscriptions to *Every Day with Jesus*, applications for courses, tickets for rallies, Christmas orders for books and tapes meant that we needed to increase our staff, if only for the weeks leading up to Christmas. David Swan (the son of Roy, our office manager), who was a valued member of our team, told us of a man in his church who might help. Paul Bexon, a Yorkshireman who had recently returned from working overseas and had not yet found a job in this country, accepted the invitation to join us.

At first Paul worked on things such as collating notes, helping to deal with the *Every Day with Jesus* subscriptions, looking after the orders that come from the Christian bookshops. Paul's skills were mainly in accountancy and bookkeeping and it was soon obvious to us that he was too good a catch to let go. Eventually we persuaded him to become a full-time member of staff, a decision that time has proved to be of great benefit to CWR. Later Paul became office manager, then Company Secretary and at the time of writing he is, next to myself, the longest serving member of CWR, with 26 years of service. He is highly regarded by all members of the Board and the staff. His wisdom, gentleness, attention to detail and his Christ-like character, mark him out as a man above the ordinary.

After several years of focusing on teaching the concepts of the Dynamic Christian Living seminar to Christians in the UK and establishing the counselling courses, I felt a strong pull to be involved in a large overseas evangelistic crusade once again. So there was great joy in my heart when, early in 1978, I set out once more to conduct a crusade in Madras, South India. The churches there had been asking me for several years to return, but the demanding seminar schedule and other meetings we had set for ourselves in the UK had made it impossible.

This time I took with me not only Eric Bowtell, but also Trevor Partridge and Sidney Barrington. Sidney had served as a chaplain in Her Majesty's Forces in India and he was overjoyed at the opportunity of returning to what he called 'the land of joyous and happy faces'. We arrived in Madras at the end of February, just before the monsoon season, when the climate is not too hot. Once again many of the city's churches had joined together to make the week-long crusade a united effort, with meetings for ministers in the mornings and evangelistic rallies at night.

Trevor, Sidney and myself presented the concepts of the Dynamic Christian Living seminar to the ministers, while Eric regaled them with his stirring songs. Many of the ministers said how rich it was to hear the different voices and gifts of the men I had brought with me in addition to my own contribution. One of them told me: 'If these men could remain here for six months and teach us in the way they have done during this week it would transform the life of the church in Madras in ways beyond all telling.'

At the end of our time in Madras the participating churches did something they said they had never done before: they cancelled their Sunday morning services to join together for one big celebration. Towards the end of that service, Henry Joseph, a pastor and also the distributor of *Every Day with Jesus* in India, asked how many people read the daily devotional. So many raised their hands that my eyes filled. I thought how wonderful it was that although I would be leaving these people in the next 24 hours I had the privilege of still ministering to them each day.

Arriving back to Britain, we hit the ground running, so to speak. Apart from the many seminars that were scheduled, there were three Holy Land tours to organise. For the first time we were taking a tour to Greece and Turkey, which we called 'In the Steps of St Paul'. Trevor and I had visited the area the previous year to survey the possibility of such a tour and, having satisfied ourselves about hotels and transportation, we decided to launch it in May 1978.

Trevor, Sidney and I led the 12-day tour, which visited Corinth, Athens, Thessalonika, Philippi and Ephesus. We found that while the tour did not have the same emotive qualities we experienced when walking in the footsteps of Jesus, everyone on the tour (most of whom had been on a Holy Land tour) said it was still a wonderful spiritual experience. In Thessalonika we experienced a minor earthquake in the middle of the night. All I remember about it was being awakened by the sound of a rumbling, feeling the bed shaking slightly and a glass on the side of my bed falling on to the floor. I was so exhausted by the constant pressures of the tour that I instantly went back to sleep. At breakfast the next morning someone jokingly suggested that as Thessalonika was adjacent to Philippi where the apostle Paul was set free from prison as the result of an earthquake, our first CWR tour could be said to be biblically authentic!

When we crossed from Greece to Turkey we stayed for several days in the port of Kusadasi so that we could explore nearby Ephesus. Each morning, before setting out to visit the ruins of the ancient city, we sat around the hotel pool looking at

Paul's letter to the Ephesians and Christ's later message to that church in Revelation chapter 2. Though Ephesus is now just a collection of ruins, it is easy to see from the exquisitely carved marble columns and statues what an important, strategic and beautiful city it was in Bible times.

The rest of 1978 was filled with seminars and rallies and other activities such as the Holy Land tours, but our main focus as we drew towards the end of the year was preparing for our New Year Rally, this time in the Royal Albert Hall. There was a certain amount of apprehension within me as we approached the last few months of the year. Would it be another fiasco in terms of numbers? Could we really fill one of London's largest auditoriums, with accommodation for well over 5,000 people? My concerns were all put to rest when, just six weeks after announcing the rally in the September/October edition of *Every Day with Jesus*, all the seats were booked. As applications for tickets continued to flow in we decided to hold an afternoon overflow meeting, and by the middle of December that extra meeting was fully booked as well.

In the months leading up to the Albert Hall rally Trevor had worked hard to bring together a 100-voice choir for the occasion. Hours and hours of effort had gone into preparation for the event and it was a tremendous spiritual success. As people flocked into the afternoon and evening meetings the atmosphere was charged with expectation. In the late 1970s there were not many large Christian events such as we know today. Spring Harvest now brings together more than 50,000 people over nearly three weeks, but in 1979 there were few occasions when a crowd of over 10,000 believers would be gathered together for a Christian event. It was without doubt the largest and most successful event ever conducted by CWR in the UK.

CHAPTER 32

AROUND THE WORLD IN 30 DAYS

In early 1979, a few weeks after the Royal Albert Hall rally, Trevor and I launched a completely new seminar in London on the subject of family life. We took the principles we were teaching in the Dynamic Christian Living seminar and applied them to relationships in the home. The one-day course covered such topics as handling family conflicts, child discipline, developing family communication, Christian sex education and building family unity. It was presented in the Friends' Meeting House to a large group of people in March and was enthusiastically received. Later we presented it in several other places such as Birmingham and Glasgow, but it never attracted the numbers that we saw in the Dynamic Christian Living seminar, so after a while we decided to discontinue it. Today when I look at the terrible problems facing families, both Christian and non-Christian, I feel somewhat sad that we didn't persevere with the Family Life Seminar, especially when those who attended testified to the transformation in their families as they applied biblical concepts.

The popularity of Dynamic Christian Living seemed to keep on growing as we presented it in a number of UK cities. Those who attended and had their lives changed talked about it to their friends. Later in the year Trevor led a second tour to Turkey, following the steps of St Paul.

Eddie Tait joined CWR at the beginning of 1979. Eddie's

background was in journalism. Late in 1978 some friends drew his attention to the fact that CWR were advertising for an editor to work on *Revival* magazine. He joined us at Hersham on a snowy day in January 1979, immediately after the Christmas break. The office heating would not work and thoughts of the warm newspaper office he had left were definitely on his mind! He was not to know it then, but he would stay with CWR for 14 years, and continues to this day working on a freelance basis.

His work involved putting together *Revival* – writing, editing and helping to plan the graphics. A main part of his work was doing interviews with leading Christians and writing features about a wide variety of Christian work. Eddie's most significant work in recent years has been to compile the Prayer Focus after it became part of *Revival* magazine, having taken it over from David Boulnois. When we launched the *Christian Counsellor's Journal* he worked for a while on editing that. I am deeply grateful to Eddie for his friendship and support during the years that I have known him, and in particular for the help he has given me in producing this autobiography.

During 1979, articles were appearing in secular and Christian magazines on what was called 'a counselling explosion'. A UK television channel did a documentary on the topic, indicating that in the Western world more and more people were applying for training in counselling as they saw their friends and acquaintances fall prey to the increasing stresses and strains of daily living. This led us to launch *The Christian Counsellor's Journal*, which supplemented our counselling courses and gave helpful articles and features on all aspects of the Christian approach to this subject.

In November, all of us at CWR were deeply saddened by the death of our good friend and colleague, Sidney Barrington.

Sidney was one of the most courteous, gentle and

contemplative men I have known, and I loved him deeply. It seemed to me, as well as to many others, that when he died a light went out in the CWR family. His wife, Janice, faced the loss of Sidney with remarkable courage and continued to assist us with the counselling courses, eventually coming on staff as a part-time counsellor. We greatly valued her contribution to the ministry, which she faithfully fulfilled until she married John Aston, another friend of CWR, some years later.

Just after Sidney's funeral Trevor and I flew to Berlin to present the Dynamic Christian Living seminar in an evangelical church in the centre of the city. Although it did not stop us effectively presenting the seminar, we were both conscious of a heaviness in our spirits. Sometimes we would sit together in the hotel and say nothing to each other because of the grief that pierced our souls. Both of us had seen great potential in Sidney's involvement with CWR and it was not easy to come to terms with the fact that he was no longer with us. But Trevor and I took comfort from the fact that although God may bury His workmen He always carries on His work.

During 1980, Trevor and I made a decision to travel around the world together and minister in the different countries to which we had been invited. Our first stop was Singapore where we held meetings under the auspices of a group who were distributing *Every Day with Jesus* there at the time. Circulation was quite small and we were largely unknown, but we were able to address a number of meetings and to conduct a brief introductory course on Christian counselling. Christians in Singapore are deeply committed to Scripture and they appreciated our strong biblical approach to counselling. One of the key people we met at that time was James Wong, an Anglican curate (now a canon), who became a great friend. Over the years since then he has sponsored many key meetings and events for us in Singapore.

From there we flew to Australia. First stop was Perth, where we met a number of the families who had moved there from my church in South Kirkby. It was wonderful to see them again after 25 years, some having become grandparents.

From Perth we flew to Adelaide, where we met up with Steve Stevens, who had worked with me in CWR's travel department in the early 1970s. Steve was now involved with the Australian Festival of Light, an organisation dedicated to lifting the moral state of the nation. But it was in Hobart, Tasmania, that the main purpose of our visit to Australia took place: conducting a Dynamic Christian Living seminar. The venue was an Anglican church. The vicar, Robert Legg, had been an *Every Day with Jesus* reader for some time and testified to being greatly influenced by it. His congregation gave us a wonderful welcome and the time we spent ministering there, with an interdenominational rally as a finale, are days that live on in our memories.

Trevor and I then flew across the Pacific to Hawaii, having our first experience of crossing the International Date Line and gaining a day. Most of our stay in Hawaii was spent relaxing – with one important exception. We visited the Youth With A Mission University of the Nations on one of the islands because our vision at the time was very much focused on setting up a similar education establishment in the UK, albeit on a smaller scale. But after visiting YWAM's university our enthusiasm rocketed and we decided to look for a suitable property to start the project once we got home.

Trevor and I parted company in Hawaii. He flew to visit friends on the west coast of America and I attended a week-long Institute in Biblical Counselling in Boca Raton, Florida, at the invitation of Dr Larry Crabb, with whom I had been in correspondence since reading his books, *Basic Principles in*

Biblical Counselling and *Effective Biblical Counselling.*

When I had done the counselling training course at Rosemead in 1978 I kept hearing the name of Larry Crabb and was told that he was an up-and-coming psychologist, known for his strong stand on Scripture. 'He is the man of the future in relation to Christian counselling, the man to learn from if you want to follow a true biblical model for helping people,' a visiting lecturer at Rosemead told me. I found his books superb and my heart resonated with everything he was saying. The more I read the more I wanted to meet this man. When I wrote to him asking if we could meet while I was in the United States he told me that he was conducting a course during the time I was passing through and invited me to be his guest for the week. 'If you can get here you can have a free place at the course,' he said.

Although I had gained a good deal from the Rosemead course, I had not regarded it as a truly biblical model for counselling. But Larry's course was different. As I sat and listened to him during that week in Boca Raton I kept saying to myself, 'This is what I have been looking for all my life!' Larry comes from a Plymouth Brethren background and has a sound grasp of Scripture. Although he is a psychologist, the basis of his teaching on counselling is drawn mainly from theology. The chief difference between him and some other Christian psychologists I have listened to is that, instead of imposing counselling ideas on to the Scriptures, he exposes them from within the word of God itself.

'People are made in God's image,' said Larry, 'with four aspects to their being – personal, rational, volitional and emotional.' I saw so clearly when he expanded on that idea why I had not been fully satisfied with my own counselling approach. I had focused only on the parts of people's personalities where there were clear symptoms, such as wrong thoughts or anxiety, rather than considering that other parts needed to be looked at as well, for what happens in one part of the personality affects all the others. What we think about affects the way we feel, and how we feel affects the way we choose, and how we choose depends on our evaluation of what gives us a sense of inner intactness and a deep settled peace. That one concept alone gave me the foundation on which I knew I could redesign our counselling course and bring it closer to a more biblical model.

I could hardly contain my excitement when I came away from Larry Crabb's course. 'Whatever has happened to you? You look as if someone has given you a million dollars,' said Enid when I arrived back at Heathrow airport. 'Oh, I have got more than a million dollars,' I said. In fact I had some priceless ideas on which to reconstruct our counselling course, which I believed would be more effective in helping people with their problems, and would help CWR to make an even bigger contribution in the area of biblical counselling.

Within days of returning home I began to plan a new counselling course. I took the basics of Larry's course and developed the four areas of functioning that Larry expounded – rational, volitional, emotional and personal – and added what I considered an important fifth dimension: the physical. I am convinced that some psychological/spiritual symptoms stem from problems in the physical area of a person's being, affecting their moods and behaviour. All counsellors need to be aware of this. For example, I have come across people suffering with bizarre thoughts that were due not to any psychological difficulties, but caused by something happening in their physiology.

Trevor was also enthusiastic about what I had learned on Larry Crabb's course and he, too, realised as we prepared to present future Institutes in Christian Counselling that we now had a model far in advance of what we had been teaching previously. It took several months of work to get it ready, but the first time we taught it we knew that this was where we had been trying to get it to. It had tremendous impact on our students as they saw a clear biblical model for counselling emerge day by day on the course. One who attended it said, 'I have learned more about how people tick from this course than I ever did in my training in psychology.'

Trevor and I were more determined than ever to find suitable premises for a Christian training centre and to establish a training programme that would eventually lead to diploma and degree status. (Today, of course, it is accredited by Brunel University and is part of the London School of Theology degree course in theology and counselling.)

Towards the end of 1980 Trevor and I finalised plans for a series of round-Britain rallies for the following year. Encouraged by the attendances at the Royal Albert Hall in 1979 and the increasing attendances at all our courses, we felt that this was the time to organise a UK tour called 'Gathering Together unto Him'. A few years earlier an American group had come to this country with a successful programme called *Come Together*. It largely consisted of singing worship songs based on Scripture and it captured the imagination of many British Christians. There were few large gatherings of several thousand Christians at that time and there is something about meeting together in a large auditorium that is especially pleasing to those where church life is numbered in dozens rather than hundreds.

Trevor and I felt that the mood was right for a number of large rallies dedicated to the praise and worship of God and the ministry of the Word. This meant Trevor once again taking on the role of organiser and administrator of the programme, training a choir, arranging various musical groups around the country to link with us. He did it superbly.

Our plans were to launch the programme in the Albert Hall

in January and then take it to other cities in the UK. Up to that moment it was the largest programme we had envisaged for CWR, so as we turned towards 1981 there were in our hearts mixed emotions. Would we fill some of the biggest halls in the country, and reach as we intended to 25,000 people? Time would tell.

CHAPTER 33

A DREAM IS REALISED

The first of the Gathering Together unto Him rallies held in London's Royal Albert Hall was once again a tremendous spiritual success. The hall was packed with people from all denominations, many of them *Every Day with Jesus* readers. As well as being a helpful spiritual aid, we have also found the bi-monthly publication a wonderful advertising tool. In the early 1980s we found that that we could fill some of the largest auditoriums in Britain through an announcement in *EDWJ*, saving the cost of advertising in other publications.

While writing this autobiography, I looked back through the pages of the 1980 editions of *Every Day with Jesus* to read the announcements for the Gathering Together unto Him rallies. I was intrigued to see that tickets for the Royal Albert Hall meeting were just 50p! Today it would be impossible to cover the cost of a meeting many times that figure in that auditorium.

The joyous atmosphere of expectancy at the launch of Gathering Together unto Him is impossible to describe. Behind Trevor – who was leading the meeting – myself, and a group of musicians was a 100-voice choir brought together through Trevor's persistent efforts. It was at this gathering that we first announced our intention to develop a Christian university in this country. People clapped and cheered for several minutes – an amazing response.

After I had preached, hundreds flocked to the front to

rededicate their lives to Christ, while some came to Christ for the first time. It was a most wonderful evening from that point of view and the feedback we received was positive and complimentary. Everyone we spoke to thought it had been a tremendous time – except Trevor and myself.

We said little to each other at the end of it, but I could tell from Trevor's demeanour that something was bothering him. The next morning he telephoned to say that he had not been happy about his contribution the previous evening, whereupon I told him that I had not been happy with my own contribution either. Both of us have high standards in almost everything and falling below them is not easy to come to terms with. We spent quite a time that morning trying to console one another and get things into perspective. Eventually we drew comfort from the thought that although we were not thrilled with our own contributions, God had been glorified and the people blessed.

But everything went well at all the other rallies around the UK. We came away from every one of them deeply thankful that everything had gone the way we expected. Nearly 50 singers travelled with us, giving up their time and often returning home at 3 or 4 o'clock in the morning. Trevor and I were really humbled that these people would put so much effort into supporting us with no financial reward. As in the Royal Albert Hall, people came forward at the end of the meetings to rededicate their lives to Christ or to surrender to Him for the first time.

Throughout 1982, in between the rallies and other activities, we spent a good deal of time visiting properties for sale in the London area which we thought might be suitable for establishing a Christian university. The conference centres we had used for our courses such as Fairmile Court in Cobham, The Hayes Conference Centre in Swanwick and Pilgrim Hall in Sussex, provided wonderful facilities for our courses, but we longed for a place where we could arrange such events at times when they were more suitable for us, rather than fitting into someone else's schedules.

In between looking for property, Trevor and I made a number of changes to our seminar programme. We felt that God was leading us to wind down the Dynamic Christian Living seminar and put it on to video. The seminar had been used by God to change people's lives in a powerful way, but with our deeper understanding of people and their spiritual needs we felt the need for a bigger and wider perspective. With our counselling courses focusing on the many different causes behind behaviour we needed new seminars that would reflect the change of emphasis in our teaching.

The result was that we launched two new seminars entitled 'How to Help a Friend' and 'Building a People of Power'. The former was a one-day non-residential seminar that focused on giving people suggestions and ideas on how to come alongside hurting people and offer them spiritual and emotional support. Many people in the Christian church would never see themselves as counsellors, but would like help on saying the right things to people who are in trouble – and how to avoid saying the wrong things. Building a People of Power was also a one-day course, focusing on the key principles of effective praying. When launched these two seminars were well attended in many cities throughout the UK.

The success of the 1981 series of Gathering Together unto Him meetings prompted Trevor and myself to consider another series of rallies around the UK in 1983 – this time evangelistic. We had been very successful in bringing together large numbers of people in praise and worship of God, but could we now bring together the same numbers of people for an evangelistic event? A resounding 'Yes!' was the answer as the Come Alive rallies proved to be a great success.

We launched the programme in the Westminster Central Hall, London, in January and then visited nine other cities before ending the tour in November back in London at the Wembley Conference Centre. Once again a choir was trained under Trevor's supervision and travelled with us to provide support. We saw hundreds of people come forward at the end of each meeting to surrender their lives to Jesus Christ. As far as the UK is concerned, it was one of the most fruitful years in terms of seeing people come to Christ that we have ever experienced in CWR. We did not realise it at the time, however, but this was the last year we would hold such a series of rallies in Britain. The years ahead would hold something quite different for us.

Meanwhile, we continued to scour the London area looking for property. By the summer of 1983, having had our offers rejected on a number of properties that appeared to us to be eminently suitable, we felt a little jaded. Would we ever achieve our dream?

One day, in the late summer of 1983, I received a letter from Maryelle Andrew, an *Every Day with Jesus* reader in Farnham, Surrey, suggesting that I should take a look at a large property that had recently come on the market near her home. It was known as Waverley Abbey House. Farnham is only about 20 miles from Walton-on-Thames, where I was living, but as I was suffering from 'visitation overload' I did not do anything about it. Some weeks later, however, I got a second letter from Maryelle asking if I had been able to look over the house. Spurred on by her persistence, I drove down there one September day. I was surprised that there were no 'For Sale' signs, but as I walked on to the grounds of the property I sensed something in my spirit that I had not sensed when visiting other properties – a feeling that this was most definitely the place where our dream would be realised.

The house was built in the eighteenth century by the then Chancellor of the Exchequer. It took its name from the ruined abbey nearby. Cistercian monks had built Waverley Abbey in the twelfth century after coming over from France to establish a Christian work in the area. During the First World War the house had been used as a hospital. Set in about 20 acres of beautiful grounds with its own lake, it had in more recent years been used as an up-market old people's home, but now it was disused and badly in need of repair.

I eventually tracked down the elderly owner to a small room in the stable block. When I enquired if the building was for sale I was told that it was under offer. I felt somewhat disappointed, especially because of such a strong feeling I had earlier that this would be the place where CWR would finally settle. I told Trevor and David Rivett about it and then wrote to Maryelle to inform her that although I had visited the place it was under offer and it looked as if it was not for us. Several weeks later she wrote again to say that she had heard the sale had not been finalised and that the owner had been taken to hospital suffering from cancer.

I took Trevor with me to look it over again. There we learned that the owner had died and the sale of the house was now in the hands of his executors. Trevor and I talked the matter over with the CWR Trustees and we felt that the next step should be to ask our solicitor, Graham Ross-Cornes, to approach the executors to ascertain the current position on the sale of the property. He soon came back to us to say that there were two other offers before the executors, but they would be open to receiving a third. As we prayed about it we came to the conclusion that we should offer £325,000 for the property. We sensed that the other bids might be higher, but we wanted to see the Lord's hand at work securing the property for us in the face of the competition.

We had already opened a special account for the possible purchase of a property and it had reached £81,000. If our offer was accepted, how would we raise the balance of £244,000? There was no time to make an appeal as the executors were meeting in a few days' time. We felt that our own bank would not be interested in lending us the money, but our attention was drawn to the Christian manager of a bank in Guildford, Robin Watson. We told him about Waverley Abbey House and our vision for a Christian training centre, for which we might need a short-term loan of £144,000 fairly quickly. We explained that we would seek to pay off the loan by an appeal to CWR's prayer supporters.

After mulling it over for a while, Robin agreed to our proposal and we instructed Graham Ross-Cornes to meet the executors on the day they planned to consider the various bids. At that meeting he put our offer on the table, making it clear that if they accepted our offer they would receive the money right away. He then left to allow them time for discussion. When they called him back in they told him that although they had received higher offers, the fact that the money would be forthcoming right away had caused them to vote in our favour. Graham told us that he felt the Lord's presence with him in a very special way during that meeting and was intrigued by a remark from one of the executors, who said, 'You must have someone up there working for you.'

In late November, soon after hearing the news that our offer had been accepted Enid, Trevor, Graham Ross-Cornes, David Boulnois, David Rivett and myself met in the grounds of Waverley Abbey House, formed a circle, joined our hands together and gave thanks to God for the property coming into our hands. We quickly informed our supporters that we had decided to buy the property and set a deadline of three months to repay the interim loan to the bank. Our dream had been realised, but now came the real challenge. Would the money come in so that when the house was opened to the public we could announce that it was entirely free of debt? We had to leave that issue in the hands of God.

Meanwhile, we were preparing for the launch of an important new dated publication entitled *Through the Bible Every Day in One Year*. This was advertised in the November/December edition of *Every Day with Jesus*. We invited people to enrol in a one-year reading programme that would take them through the whole Bible in the year 1984. The programme was due to begin on 1 January and was a bi-monthly part work. It was designed to take people through the Bible chronologically, that is, beginning not in Genesis 1:1 but in John 1:1 and then following Bible events as they happened.

We had anticipated that about 10,000 people would enrol in this Bible reading plan but during the last few weeks of 1983, much to our astonishment, we were swamped with over 30,000 applications. When the staff returned after the Christmas break mail was arriving by the sackful and created a great storage problem for us.

Early in 1984 Jeannette Barwick joined our team. She not only became a key player in CWR but also a tremendous support to my personal ministry. Jeannette told us that after writing her application she felt prompted to deliver it by hand; if it had been put in the post we may not have come across it for several weeks, due to the heavy backlog of mail. Because we received her application in that way Jeannette was immediately interviewed, and she came on staff almost right away and was able to assist us at this very busy period. Within a few months she was working as my personal assistant.

The first three months of 1984, when we were hoping to

receive all the money we needed to complete the purchase of Waverley Abbey House, was an anxious yet encouraging time. We had announced to our supporters that the house was now in our hands but we needed half a million pounds in order to repay the loan to the bank and to have some funds available for alterations and decorations. The gifts began to flow in from far and wide in varying amounts. The largest gift was £20,000 from a Christian trust and the smallest less than a pound from two children. They saw the picture of Waverley Abbey House on our appeal brochure and asked their mother if they could open their moneybox and send us what was in it.

Around 8,000 people donated to the project and by April £500,000 had come in. We were able to repay the bank, and we had £350,000 to begin repairs and alterations. While the purchase of the house had been an exercise in faith, the renovation stretched us even more. At first our intention was to brighten the place it up a bit with a coat of paint, but our architect, Ray Hall, a Christian, put to us a much more imaginative plan for remodelling the whole place so that each of the three floors had a specific focus and function. The ground floor would be for reception, dining and leisure facilities; the first floor, with its large lecture rooms, for teaching and training; and the second floor for sleeping accommodation.

The view of the Trustees and the Board of Management was that these suggestions would involve us in a much greater cost than we had first anticipated and would hold up the opening of the house for a year or two. Nevertheless, it seemed right to follow our architect's proposal. It would enable the house to be developed to its fullest potential. Once this was decided Ray Hall set about the task of finding a builder and getting the work under way.

I was unable to be involved as work proceeded, except at executive level, because Enid's health had begun to deteriorate and she needed much of my attention. Trevor took on the task of negotiating with the architect, the builder and the local authorities, which involved him being on site almost every day of the week. It was a massive assignment to undertake and it says a lot for Trevor's character and determination that he did not shrink from it.

CHAPTER 34

REFURBISHING AND HEALING
OF A RIFT

W̲e were not long into the refurbishing of Waverley Abbey House when a problem arose between Trevor and myself that threatened not only our personal relationship, but also the whole future of CWR. I had begun to feel that Trevor was moving ahead and making important decisions about Waverley without consultation, so one day I confronted him about this – not, I'm afraid, in as brotherly a way as I should have done. We had not had a major disagreement in the 10 years that we had been working together, but in this rift the difference of opinion, certainly on my side, was sharp and contentious.

I wondered what this would mean for CWR. Would we have to abandon the work on Waverley Abbey House? Did it mean that the organisation might have to be dismantled and that I would return to conducting evangelistic crusades and writing *Every Day with Jesus*? In the end what saved us was our strong commitment to Jesus Christ and the truths of Scripture. Though for a while we found it difficult to talk to each other, we knew that we had to resolve our difficulties in a scriptural way and apply the principles we had been teaching others. There was a great deal of pain in our hearts as we pursued our various tasks, but we knew that we would have to work through this towards reconciliation. We were able to keep the knowledge of our disagreement away from the staff, although I did share it with some of the other trustees. They, of course, were deeply concerned and urged us to resolve our differences as soon as possible.

For several weeks Trevor and I met to share our mutual concerns and seek to find a way of being reconciled. This involved analysing where things had gone wrong, how to avoid such a problem in the future and above all seeking to bring our relationship to where it had been before. Apologies were made, forgiveness sought, tears were shed. Eventually we were able to hug each other and bring our relationship back to its original footing. Then we called our staff together and told them what had happened between us, much to their astonishment. Many of them said they were touched by the way we had handled the situation. The Christian message is all about reconciliation and we knew that unless we practised what we preached we would have lost all our credibility as servants of the Lord Jesus Christ.

I shudder to think what course our lives would have taken had we not worked through our problems. I am glad to say that after we were reconciled there was never the hint of another rift during the rest of the time we worked together – nearly 15 more years.

It was just after our reconciliation that we felt it would be helpful if David Rivett joined us full time to form a three-man executive. Trevor and I were used to bouncing ideas off each other, but now David's financial experience and expertise brought another important dimension to our executive discussions and decision-making. We also found, as Scripture so wonderfully puts it, 'A cord of three strands is not quickly broken' (Eccl. 4:12). Apart from being a fine Christian David is a great encourager and was a wonderful support to Trevor and myself in the years that he worked with us in CWR.

It was in that year, 1984, that Billy Graham visited this country for what was called Mission England. It was held in the North of England, with live relays to other UK cities. A few months before Mission England began, I was approached by the members of the Billy Graham committee for the South East of England, based in Southampton, asking if I would help in preparing Christians to give basic spiritual care for those who would be converted in the mission. They asked me if I would build and present a seminar on this theme.

The seminar I produced was simply called 'Caring'. It has always been a strong conviction of mine that one of the most important ministries of the Christian church is that its members should care for one another. So I was glad to have an opportunity to put my thinking on this subject into a seminar.

The first time I presented the seminar at Southampton University it was overbooked, so we repeated it twice. The local newspaper reported that these were some of the most popular Christian seminars Southampton had ever known. People were so hungry for this kind of teaching that they begged for more. One group said to me at the door when I was leaving, 'You have just touched the surface of this issue. There is so much more to be said. Now that you have whetted our appetites, will you take us further?' This earnest request caused me to write two more seminars that took people much deeper into caring.

The success of the first Caring seminars in Southampton led me to hold one in Swindon. Several people from the town had attended the seminar in Southampton and wanted to bring it to their own locality. Once again the response was overwhelming.

Greatly encouraged, I decided to hold a seminar in the Westminster Central Hall, the venue of our first Life in a New Dimension seminar in 1973. Once again it was overbooked and I ended up holding three seminars, with a total of around 5,000 people attending.

It was around this time that we felt the need to establish a separate counselling centre and we found premises close to Walton Baptist Church in the centre of Walton-on-Thames. Jeanette took care of the administration and Janice Barrington, along with a new member of staff, Ian McConnachie, handled the counselling appointments. Both Janice and Ian assisted us on the Institute in Christian Counselling and were a tremendous help to us during those early years of our counselling training programme.

Shortly after this, the CWR general office moved from Hersham to Sunbury-on-Thames to larger premises with our own warehousing facilities. This enabled us to accommodate the wider range of publications CWR were now producing for the whole family – *Early Days with Jesus*, *Topz*, and *Young People's Every Day with Jesus* as well as *Every Day with Jesus* and *Through the Bible Every Day in one Year*. It was during this period also that a decision was made to move away from the idea of CWR being run by trustees and for it to become a charity limited by guarantee. The first directors of the new company were Enid, Trevor Partridge, David Rivett, Geoff Winson, Maurice Paine, Gill Morgan, John Hoskins and myself.

Meanwhile, Enid's health was failing fast. There were times when the offices were in Hersham that she would go to the office and after she left Roy Swann would gather the staff together to pray for her, because of how ill she looked. Enid had never been brimming with health. All her life she had been troubled with pernicious anaemia and food allergies. She couldn't keep certain foods down and had lived on a very selected diet.

At one point I had taken her to see a specialist. As soon as he set eyes on her he said: 'I think you are suffering with Simmond's disease.' We found out afterwards that Simmond's disease is a problem that arises within the pituitary gland. A distressing feature of this disease is that it affects the physical appearance and leads to premature ageing. Enid at that time looked about 10 years older than her actual age.

For some time she was looked after by a specialist in this disease, Professor Marks of Guildford, who later referred her to the Middlesex Hospital in London, where she was treated as an in-patient for about three months. A number of nurses there were Christians and *Every Day with Jesus* readers. The treatment at the hospital relieved her symptoms for a while.

Enid suffered troublesome pains in her abdomen in 1985 and stomach cancer was diagnosed. She was operated on in early April of that year at St Thomas's Hospital, London. I accompanied her as they wheeled her to the operating theatre. The surgeon stood at the entrance to it dressed from head to foot in green and wearing a mask. As we met he said, 'Don't worry, Mr Hughes. Your wife is in good hands. You might like to know I am an *Every Day with Jesus* reader and so are several nurses who are with me in the operating theatre today.'

Our wedding anniversary, which was on 10 April, was celebrated there in that hospital. After the operation the surgeon said that they had removed all the cancer but her life expectancy was uncertain. She had recovered sufficiently by July 1985 to be able to take a trip with me to the USA and Bermuda, but when we returned she was unable to contribute any more to CWR and spent the next year mainly housebound.

Around this time I wrote my first book, *Marriage as God Intended*, and had engaged Edward England as my literary agent. Edward visited us at home one day and suggested that Enid keep a journal on her thoughts and feelings about her illness. She made a start and wrote about 3,000 words, but after that she was too ill to continue. Much of what she wrote is recorded in John

Peters' biography of me. Her comments were full of her love for me, and concern that her illness was interfering with my work for the Lord. I reassured her many times that the Lord wanted me to make her my first ministry and that He regarded all I was doing for His church as secondary. I think I eventually succeeded in assuring her of this.

The time Enid was in hospital for her stomach cancer operation coincided with the presentation of one of the Caring seminars at the Westminster Central Hall. During one of the sessions I happened to remark that my wife was lying in St Thomas's Hospital just across the River Thames with what had now been diagnosed as a terminal illness and that I was feeling somewhat sad and disconsolate. To emphasise the point I was making that when people are hurting they need to know you care for them before starting to give them texts from Scripture I said, 'The reality is that while I am teaching you this material my own heart is hurting. Imagine you are sitting with me in your church and I open up to you as to how I am feeling, what would you do with me?'

People began to shout out Scripture texts, but I said, 'No, I don't want those now.' There was a hushed silence. People seemed nonplussed at the fact that as a Bible teacher I rejected the idea of giving me texts. I explained, 'Anyone can give Scriptures to people and there is a time and place for that, but what I need at this moment is something different – not a succession of texts but the knowledge that someone cares.' They quickly got the point. Some in the audience started shouting out things like, 'We love you Selwyn.' And 'Come down from the platform and let us give you a hug.'

I made the same point in all the other Caring seminars and when doing so in the Birmingham Methodist Central Hall a rather tall man ran down the aisle from the back of the hall, leapt up on to the platform and gave me one of the biggest hugs I have ever received in my life. After he had returned to his seat I said, 'Now I feel cared for!'

After the seminar in the Westminster Central Hall concluded I crossed Westminster Bridge to visit Enid in hospital, and found that her room was filled with flowers. She was puzzled. 'I can't understand why the nurses suddenly walked in with all these flowers,' she said. 'I wondered for a moment if God had gone into the flower business!'

I explained that I had talked about her being in hospital during the seminar and doubtless some people had gone out during the lunch break to visit a nearby florist and order flowers be sent to her. Tears filled her eyes at that moment as she was moved by the fact that so many cared. And in caring for her the people made me feel cared for, too.

While I was busy with the Caring seminars and visiting Enid daily in hospital or caring for her at home, Trevor was supervising the refurbishing programme at Waverley Abbey House. It took over three years to bring it to the condition we wanted. Trevor's task was made all the more difficult by the house being a Grade II listed building, which meant that the major changes had to be negotiated at every stage. In fact, English Heritage, the authority overseeing listed buildings, had to be consulted over most of the alterations, taking a great deal of time and slowing down progress of the work.

At one stage it was discovered that there was dry rot in the walls and a large amount of wood had to be completely removed. So many problems came to light during the renovation that one surveyor said an ideal solution would be if the building were to go up in flames; then we could collect the insurance and build again from scratch! Although CWR supporters kept sending in donations there came a time when the money ran out completely, causing us to lay off the workers for a while. It didn't help matters when we received a cheque for half a million pounds, and then found out through the bank that the person who had sent it didn't actually have that much money. She wanted to encourage us to believe that one day such a sum might be sent to us, but despite her motive it did not raise our spirits. When some money did come in a contractor falsified the amount on a cheque we had given him and took £10,000 from our account. It took two years to recover it.

I watched as Trevor began to sink under the weight of all this. It took a heavy toll on him. Grey streaks began to appear in his hair and I wondered at times whether he would be able to survive all the problems. He told me that one day when he was feeling somewhat jaded, he took his future wife, Debbie Hartland, to Windsor Great Park. Lying on the grass staring at the sky he felt really tempted to give it all up. Then a family came and sat down to picnic nearby. The two little boys started singing, 'Ah, Lord God, Thou hast made the heavens', with the refrain, 'Nothing is too difficult for Thee ...'. Tears ran down Trevor's face as he felt the Lord ministering to him through those words. When he got up he was gripped with a new strength and determination. I never cease to be amazed that in the moments of deepest despair God brings words of encouragement that scatter the clouds of gloom and cause the sun to shine through again.

CHAPTER 35

THE LOSS OF MY WIFE

———————

Early in 1986 hospital tests revealed that Enid's cancer had returned – this time in her liver. This meant more treatment at St Thomas's hospital. Eventually her doctors told me that they could do nothing more for her and thought she had no more than three months to live. My immediate problem was whether to tell her this or not. Opinions vary on this subject. Some say that informing a person that they may have only a short time to live may interfere with their psychological wellbeing. And of course there are many instances where doctors have told people they have just months to live only to see them recover. I know without a shadow of doubt however that the discussion I had with Enid about her illness being terminal and that she had just months to live was the right thing to do. She had no fear of death and when I shared with her the news that she had only a little time left the information didn't seem to faze her one bit.

Several days before Enid died, my mother and sister came up from Wales to help me. I wanted to nurse Enid to the end and for her to die at home, and a nurse came in daily to attend to the things I was unable to do. However, there came a moment when I wondered whether she needed more professional care than I was able to give. I asked two nurses from a nearby hospice in Walton-on-Thames to give me advice on this matter, but before anything could be done Enid fell into a coma and within a few hours had died and gone to be with the Lord whom she loved and had served so faithfully.

Just before going into that coma, however, she said something to me that will live for ever in my memory. She turned to me one night after we had prayed together and said, 'Thank you for helping me to understand how deeply loved I am by God by the way you have loved me and cared for me.' She said that she knew I taught in my marriage seminars that the way a couple relate to one another in marriage with touch, tenderness and affection, gives them a clearer picture of how much they are loved by God. The feelings they get through their loving relationship with each other helps them understand more vividly how God feels about them. 'Marriage,' I have often said, 'is where the fact of God's love is turned into feelings.' Before she lost consciousness I responded to Enid by saying, 'And thank you, too, for helping me understand more clearly how much God loves me by the way you have related to me.' Those were the last words between us.

I telephoned our doctor to have him come and confirm her death and then rang my son, David, whose printing shop was just a few miles away. He contacted Trevor and they arrived within minutes of each other. At such times family and friends are so precious. It's not what they say but who they are that can be so comforting.

Enid's funeral service was held on 7 August 1986 at Walton Baptist Church. Trevor and my old friend, Vic Ramsey, conducted it. Vic's wife, Jan, was also there, as well as all our staff and a host of friends. Enid's sister, Joan, and some of her family came up from Cornwall, as well as my father and my sister's family from Wales. Steve Powell, a young man from Wales who had recently joined our staff and was to play a vital role in CWR for many years, played the organ. I was interested to see several shopkeepers and assistants from Walton-on-Thames among the mourners. One of them told me afterwards, 'Your wife was one of the friendliest people I have ever known. We are going to miss seeing her coming in and out of our shop very much, I promise you.'

In his funeral address Trevor highlighted some of the key moments in Enid's life, and said that due to the age difference he looked upon Enid like a mother. I know that she, in turn, loved him dearly. When Trevor and I had that rift Enid hurt almost as much for Trevor as she did for me. He said that she was also a 'mother' to all the girls on the staff. Each year she would look out for Christmas presents for the staff and always tried to buy a present that matched their personalities. Enid was never at home on a platform, but loved to work behind the scenes. She felt more comfortable in a one-to-one situation with people. Vic commented on the long and close friendship he and Jan had had with Enid and how sad they both were that she was no longer with us. He pointed out that I would not have been able to achieve as much as I did were it not for her. I entirely agreed. The service was followed by a short committal service at Randalls Park Crematorium.

As a pastor, I had been involved with scores of people in their bereavement, but I never realised how the death of a loved could affect a person until I passed through it myself. The day after Enid's funeral I took my car to the garage to fill up with petrol and stood there, completely disoriented for several minutes trying to remember how to do it. I completely lost focus, and for several days afterwards it was as though I was walking through a dream. It felt as if something had been ripped out of my soul, for I loved Enid dearly.

At the weekend I drove down to Wales with a friend, not to visit my family but just to see the village where I had been brought up and especially to visit the Mission Hall where I had given my life to Christ. I have often wondered why I felt this gravitational pull to return to my roots in the days following Enid's funeral. I still don't understand exactly why, but I found the experience strangely comforting.

Facing me the following week was the completion of the next edition of *Every Day with Jesus*. I had begun it a few days before Enid's death, but now the deadline for completion was fast approaching. I switched on my word processor one morning and sat for hours before a blank screen. Nothing came. I thought about what another writer said when his brain didn't seem to work: 'In the morning I wrote one sentence in which I placed a comma; in the afternoon I took the comma out.'

For several days I was unable to write a thing. I turned to a book called, *Shadowlands*, about C.S. Lewis' loss of his wife to cancer, and read: 'Why love if losing hurts so much? I have no answers, only the life I have lived. The pain now is part of the happiness. That's the deal.'[1] I found those words deeply moving. It brought home to me more clearly than ever before that the hurt one feels when a loved one dies is because that person brought you so much happiness. Lewis was right. As another writer puts it, 'Pain is inextricably woven into the fabric of love.'

My chosen theme for that edition of *Every Day with Jesus* was the indispensability of Christ. After a few days of being unable to write anything meaningful I had just begun to get going again when I received a phone call from my sister to tell me that my father had died from a massive heart attack. He had been travelling on a bus to another village when he slumped over his seat and although an ambulance came quickly he was dead on arrival at the nearby hospital. Among his belongings returned to my mother was a copy of *Every Day with Jesus* on which he had written his own personal thoughts.

I seemed unable to grieve for my father. As I watched his

coffin being lowered into the ground at a cemetery near Bargoed I thought, 'Why am I not crying? Why do I not have feelings of grief over my father's death?' I think it was because there is only so much grief one is able to bear, and as I was still deeply grieving over Enid's death the defence mechanisms of the personality came to my aid and said: 'You are handling as much grief as you can bear at the moment. We will see to it that you don't feel any more.'

I returned to writing on the indispensability of Christ a few days later. I was attempting to show that there are many areas of life where there can be no satisfying substitute for Jesus. I had dealt with the alternatives people turn to when facing problems, such as alcohol, nature, art and literature, making the point that none of these things can satisfy and help to heal the pain as Jesus can. It occurred to me that another area of life in which there is nothing or no one who can take the place of Jesus is bereavement. So I wrote:

In our examination of the areas of life in which there can be no safe and satisfying substitute for Jesus, we arrive today at the issue of death and bereavement. Sooner or later everyone has to grapple with the fact of death – it is the common experience of the human race. Whether it is the thought of one's own exit from this world, or the loss of a loved one, we cannot avoid the fact. Many writers, philosophers and poets claim that the greatest of all fears is the fear of one's own death. And a lot of people fail to live their lives effectively because of this fear. Over the years I have often given advice to those who have been bereaved; now I have had the opportunity to test that advice in my own life. On the evening of the day my wife died I picked up an old copy of *Every Day with Jesus* in which I had written a section on bereavement. I read: 'Make up your mind that grief is bound to come to you and when it comes be prepared and willing to feel it – really feel it. Don't dodge it, sidestep it or repress it. Let it sweep over you. Remember, when you are prepared to face a feeling and not run away from it, really feel it, then you are in charge of it, and it is not in charge of you.' I responded to my own advice, went down into the feeling and found there the sweet comfort of Christ assuaging the pain and softening the hurt. It hurt, but not half as much as it would if He had not been there. I feel deeply sorry for those who lose a loved one and do not know the comforting presence of Jesus. It is this that helps shorten the period of readjustment. Now I can testify, not just from a theoretical base but from an experiential one, that there is no substitute for Jesus in the hour of bereavement.

Written at a time of such personal grief and sadness, those notes had a more than usual impact upon my readers. When that edition came out I was besieged with letters from all over the world telling how my words had touched people's lives. How true it is that when one writes out of one's pain one is sure to reach the pain of another.

During the weeks following Enid's death I received hundreds of letters of condolence from those who had heard of her passing. I was especially moved by one comment: 'One can see farther through a tear than a telescope.'

No matter what situation we find ourselves in, God gives grace not only to comfort, but to increase our contribution to life and to others. God gives most when most is taken away.

Yes, it is true: one *can* see farther through a tear than a telescope.

One of the things that I found quite remarkable was the fact that from May 1986 to the time when Enid died I had no ministry engagements in my diary and I did not have to leave Enid for any significant time. Soon after her funeral in August 1986, and sooner than I was really emotionally prepared for, I had to take to the seminar trail again. Venues for the Caring seminars in Grimsby, Nottingham, Preston, Bristol, Manchester, and several other smaller places were booked at least a year in advance, and although my heart was heavy with grief it was something I had to do. During those first few months of my bereavement the most difficult part of presenting these seminars was the last half-hour where I challenged people to commit themselves to care for others even though their own hearts might be breaking.

I never had any doubts about the truth of what I was saying, but now it was something I myself had to put to the test. As C.S. Lewis has pointed out, it is one thing to believe that a rope could hold you if you had to be suspended by it, but it is another thing when you have to put your belief into action. 'You will never know how much you trust a rope to hold you,' he said, 'until you are hanging by it.' Enid's death meant it was no longer possible for me objectively to make the point that we need to move towards others even though our own hearts might be breaking; now I had to be living proof of what I was saying.

The illustration I used was one I got from Dr Larry Crabb: picture yourself standing on the edge of a cliff looking down into a deep abyss. The abyss represents your fear of being unable to cope with a situation and of being dashed on the rocks of desolation. Now visualise a strong rope tied securely to your waist, a rope that represents God's love and which is held in the divine hands. While you remain on the cliff the rope hangs limply around your waist, and it is the cliff, not the rope, which is supporting you. The only way you will know whether the rope holds or not is to jump off the cliff and trust yourself to it. I promised people that whenever they moved towards others to care for them, even though their own hearts might be hurting, they would not be dashed on the rocks of desolation, but would be supported by the unbreakable rope of God's love.

I came to experience the truth of those words in a way I had not done before. As I continued to give myself to encouraging others when my own heart was filled with so much grief, I stepped off the cliff, so to speak. I felt the rope of God's love entwine itself around me tighter and tighter and keep me from being dashed against the rocks of despair. This did not prevent tears from flowing down my face as I spoke and my voice breaking a little, but I was able to testify that the same rope of love that held me would sustain anyone else who would trust it.

It took about six months before I could present that final concept of the seminar without my voice breaking and the tears coming, but I came through it with a deeper conviction than ever before that when we move towards others to care for them in their hurts even when our own hearts may be breaking, divine resources go to work. As our Lord Himself put it, 'It is more blessed to give than receive.' Christ constantly reached out in love to others even though His own heart was in need of succour and encouragement. His experience in the Garden of Gethsemane bears eloquent witness to that fact. And then, of course, there was the cross. Skewered to those timbers of torture and in great physical pain, He found time to think of others and pray, 'Father forgive them, for they know not what they do.'

I am grateful beyond words for the care and support given to me during that time by Jeannette Barwick, my loyal and faithful personal assistant, and the members of the team who travelled with me. Christ's love flowed through them to me in ways that strengthened my spirit and helped to heal my hurting soul.

As we moved into 1987 our attention became focused on two things, the launching of the Partnership Programme and the opening of Waverley Abbey House. For some years Trevor and I had considered developing a scheme through which we could bring those who were interested in CWR's ministry into a closer relationship with us. Gradually the idea of a partnership programme evolved and a Bible text that inspired us to go ahead with the idea was this: 'So they beckoned to their partners ... they came and were astonished' (Luke 5:7).

With the help of David Poyser we put together a full-colour fold-out leaflet, indicating our plans for Waverley over the next ten years, and inviting people to join us as partners through regular financial giving and prayer. Hundreds responded at once to our appeal and over the months the numbers reached close on 2,000. Our partners, with their regular giving and prayerful interest, are responsible for much of the growth and development of our ministry over the years. There are no words adequate to describe my appreciation, and that of all of us at CWR, for the wonderful strength and support this group of special people have been to us over the years. As a mark of my own respect and gratitude I chose to dedicate this autobiography to them.

1. Brian Sibley, *Shadowlands*, Hodder & Stoughton, 1998.

CHAPTER 36

THE OPENING OF WAVERLEY

After nearly four years of refurbishing and renovation work on Waverley Abbey House the time came in 1987 for its official opening. Although at first we found it difficult to project an opening date due to uncertainty about when the work would be finally completed we decided to announce August Bank Holiday Saturday as the big day.

Trevor and I continued to present the Caring seminars in different cities throughout the UK and we had engaged a new member of staff to help us coordinate the programme – Colin Nelson. Colin proved himself to be a great asset at that time, setting up the halls in the way that was necessary for seminar presentations. He went on to become our international coordinator and has been at my side supporting me in dozens of different countries of the world. I have often said that if I am assured that the Lord would be with me, and Colin Nelson at my side, I would be prepared to go anywhere in the world. Colin's wife, Andrea, also has played a part in CWR's ministry at different times over the years.

During our discussion as executive directors about the opening of Waverley Abbey House we wondered whom we could we ask to conduct the opening ceremony. Jeannette came up with a name that met instantly with everyone's approval – George Thomas, Lord Tonypandy, former Speaker of the House of Commons.

I had never met him personally but I knew he hailed from Wales, was the son of a miner and, like myself, was staunchly against Welsh nationalism and devolution. His full name was Thomas George Thomas, earning him the nickname in the valleys of 'Tommy Twice'. He was also a well-known Methodist layman and almost every Sunday could be found in a church preaching, as he put it, 'the word of life'. His distinctive Rhondda Valley accent when calling 'Order! Order!' in the House of Commons was known even to those who were not interested in politics. Our invitation was accepted with enthusiasm.

A few months before the opening we wondered whether we would have to postpone it. Though the renovations were almost completed there were still many other things needing to be done – decorating, choosing furnishings and fittings, curtains, drapes and so on. At an informal meeting between our architect Ray Hall and Ruth Crow, who specialised in the décor of large country houses, he asked her if she would be interested in assisting with the interior of Waverley Abbey House. Ruth had just retired to the house of her dreams in Suffolk and initially was unenthusiastic about embarking on such a project. However, she felt the Lord say to her, 'I've given you your house. I want you to do this house for me.' What a marvellous job she did! She approached every room prayerfully, considering what it would be used for and choosing what we all considered were the right colours and furnishings for each. Honesty compels me to admit that there were times when some of us stood in a room that was being decorated and wondered whether Ruth had made the right decision, but when we saw the finished results and the curtains were finally hung, the whole room took on a new perspective. It is a tribute to Ruth's work that now, 16 years later, much of the original décor remains as fresh and as appealing as it looked on the day of the opening. She willingly donated all her services to

CWR – an incredible saving to the ministry.

The Farnham Society, one of the largest and oldest conservation and amenity societies in the country gave us a certificate after the completion of Waverley congratulating CWR on the restoration work that had been done to the House.

A few weeks before the opening I moved from Walton-on-Thames to a flat in Farnham, just five minutes' drive from Waverley Abbey House. The ease with which I was able to sell my previous flat (the home Enid and I had shared for close on 20 years) and to buy another one so close to Waverley Abbey House was astonishing. I am quite sure that my heavenly Father had His hand very firmly on that matter.

The day prior to the official opening of Waverley all our staff came down from Sunbury to help us complete everything. It is quite amazing the things that were accomplished in that one day. The place became a veritable hive of industry as people took on the different tasks allotted to them. Carpets had to be laid and vacuumed, every room dusted, windows cleaned, flower beds weeded and 101 other jobs attended to. Our staff threw themselves into the task with great energy and enthusiasm. How I wish those frenetic activities could have been captured on video. My contribution was to make cups of tea for everybody – a service that seemed greatly appreciated.

Tarmac had been laid on the area in front of the house only a few days before the opening and we wondered whether it would set in time. We had visions of people wandering through the house leaving bits of tar on the brand new carpets. But we dealt with the problem by laying hessian matting to the front door of the house. A stage was erected in the field facing the front of the house for a short open-air meeting before the actual opening ceremony, and a marquee seating 500 was set up in the grounds in readiness for the evening celebration.

One of the novel ideas we had for the opening day was to drape the house from side to side with wide yellow ribbon and tie it in a bow at the front to convey the idea of God's gift to us. This operation was to left to the morning of the opening day and George Thomas arrived at about 10am as some of the staff were doing it. He at once joined in to help, and when I arrived at about 11am he greeted me with: 'Fee fi fo fum, I smell the blood of a Welshman!'

The opening celebrations started at 2pm and hundreds of people gathered on the field opposite the front of the house for a short ceremony chaired by David Rivett. Alongside me on the platform were George Thomas, Trevor Partridge, Gilbert Kirby (former principal of London Bible College) and the Mayor of Farnham. Phillip Hillsdon and Andy Neeve provided the music, and after we had sung a few songs of praise and worship to God Trevor spoke of the struggle it had been to bring the house to the condition it was in that day. I followed by describing the day as probably one of the greatest milestones in the history of CWR.

Then came Lord Tonypandy who, after a few humorous references to his Welsh ancestry, went on to say: 'For CWR, this is a watershed day.' Then for a few minutes his voice took on the timbre of a prophet as he declared: 'This place will be a powerhouse for the Lord Jesus Christ in the unfolding years which are yet to be revealed. It will be used to train tomorrow's leaders in the Christian world, which will be so different from the world it is today. We can be sure of this: in a hundred years from now, when other folk will be here celebrating this day, the need of people and the challenge of the gospel will be the same as it is now.'

After the speeches, we gathered around the front door and George Thomas cut the ribbon and declared the house open. For several hours visitors were taken on conducted tours. Tea was provided for about 100 special guests in the Waverley Room – men and women who in one way or another were very close to us and supported CWR's ministry. At this point George Thomas had to leave to drive north for a Sunday preaching appointment. I handed him a cheque to cover his expenses for the day, but he promptly signed his name on the back and handed it to my two grandchildren, Leighton and Sheryl, as a souvenir of the day. Before leaving George said he would like to become a CWR partner. We gave him a Partnership form and were overjoyed to receive it back duly filled in a few days later.

In the evening we gathered in the marquee for song, worship and celebration. The meeting was chaired once again by David Rivett. Trevor expanded on the history of the house and explained more about the difficulties he had faced in bringing it to its present magnificent condition. A number of people who had been involved in the refurbishing were singled out for special thanks. First the architect Ray Hall, whose vision for the House had inspired us to delay the opening for a few years so that it could be developed to its highest potential. Then Len Cooper, the Master Builder whose tireless efforts in overcoming the many problems was deservedly highly commended. Ruth Crow, whose skill in choosing the right décor for every room, was thanked profusely for her labour of love and it was the opinion of every one who had viewed the House earlier that it was the décor that had impressed them more than anything.

Later in the meeting when I brought a devotional message based on the story of the woman in the Gospels who broke the alabaster box of ointment on the head of Jesus, I said that all the effort and time that had gone into the refurbishing of the house to bring it to a state of great excellence, was our gift to Him. The following day, Sunday, had been declared as an Open Day, when people who could not be there on the Saturday were able to come in the afternoon. The Bank Holiday Monday was our final celebration, when again we had a service in the evening. This brought to a close what, for me, was one of the great moments in CWR's history.

Although the house was now ready for residential courses we had not been able to advertise a full programme in advance because we needed to be certain that no unforeseen problems would interfere with our opening date. So just three counselling courses and several other small events were held there during the remainder of that year. The week following the opening Trevor and I sat down to plan a full programme for 1988. This was designed to fill the house for almost every week and weekend of the year.

Our first counselling course at Waverley in mid-September was a wonderful occasion. We had been so accustomed to conducting these courses in other people's conference centres that it was sheer joy to be able to have the freedom to arrange everything to our own timings and requirements. Our second counselling course scheduled for late October had to be cancelled due to southern Britain being hit by one of the worst night of storms in living memory. At least 13 people were known to have died and many dozens injured by falling trees and buildings. I went to bed on Friday 16 October 1997 after listening to BBC weatherman Michael Fish reassure viewers that the deep depression strengthening over the Atlantic would track along the English Channel and would miss Britain altogether. Instead it cut a swathe of destruction right across the south of the country.

The storm didn't disturb me when it broke, but when I awoke about 6am and turned on the television an announcer was warning people in the south to stay at home as hundreds of roads and railway lines were blocked by fallen trees. Winds had reached 94 mph in London, he said, and 110 mph in the Channel

Islands. I looked out of my window and saw trees fallen across the street. I immediately wondered what had happened to Waverley Abbey House. Unable to drive there because of the fallen trees, I walked, although it took me over an hour instead of 20 minutes. Fallen trees blocked Waverley Lane, the road that leads from Farnham to the house. After clambering over what must have been 20 or more of these I arrived at the house to discover, to my relief, that although a few trees had fallen there, no serious damage had been done to the house itself. It took well over a week for the electricity supply and telephone system to be reconnected, so the counselling course planned for the week after the storm had to be postponed. Bearing in mind that the storm cost an estimated £1 billion in repairs and clear-up costs, and 15 million trees were lost, we were fortunate that Waverley Abbey House escaped so lightly.

On 5 November of that year an event happened that almost ended my life. I was returning from speaking at an evening meeting in a church in Sutton, Surrey, and travelling on the A3 near Chessington, when I suddenly encountered an unexpected swirling bank of dense fog. One or two cars ahead of me had already crashed into each other and I in turn crashed into them. Within seconds a car crashed into the back of mine and as there was a likelihood of more crashes I got out of my vehicle. As I reached the side of the road a car travelling at speed swerved to avoid crashing into the other cars, but headed straight towards me. I managed to hurl myself on to the grass verge and it narrowly missed me as it careered into a nearby field.

Within minutes the police and ambulances arrived on the scene but fortunately there were no fatalities. My car, as well as others, was a write-off. Feeling no immediate physical effects, I walked for about a mile to a telephone box to call Jeannette Barwick, who lived just a few miles from the crash scene. She collected me in her car and took me, on the advice of the ambulance men, to Kingston Hospital for a check-up. On the way there I began to feel some pains in my chest. The subsequent examination discovered a few cracked ribs. Police at the hospital with other casualties from the pile-up told me that the A3 in the direction of my home was impassable.

Jeannette took me home with her and she and her daughter looked after me for a few days until I was able to move again. Later my son, David, picked me up and took me to my flat. That experience effectively put me out of action for a few weeks but I was able to fulfil the few remaining seminar engagements though I had to remain seated to do so.

As the year ended I knew there was so much to thank God for – the opening of Waverley, protection from the storm and my deliverance from an accident that could have caused my death or serious injury. I had been spared to live another day.

CHAPTER 37

WAVERLEY – THE FIRST
THREE YEARS

Trevor Partridge and I approached 1988 with mixed feelings – excitement at the opportunity of implementing our ideas for Christian education and a certain amount of apprehension about whether it would work. Our week-long counselling courses had proved an unqualified success and we were confident they would go from strength to strength, but it remained to be seen how the other courses we had planned would fare. We had produced an ambitious brochure entitled 'Waverley Abbey House – The First Year', which advertised a variety of courses – 27 in all.

We planned that our first year would take up about 50 per cent occupancy of the house – a goal we knew would be difficult to meet, but we figured that sometimes you have to aim for the moon but be content just to hit the lamp post. A few of the courses did not materialise through lack of take-up, but as we saw our first year as an experimental period we were not too disappointed with the results. Trevor and I did the teaching on almost all of the courses, assisted in some sessions by members of our staff and other lecturers whom we brought in occasionally.

Often Trevor and I would find ourselves writing the printed notes for the courses just days before the event. Almost everything we did was a new course for us and it is a testimony to God's grace and help that we were able to get through that first year without it affecting our health. Often we would finish a week-long course on a Friday morning and begin a weekend course the same evening. In addition to this there were the Caring seminars that had been planned a year in advance. We decided to share some of these presentations, which were held in different cities throughout the UK.

Though exhausting, the work was extremely fulfilling. The vision we had carried for years was now being realised and we were both thrilled with the dynamics of experimenting with new courses. After every course had finished we met to consider its strengths and weaknesses and to determine what should be left out and what new concepts and ideas should be built in for the next presentation. Some courses had a short life and others a much longer one. Slowly it began to dawn upon us that although we would have liked to develop courses that related biblical principles to almost every profession or vocation, it was physically beyond us.

It was in the summer of the first full year of the courses conducted at Waverley that Jeannette put to the executive directors a proposal that we should include some special events for women. Before Waverley opened Jeanette had felt God's leading to establish a ministry to women. Trevor, David and myself encouraged her to move in this direction, with the result that the women's ministry at Waverley has grown and developed and at the present time is influencing thousands of women both in the UK and other parts of the world.

As the weeks and months went by Trevor and I felt the need to give ourselves to pioneering a smaller number of in-depth courses that were more directly connected with the helping professions. So we decided that the following year we would run a one-year course on counselling (one day a week spread out over three terms of 12 weeks) and take people deeper into the subject than we had ever done before. I decided at that stage that I would commit myself to spending the next three years focusing mainly on the courses at Waverley and declining most of the invitations I received from across the UK and overseas.

Before that first one-year counselling course began in 1989, Trevor and I were joined by Jenny Trust, a qualified psychologist. She was someone who, like ourselves, was thoroughly committed to the authority of Scripture. Jenny had been to a number of CWR activities and had become a very close friend of ours. She had been in the nursing profession and had then done a course at the Bible Training Institute, Glasgow. After graduating she became involved in Christian ministry in an Anglican church in Brighton. Jenny then pursued further training as a clinical psychologist. We had always kept in touch with her, and it had always been our hope that she might work with us one day. After she had completed her training as a psychologist, and had done some work as an intern, we invited her to come and help us take the counselling training to a higher level. Terry Virgo and the elders of the NFI (New Frontiers International) church in Brighton, where she was then a member, kindly agreed to release her to us. We appointed Jenny as course tutor for our one-year Institute in Christian Counselling.

In the midst of the teaching and training programme at Waverley, a very happy event took place in the autumn of 1989 when Trevor and Debbie were married. The service was conducted by the Revd. John Innes at All Saints Tilford, just a few miles from Waverley. Debbie's father had died years previously and when she asked me if I would give her away I remember feeling very mixed emotions. Although I loved my two sons David and John I had always wanted a daughter. I had seen Debbie grow and develop from a girl into a beautiful young woman and both Enid and I looked upon her as our own. Prior to the wedding I went through some of the emotions a father must go through as he prepares to hand his daughter to another man.

Our first one-year course at Waverley was launched in January 1990, and it was fully booked. We met every Monday for the whole day, beginning with devotions and lectures in the morning, with the afternoons being taken up with group work and special assignments. Every week the students were given homework assignments and soon the course began to take on a professional feel. Many of our students who had completed degree courses in tertiary education said the course was as well laid out and presented as any they had experienced at university or college.

Three people who helped us greatly in the early development of the courses at Waverley were John and Mary Wright and Ian MacConnachie. All three had contributed to our ministry in the counselling centre in Walton-on-Thames and when we opened Waverley Abbey House they helped us establish our ministry in this new place, Ian staying only for a short time until he moved with his family to Scotland. Mary's contribution was largely dealing with the many letters and calls that came to us from people with problems, asking for help and advice, as well as group facilitation. John, at that time a retired public school master, was invaluable in helping us lay down a sound administrative foundation for the one-year counselling course. I came to regard John as a very dear friend and I missed him greatly when he died suddenly several years later.

A few weeks into the one-year course we began to see the potential for it to become a regular and on-going feature of our training programme, so we launched a second course in September of that year to bring it in line with the academic year, again with a full complement of students. So for three months we were running two one-year counselling courses on the same day.

Before the second course began we added another person to our training team – Simon Gibson. At the time he was a pastor on the south coast and had already been working with us for a year as a visiting lecturer. He too proved to be a great acquisition to the team. I first met Simon when he visited me at our counselling centre in Walton-on-Thames in 1985 when he was based in Bristol. Not long after he joined us he wrote a thesis on the CWR model of counselling for his Bachelor's degree. Later he gained his Master's and later still a PhD. His contribution to the counsellor training ministry at CWR has been enormous and has continued to the present day.

It was a wonderful moment when we celebrated the end of our first one-year counselling course. Our top student that first year was Nigel James. He had a photographic business but was tremendously keen on the subject of counselling. Nigel had become a Christian at a crusade that Trevor and I conducted in The Dome, Brighton, in 1982. Over the years Nigel has grown closer and closer to us. He eventually became a valued member of staff and today is Training Course Co-ordinator.

Around this time two personalities came on the CWR scene who were destined to play vital roles in the development of the ministry. One was Sean Gubb and the other Mick Brooks.

Sean was a graduate of London Bible College (now the London School of Theology) and has contributed to the ministry in several significant ways. He has helped greatly in the shaping of the training programme and has established strong links and partnerships with other Christian organisations such as, the Evangelical Alliance, London School of Theology, the Association of Christian Counsellors and Spring Harvest.

Mick came from a background in psychiatry and after studying at CFNI Bible College in the USA, he became Dean of

Students in the CFNI College in Jamaica. Since joining CWR he has contributed to various aspects of the training programme including being course tutor for the Basic Biblical Counselling Course for many years. He has also done some significant work in the publishing department and has helped to maintain relationships with international publishers.

A big event that took place in September 1990 was the celebration of the twenty-fifth anniversary of CWR. Hundreds of people gathered with us in a marquee at Waverley to celebrate the years of successful ministry. Gerald Williams, the well-known tennis commentator and a good friend of Trevor and myself, was the guest of honour. He interviewed us, focusing on the special relationship we had enjoyed for so many years. One of the questions he put to us was: 'You have worked together for some time, but do you really like one another?' A summary of our answer was – 'More often than not!' Trevor and I knew beyond any shadow of doubt that we had been teamed together by the Lord to fulfil a special purpose. Despite those moments when our habits and idiosyncrasies might have irritated each other we were conscious of the fact that we had been called by God to work towards some divine goals – a fact that held us together when other things might have driven us apart.

In 1990 we decided to close down the offices in Sunbury-on-Thames and relocate in the East Wing at Waverley Abbey House. This was done not only for economic reasons but also to enable our whole team of nearly 50 people to be together in one place. Gerry and Barry Bacon, a father and son who had been involved in the restoration of Waverley, were kept on on a full-time basis after the house had been opened to maintain it. They spent a good deal of time preparing the East Wing for the arrival of the team. Our joy knew no bounds that we were together again and we celebrated it with a special time of prayer and devotions.

We found being together like this helped us to operate the whole ministry in a more cohesive way, especially in relation to the development of our publications. Reference here must be made to Matthew Taylor, who in the years since moving down from Sunbury has built and developed a most creative and effective team responsible for the design and production of all CWR's publications. Many consider that the design and appearance of our publications have put CWR among the leaders in this field, and much of that is due to Matthew's commitment to excellence and his leadership in this area of our ministry.

I cannot remember ever feeling so fulfilled as I did in those first few years following the opening of Waverley Abbey House. I remember thinking to myself that this was what I was put on earth to do – preaching, teaching, writing and building courses that help people develop as true disciples of Jesus.

After giving my undivided attention to Waverley for three years, however, I began to feel that it was time to plan an overseas training programme and take to other countries the teaching that had been worked out in the many courses delivered at Waverley. The fact that I was now single made it easier for me to give myself to other countries in this way and also provided me with an outlet for my natural and spiritual energy.

First we began to take the Caring seminars to different countries beginning with Australia and New Zealand. One couple who became great personal friends as a result of visiting Australia were Robert Colman and his wife Carol. Robert is a wonderful singer and acted as song leader in some of our Caring seminars during our first presentations in that country. Hardly a week goes by without us making contact with each other by email. We then took the Caring programme to Singapore, Malaysia, Sri Lanka, Canada, Ghana, Uganda, Kenya and South Africa. The visits were stretched out over several years and in addition to visiting these countries with a basic team consisting of Trevor, Jeannette, Colin Nelson and myself, there were occasions when Colin, David Rivett and I visited other countries such as India, Nigeria, Russia and Sri Lanka for various types of ministry engagements. Those years, spent laying down a strong foundation for helping people with their problems in the various countries we visited, were not only thrilling for everyone of the team who participated but also deeply appreciated by the churches in the different nations. In all these countries we had great friends who helped us promote the courses. How I wish I had space to mention all their names but I feel I must identify the following who have given us outstanding help and support: Rev Lawrence Yap in Malaysia; Canon James Wong in Singapore; Remi Ayida and the FBFM Committee in Nigeria; Neville and Ruki Mendis and Hilary Fernando in Sri Lanka; Henry Joseph and his sons Finney and Alex and Samson Gandhi in India; and Pastor Gary Skinner and Olivia Kyambadde in Uganda.

Meanwhile, back at Waverley, things were developing so fast that we felt it necessary to appoint a Chief Executive for the organisation. Trevor, David Rivett and I felt that our function as a three-man executive meant that we were spending so much time on running the organisation that that we could not give ourselves more fully to other important aspects of the ministry. A Chief Executive Officer, responsible for the day-to-day running of CWR, seemed the solution.

Interviews were set up with a number of candidates, and we finally settled on Patrick Hibbin. He took up this important new position in May 1994. As he could not immediately move from Yorkshire into the Farnham area he stayed at Waverley from Monday to Friday and went home every weekend.

Patrick had held several key positions in business, and had excellent qualifications. His appointment left Trevor, David and me feeling greatly relieved that at last we could get on with what we really needed to do. Although Patrick was responsible directly to the Board, we met with him during the first few weeks of his employment to brief him on the history of CWR and acquaint him with the rationale for many of the systems and procedures that we had put in place. Our intention was that once we had put him fully in the picture we would leave it to him to run the organisation as he saw fit.

However, Patrick began to introduce changes which caused the three of us some concern. Having spent years laying down the foundations for the work at Waverley Abbey House we were somewhat exercised in our spirits that things were being suggested that might undo what had been accomplished. Every Chief Executive likes to have a free hand to run things as he sees fit, and when we began to share with Patrick our concerns he came eventually to feel that there was no future for him at CWR. He resigned with effect from September 1994. Sadly we said goodbye to him and faced the fact that our first CEO appointment did not turn out the way we had hoped.

This whole experience greatly concerned the Board members and we spent many hours discussing it before deciding on the way ahead. Two of the Board members resigned because they felt that Trevor, David and I had not handled the situation in the way they would have liked. Eventually, after much prayer and discussion, the Board decided that, before advertising for another CEO, and as an interim measure only, Trevor should be invited to fill that role. David and I met with Trevor and encouraged him to go ahead. We felt that his knowledge of CWR, his long experience in the organisation and his organising ability made him a suitable candidate for the post. We knew, of course, that Trevor's acceptance of the position would involve him in some personal cost, inasmuch that his time would be more taken up with administration than ministry.

With characteristic thoroughness and enthusiasm, Trevor began to throw himself into the task of running the organisation, this time as the sole decision-maker, while David and I gave him as much support as we could. I thought it was an ideal arrangement, although we did miss our times of meeting as a triumvirate. With hindsight, the decision we made at that time, though it was the right one, nevertheless meant that something had been lost in terms of our relationships. It was not something we missed deeply at that time but while the new arrangement clearly had some clear advantages, the fact that we were not working so closely together had some disadvantages also.

CHAPTER 38

MY BATTLE WITH CANCER

While Trevor began to focus on being CWR's Chief Executive, overhauling the administrative systems to gain greater efficiency, directing the affairs of the organisation and planning for the years ahead, I was much freer to concentrate on the work that I love best – writing, teaching and preaching. Administrative work and committee meetings do not greatly appeal to me. This kind of work is necessary, but given a choice I would much prefer to be sitting at my computer or conducting a seminar.

Trevor's new role meant that, sadly, he was seen less in the lecture rooms, but he did join us as part of the team on some occasions when we travelled overseas for the presentation of different seminars.

During the first few months of the year I began to experience some physical problems that at first were difficult to trace to any particular source. Everything I did – writing, teaching, preaching – left me exhausted. At first I did not seek medical advice but by the middle of the year I was experiencing so many difficulties that made it necessary to see my doctor. He gave me a full examination and ordered a blood test (called a PSA – Prostate Specific Antigen), which analyses the degree of cancer that may be in the prostate.

A few days later my doctor told me that my PSA was in the questionable zone – high, but nothing to be unduly worried about at that stage. The PSA reading can be elevated and driven up by an infection, so a high PSA doesn't necessarily indicate cancer. He said he would arrange for a more detailed test with an urologist. At my initial interview with the urologist I told him that I was about to embark on an overseas lecture tour but he thought it unlikely that that there would be complications while I was abroad. 'Immediately you return,' he said, 'I would like to arrange a biopsy, which means taking a sample from the prostate gland.'

While I was in New Zealand with the team presenting a counselling course I could not help thinking to myself: have I fallen victim to prostate cancer? This form of cancer, I was told, kills about 10,000 men a year in the UK, so regular blood screenings for prostate specific antigens are recommended for men over 45. It is not easy coming to terms with such a killer. When I got home I had a biopsy at Frimley Park hospital – an uncomfortable but not painful experience. As I had read on the Internet that cancer could sometimes be missed in a biopsy, I asked the urologist to take as many samples as necessary, even though it lengthened the procedure a little. A few days later I met the urologist again and he said: 'Your biopsy results have turned out positive.' Associating 'positive' with 'good' I felt relieved for a few seconds – until I realised what he was really saying. Then the weight of it hit me: I had prostate cancer.

The urologist did a drawing of the prostate, showing me that the cancer was found in one area but not the other and then he went through the treatment options, explaining how I should go about making a decision on the best treatment. One of my concerns was whether or not the cancer had spread beyond the prostate, as for some time I had been experiencing a nagging pain in my back, ever since slipping coming off the platform of a church in Australia. The urologist arranged for me to have an

X-ray, which showed there was a hairline fracture at the base of my spine that appeared to be healing up nicely. I was greatly relieved.

I was referred to an oncologist (a cancer treatment specialist), who told me that there are three basic treatment options: surgery, hormone therapy and radiation. Surgery involves the removal of the entire prostate; radiation blasts the affected area and hormone treatment by injection slows down the production of testosterone. Each treatment has its pros and cons and many factors need to be considered, such as the size of the tumour, how aggressive it is, and the patient's age and lifestyle. My oncologist, Dr Robert Laing of the Royal Surrey Hospital, Guildford, recommended three months of hormone therapy followed, after a break, by a month of radiation. 'First,' he said, 'we will starve it, then we will fry it.'

I was warned of possible, including urinary, problems, fatigue and a degree of pain. The side effects I experienced were hot flushes (such as women get in the menopause) and a certain amount of fatigue, but not enough to hinder my programme of writing, teaching, preaching and travelling.

After four months of hormone therapy came the next stage – radiation treatment. This began in early 1996 and I found it much more difficult to cope with than the hormone therapy. It involved attending hospital five days a week for a month. First there was an investigation to locate exactly where to direct the radiation. The daily treatment involved lying under a machine which focused on the prostate gland with a few bursts of radiation for about 30 seconds.

The course of treatment ended a few days before I was due to present the morning Bible studies at the Easter People celebrations in Blackpool. The event always begins on the Tuesday after Easter, but on the Bank Holiday Monday I was in such pain and discomfort that I was on the point of ringing up to cancel my visit. Although it was a Bank Holiday, several desperate enquiries enabled me to telephone my oncologist at home. I apologised for troubling him and he arranged for me to obtain a special prescription for dealing with the pain from a hospital in Guildford. Within hours of taking the medication I felt fit enough to make it to Blackpool.

I felt apprehensive, not only about the week in Blackpool, which is always a most wonderful event, but also about the following week in which I was booked to speak at a Christian conference for students in Slovakia with John Stott. But the medication worked there as well as in Blackpool and within a few weeks the problem cleared up, with no further complications. The conference in Slovakia was organised by a group of Christian students in conjunction with European Mission and Gary Cox, my good friend from Eurovangelism. Gary drove me and Colin Nelson, my faithful colleague and friend, from Hungary up into the hills and we came eventually to a wonderful conference centre not far from the Polish border. I found that my condition did not affect my ministry there in any way, although the medication I was obliged to take did have a slightly adverse effect on my energy levels.

Being busy with my writing and preaching schedule in the months that followed actually helped me to get over the side effects that were residual to my cancer treatment. It would not be true to say that there was no fear in me, but I have always believed in being honest and facing the fear. Once again, the support I got from Jeannette and the staff at CWR was tremendously encouraging. Nothing was too much for them and they all excelled themselves in upholding me through those difficult months. I was also grateful for my many friends around the world who prayed for me and sent me words of comfort and consolation. Many people who contacted me had dealt with cancer and I found their advice extremely helpful. Some people diagnosed with cancer feel they have to hide it – that it will feel less real if no one knows about it, or that their friends will pity them. In fact, the fear gets worse when it is hidden.

Yet no matter how open one is about a life-threatening illness, ultimately everyone has to face it alone. People can help deal with the symptoms and sympathise with the condition, but there are still nights when one wakes up frightened. The way I face fear is by acknowledging its presence, reminding myself that a sovereign God knows all about the situation, and opening myself to the grace which He promises to provide for every one of life's difficulties.

At the time the urologist told me I had prostate cancer I was writing an edition of *Every Day with Jesus* on heaven. I remember thinking to myself, 'Maybe it won't be all that long before I'll be there!' I confess however, that I did not share the apostle Paul's desire when he told the Philippian converts that as far as heaven was concerned he was eager to go but willing to stay. I was *willing* to go but *eager* to stay. Heaven figured a good deal in my thinking during the period of treatment I went through and the concept of eternity came alive in my heart in a way I have never before known. Since then the prospect of one day being in heaven has been a tremendous strength to me.

During the treatment, which altogether took about five months, I felt the strong, supportive hand of God in the most wonderful way. I did not miss a single service at which I was booked to preach, and also on occasions travelled overseas to speak at meetings in Malaysia, Kuching in Borneo, Africa, Canada and Singapore. I was grateful for the support of Dr Peter Tong in Malaysia, whom I had met many times during my visits there, and who sent me all kinds of medication designed to fight cancer. This helped me tremendously. He asked all the businessmen in his fellowship to pray for me and sent me encouraging letters all the time. He was a great inspiration. He himself had struggled with cancer and greatly benefited from the various kinds of medication he sent me.

I am grateful for the expert and excellent medical attention I received, and through it have had my conviction reinforced that God not only heals directly but also utilises the discoveries of modern-day medical science. Regular check-ups showed that my PSA blood test had come down to normal and although I was not told that I was clear of cancer, it was obvious that it was in remission. The feeling of fear that accompanies cancer expresses itself in a variety of ways. Every little ache and pain conjures a worst-case scenario. I would feel twinge in my foot or knee and wonder if the cancer had started up again and had spread to other parts of my body. Regular testing proved that it was not so.

It was a wonderful feeling to be able to continue with my writing, preaching and teaching without the prospect of my prostate cancer being life-threatening. I continued to divide my time between Waverley and other overseas visits while Trevor focused on the administration of CWR, establishing more efficient systems, and planning for the future.

In 1996 we said a sad goodbye to Jenny Trust who felt that having given six years to CWR that it was time to move on to take up work as a community psychologist. Jenny's contribution to the counselling training at Waverley Abbey House had been enormous and everyone on the training team felt her loss most keenly.

A key role that was created during Trevor's tenure as Chief Executive was that of a training manager who would also be responsible for the running of the house. This role was filled by Paul Grant – a retired headmaster who had grown close to us as a voluntary worker in the years prior to his appointment. Paul and his wife Eileen had attended the one-year counselling course in the early nineties. Eileen did the 1992–93 course and Paul did the same course the following year. Both Paul and Eileen worked with us in various ways following their completion of the courses and when the time came to make the appointment of a training manager, Paul was the obvious choice.

Paul's background in education made him an excellent candidate for the role and more especially because, after preliminary soundings in the mid-90s with London Bible College, a plan began to develop for a partnership between LBC and CWR to develop courses up to BA degree level in theology and counselling for validation by Brunel University. Paul's knowledge and experience of the world of education were a tremendous help to us in working through the accreditation process. The sterling work he put into this project helped lay down a programme of training that took CWR into a completely new dimension.

All this was made possible through the determined efforts of the Principal of LBC, Dr Derek Tidball and the enthusiastic support of Dr Peter Hicks, Director of Ministry. Credit also must be given to Nathalie Hallervorden – a highly qualified and practising counsellor from Germany (a USA graduate) who joined the staff in 1999 as a full-time tutor, and to Ron Kalmier, another highly qualified contributor brought over from Australia as a member of staff, who helped greatly in the link between CWR and LBC. Norma Parrack also was a key player, and between them all the foundations were securely laid for the future of counselling training under CWR.

After just over two years as Chief Executive Officer Trevor felt he needed a sabbatical, so early in 1996 we began as a Board to seek a replacement for him. After advertising and interviewing a number of candidates we were particularly drawn to a New Zealander, John Muys. He had first come to our attention in the early 1980s when Trevor and Gerry Matthewman, who was then our finance officer, attended the Australian booksellers' convention in Adelaide seeking a distributor for *Every Day with Jesus* in that part of the world. John had established a company in Australia called Christian Marketing (later to become Christian Marketing Communications Australia) and after seeing *EDWJ* and being drawn to what he described as 'the strong life application in its pages', expressed an interest in taking on the task of being CWR's distributor in the Antipodes. CMC not only became the distributor in Australia, but also later in New Zealand and Canada. The relationship has continued in the first two countries until this day.

In August 1991, John and his wife, Rosaline, came to Waverley Abbey House to report on the progress of CMC's distribution of *EDWJ* in Australia. The discussion moved on to publishing and distributing worldwide. 'John, the world is opening up to us in terms of the distribution of *Every Day with Jesus*,' I said. 'Your experience is invaluable in this regard. You have got to help us.' Later John told me that my words came home to him as confirmation of something his wife said after reading John Peters' biography of me in late 1989. The story of my life touched Rose in such a way that with a good deal of emotion she said to her husband, 'I believe the Lord wants you to help Selwyn in the work he is doing.'

The result of that meeting was that John committed himself to giving CWR 12 weeks a year to help set up an international department. He charged nothing for his services other than travelling expenses. The work involved him in visiting different countries with Colin Nelson, our international representative, giving input and advice on various styles of agreements, and helping Colin identify various partner possibilities in different markets worldwide. The fact that he had worked with us for a number of years in this capacity weighed heavily in his favour when we were looking for a new CEO. Although there were a number of other interesting candidates, we finally chose John.

John was duly installed as CEO in February 1997 and soon afterwards Trevor began his well-earned six-month sabbatical. We quickly felt the impact of John's dynamic leadership. A month after being appointed, he attended the Christian Booksellers Convention in Bournemouth and negotiated an agreement for my writings with one of America's largest Christian publishers, Broadman and Holman, which would result in some 15 books being published over the next few years.

In his first six months as CEO John initiated so many changes and new projects that one of the staff said, 'I feel as if I am caught up in a whirlwind!' Restructuring of the counselling programme was one of the things started during that time.

When Trevor returned from his sabbatical in September he found that his new role as Executive Ministry Director was under review. There were other significant issues as well, one which had to do with the future direction of the ministry. After a prolonged discussion at Board level Trevor made it clear that in the light of the changes he needed some time to review his position. Several days later he tendered his resignation and informed us that he would cease employment with CWR at the end of 1997.

It was very sad for us all, and particularly for me, that after 23 years the working partnership between Trevor and myself was to end. When the news was announced to the Christian public many thought that Trevor and I had fallen out, but that was not the case. In fact we have continued our friendship over the years and still meet up from time to time. Trevor has a full-size snooker table in his home and we enjoy playing a game and chatting about old times. After leaving CWR Trevor became involved in a business venture as well as continuing his ministry on a personal level. His wife, Debbie, stayed on after Trevor's resignation, finally leaving in 2000, having worked for CWR for 25 years, which makes her one of the longest serving members of staff. She still comes in to do some work for us whenever her help is needed, however, and Trevor continues to contribute regularly to CWR's publishing ministry.

CHAPTER 39

70 YEARS, AND STILL
GOING STRONG

———————————

One of the big events of 1998 for me and one to which I eagerly looked forward, was the celebration of my seventieth birthday on 27 April. Two days before that I was involved in an event that also gave me a great deal of personal pleasure. I was invited to South Elmsall, a small town in Yorkshire, near South Kirkby, where I had spent so many happy years in pastoral ministry, to speak at the official opening of the new church there. One of my goals as pastor in South Kirkby 40 years earlier had been to open a new church in South Elmsall, but it had never been fulfilled. So I was thrilled to participate in what I saw as a late realisation of that dream.

It was wonderful to see many of the people I knew from past days – people who had been members of my church in South Kirkby but now, like me, were 40 years older! I told them that to meet up with them again on the eve of my seventieth birthday was one of the best presents I could ever have received.

Two days later I celebrated my birthday at Waverley Abbey House, where I invited 70 of my closest friends. The CWR Board were there, of course, as were Trevor and Debbie, John and Rose Muys, Vic and Jan Ramsey, Gordon and Barbara White, Eric and Grace Bowtell, Tony and Beryl Holloway, Steve and Kay Stevens, the Special Ministries team who worked closely with me, Edward England my literary agent, my son David, his wife

Sue and my grandson, Leighton. Everyone present had added richness to my life through their friendship and support.

It is said that the only person to have two birthday celebrations in the United Kingdom is the Queen. Her actual birthday is on 21 April and her official birthday is on a Saturday in June, which varies each year. But in my seventieth year I also celebrated two birthdays – one on my actual birthday on 27 April, and the other in May when CWR put on what was called the Waverley Festival. The staff and directors thought that there were many *Every Day with Jesus* readers, partners and others who might like to join in the celebration of my birthday, so part of the Festival, on the Saturday evening of the Spring Bank Holiday weekend, was given over to that. It took the form of a 'This Is Your Life' presentation and although I was told beforehand it was to be something of that nature, the actual details were kept from me.

Gerald Coates, founder of the Pioneer churches, chaired the proceedings and the whole evening was one surprise after another. There were videos from people with whom I had been involved in the past, including friends in my youth, a fellow Bible college student, and men and women I had ministered to around the world. There was a message from Wendy Craig, the actress, who has been an *Every Day with Jesus* reader for years. Some of my family surprised me by being there and there were many others who came to the platform to say a few words. The evening ended with a firework display. It was a wonderful end to a wonderful evening and as I got into my car to go home tears flooded my eyes as I thought to myself 'I just wish Enid had been here to enjoy this.'

The other activities of the festival weekend included workshops with Phil Greenslade and Jeannette Barwick, a Sunday family service in the big tent with Ishmael, a talk by Gerald Coates on revival and one by me on discipleship. Then on

Bank Holiday Monday we launched a new seminar, Christ Empowered Living.

At my birthday celebrations in April a number of friends, with my health and personal interests at heart, said they hoped that 'now you are 70 you will slow down and take things a lot easier'. I did not have the nerve to tell them what my preaching and travelling schedule was for the next five years if God spared me! While John Muys continued to network and develop contacts around the world, I was kept busy during the rest of the year. First I ministered at the three-week counselling course at Waverley which began in late May and continued into early June. Following that I drafted a new book during July, preached at the Good News Camp organised by Don Double in Malvern during August, undertook a visit to the Philippines with Colin and Jeannette during September, followed immediately by a week's meetings in Singapore. During the autumn I presented a marriage seminar and a Revival Rally in Norwich, a Promise Keepers Rally in Vancouver for 6,000 men and also visited Ghana and Lagos with the team in November.

Two events took place during the autumn and winter of 1998 that would come to have a significant impact on the ministry of CWR in the future. The first was when John Muys met with me to discuss an idea that, initially, struck me as rather revolutionary. Because Waverley Abbey House was not being fully used he proposed that we should link ourselves with another ministry that had a similar emphasis on revival, evangelism, teaching and training. The person who best represented the ministry that would be compatible with our own, he suggested, was Gerald Coates.

I have known Gerald for many years. Trevor and I used to meet with him occasionally for fellowship when we had our offices in Hersham and he was the leader of a church in Cobham.

Gerald is a personable character but I regarded him as sometimes a little too radical for comfort. I had heard many stories about some of the things he had said and done, and while I had a great fondness for him as a brother in Christ I was a little hesitant about being linked closely with him.

John made the point that Gerald and I were two of the strongest voices in the UK in calling the church to pray and to believe for revival. Blending our voices together would make that call stronger and more powerful. This idea helped to overcome my initial hesitancy and after thinking about it for a while I agreed to the matter being brought to the Board for consideration. The outcome of these negotiations was that Gerald's ministry at Waverley Abbey House should be established under a new name and organisation. This was to avoid confusion in the minds of the Christian public that Waverley Abbey House was now a centre for Pioneer, the fellowship of church groups started by Gerald. Gerald decided on the name Kingdom Life Ministries for the operation of his personal ministry at Waverley, which came to be referred to as KLM.

It was also agreed that the new organisation would be given a three-year lease, with an option of six months' notice either way, and that Gerald and the new organisation should become responsible for the running and administration of the house, thus relieving CWR of that responsibility. A final arrangement was that Gerald should be allowed to have an apartment in the house and to be domiciled there.

Once these decisions were ratified in the form of a contract, an apartment was prepared for him, and he and his wife, Anona, moved into Waverley Abbey House in December 1998.

As soon as it was announced that Gerald was now operating his personal ministry from Waverley Abbey House, I received a number of letters from supporters of CWR strongly disapproving of the decision. Some of them were quite ascerbic. It has always amazed me how Christians can write the most bitter things and then sign their letters 'Yours in Christ'! I would have thought that being 'in Christ' meant having His mindset in all things. On the Internet I came across statements from some of the more extreme Christian ministries claiming that I had moved from my conservative position and had 'gone over on the side of the radicals'. In fact the relationship between CWR and KLM was not a partnership in the true sense of the word. Rather the two ministries simply operated from the same premises, each pursuing their own aims and goals, yet coexisting in Christian friendship and love.

The other event that was to affect greatly the ministry of CWR was the special presentation of the Christ Empowered Living seminar at Waverley Abbey House in December. I use the phrase 'special presentation' because a number of key people, some from overseas, were invited to the seminar by John Muys not just to experience, it but also to evaluate it and advise on its development. Brian Warren, leader of the Promise Keepers in Canada was there. So were Bucky Rosenbaum and Len Goss from Broadman and Holman, David and Dale Garratt, founders of Scripture in Song, from Australia, and Scott Hughes, an executive of a music company in Nashville, USA.

When we met after the seminar everyone was enthusiastic about its potential and Scott Hughes from Nashville said that his life had been impacted in a most powerful way through the presentation. Later Scott wrote this to me:

> I always knew I had problems but I never knew how to fix them. I finally learned how when I attended Christ Empowered Living. My entire understanding (mentally and emotionally) of God has taken a 180 degree turn.

That presentation later led to Scott arranging for me to present the Christ Empowered Living seminar to a large group of chief executives in the music Industry in Nashville. It also led to Broadman and Holman arranging for me to take their whole staff through the seminar at their headquarters in Nashville and later publication of the book in the USA.

As we moved into 1999 the thoughts uppermost in my mind were about how this arrangement with Gerald would work out. I was concerned that we had lost a few supporters because of it, but as many of the decisions we make in life are unlikely to please everyone I did not worry unduly. From the beginning of the year, KLM appointed a manager who took over the administration of the house, and Anona (Gerald's wife) ran the reception office. Gerald set up his own office there with a small staff and they and the CWR staff would meet regularly for prayer before the day's work began.

How and in what direction our relationship would develop we did not know, but we were prepared to do all we could to foster it, despite the predictions of some of our supporters that it would have a deleterious effect on CWR.

The advice to slow down given to me at my seventieth birthday still reverberated in my mind, but how could I slow down when my health was fairly good, my energy levels high and so much still needed to be done? The year turned out to be as busy as other years and in some ways busier. My preaching and teaching schedule in the UK was extremely heavy.

One of the most important CWR activities among all others at Waverley Abbey House during the last year of the twentieth century was preparing the 'Cover to Cover' programme. It had been a dream of mine for many years to start the new millennium by encouraging a million people to read through the Bible in one year. While there were those who argued that the new millennium didn't really begin until 2001, which of course was technically correct, most people seemed to view it as beginning in the year 2000, and we decided to go along with that. This meant a great deal of networking and preparation. Wherever I travelled during 1999 I sought to encourage people to begin the new millennium by committing themselves to read through the Bible from cover to cover. Colin Nelson and Lloyd Ashworth also undertook a special international itinerary through Asia and Africa to encourage people in the churches in many different countries to join us in this way.

One of the things that has concerned me over the years is that while many Christians are keen to read through the whole Bible, so often, after starting in Genesis and ploughing through Exodus, they give up in Leviticus. One way this problem can be overcome I have found is to read through the Bible chronologically, following the time line that runs through Scripture, beginning in John1:1, 'In the beginning was the Word, and the Word was with God and the Word was God', continuing with the story of creation and from there following the events of Scripture as they happened.

I am astonished that so many Christians *believe* the Bible from cover to cover but comparatively few have actually *read* it from cover to cover. Although we did not achieve our target of taking a million people through programme in the first year of the new millennium I felt deeply gratified when waking up on 1 January 2000 knowing that over half a million people would be beginning a journey through the Bible that day. I usually read through the Bible about once every five years. I followed the Cover to Cover programme through 2000. Since then, through the generosity of many supporters, thousands of copies of the reading programme have been distributed in the developing world.

During January and February I set some time aside for

writing the *Christ Empowered Living* book, then towards the end of March Phil Greenslade, Jeannette and I flew out to minister at a pastors' conference in Langkawi, off the coast of Malaysia, which was hosted by our great friend, Rev Lawrence Yap. Langkawi is one of the most beautiful islands in Malaysia and many of the pastors were able to be at the conference because two fine Malaysian Christian businessmen had helped with their costs. After this Phil returned home while Jeannette and I went on to Miri on the island of Borneo in East Malaysia. There, with Johnny Tan, the pastor of a fairly new and growing community of believers, we conducted several kinds of seminars in the ballroom of the hotel where we were staying to capacity crowds. We were thrilled also to meet up with an old friend, Catholic Bishop Anthony Lee Kok, who some years previously had attended a Summer Institute at Waverley Abbey House and was an enthusiastic reader and promoter of *Every Day with Jesus*.

Not far from Miri, on the northwest coast of Borneo, is the oil-rich Islamic sultanate of Brunei. The country is known chiefly for the astounding wealth of its Sultan, its tax-free, subsidised society, and the fact that (statistically at least) its 350,000 people enjoy one of the highest per capita incomes on earth. It is described in one brochure as 'a little slice of Islamic heaven'. The British High Commissioner there at the time of our visit to Miri was Robert Laing, a fine Christian. He and his wife Sybilla were avid *Every Day with Jesus* readers. Hearing that we were coming to Miri, Sybilla had telephoned us in the UK before we left and invited us to conduct a seminar in the Anglican church in the capital of Brunei. In one of those wonderful 'God-incidents', there was a 24-hour window in our programme. Flights and hotels were changed and the church in Brunei was free only one evening in the month – the very date that we could make! People known to have Christian connections sometimes encounter difficulties entering this strict Muslim community, but by following the Laing's instructions carefully we had no problem.

Jeannette and I had the pleasure of spending two nights in the British High Commission and I slept in the bedroom that Queen Elizabeth used on her last visit to the country. The small Anglican church is the only Christian centre in Brunei and the seminar on relationships I presented was enthusiastically received. Jeannette did a women's seminar the following morning, while I was given a tour of the city in the ambassador's chauffeur-driven limousine.

One of my key tasks in the UK that year was to give the keynote address at the conference of the Association of Christian Counsellors in the Hayes Conference Centre in Derbyshire. I told participants that one of the greatest challenges facing Christian counsellors today is the danger of becoming more enamoured with psychology than with Scripture. I urged them not to stray from the Bible, but to allow it to be the referee in everything and to bring all theories to its judgment bar, because it is the one reliable body of truth, the rock that stands firm and solid in the midst of a sea of post-modernism. 'The ACC,' I said, 'can be a good movement by following the best psychological insights of the day, but it can only be a great movement as it stays close to Scripture.' That applies of course not only to the ACC but to every Christian organisation.

CHAPTER 40

A YEAR OF HIGHS AND LOWS

The year 2000 began with John Muys and me ministering at a number of key events in the United States. John did a considerable amount of networking in the USA that came to benefit CWR a great deal, but one night, when he was in Charlotte, Virginia after I had left to come home to the UK, he had a heart attack, thankfully a mild one. After a few days in hospital he was well enough to return to the UK, and although he had to cut down on some of his activities, it was not long before he was up and about again.

My schedule that year was once again filled with overseas visits. Towards the end of the year both John and the CWR Board felt that as he was so enthusiastic about the development potential of the American market it would be helpful if he went to live in the USA and gave himself entirely to that part of the world. Steve Bradley, one of our Board members, was appointed to succeed him as Chief Executive Officer. Steve had taken early retirement from a significant position in business and he agreed to lead CWR for the next two years. He also chose not to accept a salary for that period – which the Board greatly appreciated. Everyone agrees that Steve's time as CEO was a major turning point in CWR's ministry. His style of management was quite different from that of his predecessors and his major achievement was in building a strong management team and focusing once more on the development of CWR's ministry in the UK.

In the late autumn of the year I began to feel a great deal of pain in my ankle and reported this to my oncologist. When one has had cancer and it has gone into remission, the worry is, as I said earlier, that it will start up again. I had enjoyed very good health in the years since prostate cancer was diagnosed in 1996, but a bone scan now showed that the cancer had spread into the bone of my right leg. Radiotherapy was recommended and although this deals wonderfully with the pain it takes a period of several weeks – six in my case – before full relief is felt. Radiation therapy directed at the painful bone lesions kills cancer cells that grow in the bone. As the tumour regresses, the local pressure against the nerve endings around the bone decreases, thereby ensuring relief of pain. Because of this treatment, and the difficulty I had in walking, I had to cancel a trip to Nigeria in November and meetings in India and Sri Lanka early in 2001.

I was still trying to come to terms with the spread of cancer when I received some devastating family news. I was about to get into bed one evening in December 2000 when the phone rang and a friend of my younger son, John, told me as gently as he could that John had died after being taken to hospital with a serious liver condition. Sadly, John's alcoholism had finally caught up with him. As I had talked to John in recent weeks I knew he was struggling with health issues and fighting a losing battle with his addiction. I wept copiously, my sorrow being intensified by the fact that it was drink that killed him. The cause of death given on his death certificate was cirrhosis of the liver.

John often referred to himself as the 'black sheep of the family' and despite the best efforts of his mother and I to dissuade him of this, he seemed to cling to this idea for the rest of his life. He had a good mind and for many years held down a steady job as a printer until his problem with drink interfered with his ability to continue in that trade.

I think one of the great sadnesses of my life is that whilst I have been able to help many people overcome their problems I seemed powerless to be able to help John overcome his addiction. However, I am glad that we were able to maintain a relationship where our love for each other remained unquestioned.

John had been living in a flat in Folkestone and because I was still suffering the effects of the radiotherapy treatment David and Jeannette went down there to console his close friends and to make arrangements for the funeral. I was able to attend the funeral a few days later on 21 December, at the Hawkinge Cemetery, Folkestone. A local Anglican minister, the Revd John Tapper, conducted the service, Trevor Partridge gave the funeral address and David Rivett read the Scriptures. It was a simple but rather beautiful service, given the circumstances, and I was deeply grateful to a number of friends from CWR who travelled to be with me for the occasion. A few days later I went down to Wales to spend Christmas with my mother and we consoled each other as best as we could.

As we moved into 2001 I slowly began to recover and was able to function once again. I spent a few days teaching on the 14-day counselling course at Waverley Abbey House during March, before taking a short overseas holiday to fully recuperate. On the evening I returned, I had just put my car in my garage and was making my way into my flat, when I slipped and broke a bone in my foot. It meant an enforced rest for another six weeks.

After I had recovered I flew to the USA to conduct several meetings and seminars and while I was in the country, John Muys and I visited the well-known Saddleback Church, about 50 miles from downtown Los Angeles, pastored by Rick Warren. I wanted very much to meet this highly successful pastor, and also a friend of ours, Bucky Rosenbaum, who was on the staff at the church. When we arrived, however, we were told we would not be able to meet up with Rick because he was in bed with pneumonia. But when Bucky phoned to check on how he was that day Rick insisted on us going over to his house to meet him. We were astonished that he wanted to see us when he was so ill, but when we got to his home we discovered why. It seems a book I had published many years ago, *How to Help a Friend*, had impressed him so much that when he started Saddleback Church he asked someone to develop a course based on it. He wanted to tell me that personally.

In October 2001 I had to face another shattering bereavement when my elder son, David, died of a massive heart attack. I was about to leave home to conduct a marriage seminar in Cheam when my granddaughter, Sheryl, telephoned to say that David had died in a hotel in Bournemouth in the middle of the night while he and Sue were on a weekend break. I had just put down the phone and had hardly time to take in the news when a knock at the door reminded me that my CWR colleague, Sean Gubb, had arrived to take me to the seminar. Sean was, of course, shaken when I told him what had happened and both of us sat down to try to work out how to handle things from that moment. It would have been impossible for me to conduct a marriage seminar under those circumstances and I knew that my first duty was to drive to Bournemouth and be with my daughter-in-law and grandchildren. Sean went to explain the situation to the people gathering for the seminar in Cheam and I made my way to Bournemouth.

I found the family deeply distressed in the room where David had died. It appears that David had had the heart attack in the middle of the night and although the paramedics had come quickly he had died before any help could be given to save him. David Rivett and Trevor Partridge were a great support and strength to me with their prayers and words of comfort. Trevor and Debbie came to my home on Sunday night, prayed with me and we had a private Communion service together, which comforted me greatly.

David's funeral was held at the Basingstoke Crematorium in North Waltham, Hampshire, on 22 October. Jonathan Frost, a local Anglican minister, conducted the service, while Trevor gave a wonderful tribute to my son's life and David Rivett read the Scriptures. I could not help observe, as I saw Trevor and David participate in the service, that this was the third time they had stood by my side when I have been bereaved – caring, concerned and compassionate. It was a great consolation. Many of the CWR staff joined us for the funeral service as David had worked closely with some of them in his role as CWR's print buyer and consultant.

I miss David terribly. Since he left school he worked alongside me in various capacities to support my ministry. In the early years he printed *Every Day with Jesus* and later for a while, *YP's* and *Topz*. He would work long hours and on many occasions would work all night to meet a deadline. He was so knowledgeable about the printing trade and had many contacts which resulted in his saving CWR thousands of pounds a year.

After his mother died he made it a point to telephone me almost every day and continued doing this until the time of his death. He was not only my son but a close friend and his passing has left a large gap in my life.

I am often asked how I coped with the loss of my two only sons within ten months of each other. I would be less than honest if I said I did not hurt. Sometimes the pain in my soul brought hot tears to my eyes. There were times when I was unable to pray, even though almost every day for close on four decades I have been forming prayers for other people to pray in the readings of *Every Day with Jesus*. I have a little plaque in my home which someone gave me many years ago with just one word inscribed on it – Jesus. During those times when I was in so much pain that I couldn't pray I would look at that plaque and quietly say the word – Jesus. In such moments God would come incredibly close to me, easing the hurt in my soul. When words fail us there is one word that never fails – *Jesus*!

Just a few weeks after David's funeral I flew to Nigeria with several CWR colleagues to fulfil the engagements that had been cancelled the previous year due to the flare-up of my cancer. Never have I been more tempted to cancel a ministry trip. I was so filled with grief I wondered how I would be able to preach and present the seminars. Then I remembered those words I had written in *Every Day with Jesus*: 'When you are most in need of comfort, reach out to others and you will find comfort yourself.' I decided to take my own advice and with Jeannette Barwick, Colin Nelson and David Markley (CWR's finance manager) flew to Abuja, capital of Nigeria, in early November 2001.

A reception committee headed by Remi Ayida, our *Every Day with Jesus* distributor in Nigeria, met us on arrival. The moment I met the reception committee and received their loving embraces I was conscious of much of the pain and grief beginning to diminish in my soul. There is a secular song that says 'Love changes everything'. It certainly does. The love and concern the reception committee showed for me for me began to produce great changes within my being. I felt my spirit rising above the grief that was deep within me.

We learned as we drove to the special accommodation arranged for us that the air-conditioned limousine we were in had been put at our disposal for the whole of our stay in Abuja by a member of the President's cabinet. We already knew that the President of Nigeria, General Olusegun Obasanjo was a Christian and familiar with *Every Day with Jesus*, but we also discovered that so too were some of his cabinet. Before we conducted the series of seminars we were invited on the Sunday morning to join the President in his private chapel. There I was asked to lead the prayers for the nation, and towards the end of the service I was surprised when the President stood up and spoke about the part that *Every Day with Jesus* had played in his life. He told how he was in prison under a previous military regime and was allowed a Bible and a copy of *EDWJ*. He strongly praised the publication and powerfully testified to the way God had changed his heart as he read the Scriptures every day.

After the service, the CWR team, along with a small group of invited guests, lunched with him in the presidential palace. I was seated close to the President and as we ate lunch I remembered George Thomas (Lord Tonypandy) once telling me about being invited to spend Christmas with the Queen and the royal family at Sandringham. As he ate Christmas lunch with them his mind had gone back to his roots in the little mining village in Wales from which he had risen to become Speaker of the House of Commons and he had said to himself, 'Not bad for a little boy from Tonypandy!' Now I thought to myself, 'Not bad, either, for a little boy from Fochriw!'

We had several meetings in Abujah and then flew to Lagos for further conferences. Accompanying us on the plane was a good friend of ours who has often helped us in our many visits to Nigeria, Cecelia Ibru.

Cecelia is a banker and told us that she had made arrangements for us to travel with her to our accommodation in her chauffer-driven car.

A banker in Nigeria runs a high risk of being kidnapped, so two police cars accompany Cecilia wherever she goes. Travelling through the traffic-infested city of Lagos can be a nightmare – we had once sat in a jam for three hours. But the 20-odd miles from

Lagos airport to our hotel on Victoria Island that evening took no longer than half an hour. With two police cars, one in front of us and one behind, their lights flashing and sirens blaring, the traffic just melted away. There was just one moment when some vehicles were rather slow in getting out of our way and one of the policemen in the car ahead of us stuck his rifle out of the window, fired a shot in the air and the traffic parted as quickly as the waters of the Red Sea did for Moses!

Our seminars in Lagos, again for pastors and Christian leaders, were organised by Remi Ayida and held in one of the halls in the national stadium. The theme of the three-morning conference for pastors and leaders was how to build a church with harmonious relationships. I have often found that relationships do not so much cause problems as reveal problems, and I endeavoured to show the large crowd of participants from all denominations how to deal with relational problems when they first appear and so stop them from becoming bigger ones. On two of the evenings we conducted meetings for the general public in the same auditorium, one night an *Every Day with Jesus* rally and the second night a talk on marriage. Nigerians are always quick and ready to respond to invitations and we had a great crowd of people come forward both nights to re-commit themselves to Jesus Christ and His purposes for their lives.

On the last Sunday of that visit I preached in the great Anglican church on Victoria Island known as The Church of our Saviour. Whenever I am in Nigeria I am usually invited to preach at the Sunday morning service there. It is one of my favourite churches and is where Remi Ayida and her family worship. There are many *EDWJ* readers in the congregation and I am always made to feel at home there. Normally the church holds two Sunday morning services but because of my visit they held just one combined service. On this occasion the service began at

8am and finished at midday. My sermon was not the cause of the long service – it lasted just 45 minutes – but rather the time was taken up with the singing of the choir, soloists, testimonies, Holy Communion, announcements, and prayers covering every conceivable need of the congregation. Five offerings were taken up in the service!

My message that morning was on forgiveness and I happened to refer to a letter I had received some years ago from a medical doctor telling me how something I said about forgiveness in *Every Day with Jesus* had changed her life. I had forgotten that the letter had come from Nigeria and when the service was over a fine-looking, well-dressed lady whispered to me, 'The doctor you referred to in your sermon this morning ... that was me!' We hugged.

Just as a reception committee always welcomes us whenever we go to Nigeria, so does a farewell committee arrange a wonderful send-off. This is usually in the form of a banquet, which at times has been attended by as many as 1,000 people. On this occasion, however, it was a smaller group, about 100. We met in a restaurant not far from the airport and after a time of singing and farewell speeches we were given a generous offering towards the work of getting *Through the Bible: Cover to Cover* into the Nigerian prisons, Bible colleges and other institutions. It is always difficult to tear ourselves away from these wonderful people and I often wonder, with my health the way it is, whether I will ever be able to return to Nigeria. Whether I do or not the Nigerian people will always have a most important place in my heart.

CHAPTER 41

MY LEGACY TO THE NEXT
GENERATION

Towards the end of 2001 the three years agreement with KLM came to an end and it was decided by the Board that CWR should resume responsibility for running Waverley Abbey House, so the lease with KLM was not renewed. However, Gerald and Anona Coates continued to live part of the time in the flat at Waverley and Gerald's ministry support team continued to operate out of an office at Waverley on a rental basis. He and Anona finally moved out of Waverley Abbey House at the end of 2002.

The year 2002 was once again filled with meetings in the UK and overseas. Visits were made to India, Sri Lanka and Malaysia. And for the first time, CWR was invited to participate in Spring Harvest – the well-established annual UK event. We were given the responsibility of organising what was called the Leaders' Track. As the title suggests, our brief was to minister to the pastors and leaders who attended the conferences, teaching on subjects especially relevant to them. The Spring Harvest programme is run over three consecutive six-day periods and is held simultaneously at the Butlins holiday camps at Skegness and Minehead. Some 50,000 people attend over the 18 days. We at CWR greatly appreciated the challenge to organise the first Leaders' Track. Mick Brooks (who later that year was appointed by the Board as Chief Executive), Trevor Partridge and Phil

Greenslade ministered in Minehead, while Sean Gubb, Jeannette and I conducted the Leadership Track in Skegness.

Immediately after Spring Harvest came another major UK Christian gathering – Easter People. Organised by Methodist minister Rob Frost and his team, this has grown so much that currently it is spread over three sites – Torquay, Llandudno and Scarborough. I had the privilege of ministering at the Llandudno event. Rob is one of the most dynamic, imaginative and go-getting Christians I have met. Just reading the list of his accomplishments and activities leaves me feeling breathless!

Two important events filled my calendar for the month of September. One was the launch of my new book *The 7 Laws of Spiritual Success* and the other was the fifteenth anniversary of the opening of Waverley Abbey House. On Friday 13 September *The 7 Laws of Spiritual Success* was launched in the House of Lords under the sponsorship of Lord Peter Archer of Sandwell. Mike Ashford, our marketing manager, felt that as the book was about the seven most important spiritual laws, there could be no better place to launch it than in the Houses of Parliament where the laws that govern our land are made. Mike approached Lord Peter Archer to see if he would sponsor the event and he readily agreed. Lord Archer came to see me several weeks before the event to discuss the details of the launch and I found him to be most charming, helpful and concerned to make the launch as successful as possible.

About 50 invited people gathered in a room in the House of Lords on the appointed day, among them members of the Press, CWR Board members and managers, booksellers, media representatives, and special overseas guests including Remi Ayida from Nigeria and David Shepherd from our American publishers Broadman and Holman. Two of my grandchildren were present also – David's son Leighton, and John's daughter,

Suzanne. They enjoyed being invited to the House of Lords and I felt very proud that they were part of the occasion.

After sharing a few refreshments Lord Archer brought the meeting to order and said how glad he was to be the sponsor of this occasion. He pointed out in his introductory remarks that the book had sold 13,000 copies before being published, and was destined to become a best-seller. When my turn came to speak I said that I can usually write a book in three months but this had taken a lifetime. It was a truly wonderful occasion and I was glad to be surrounded by my friends and family. Afterwards many of the group were given a guided tour of the House of Lords, which was a great experience, especially for the overseas visitors.

The following day we celebrated the fifteenth anniversary of Waverley's opening in a large marquee on the lawn. We had lunch with our partners, an afternoon meeting outlining the ministry, followed by workshops led by Phil, Jeannette and myself. In the evening we had a grand celebration with about a thousand people in attendance.

I began 2003 with a concern that this was the year I had committed myself to write my autobiography. It was needed by CWR for publication in 2004 and the aim was to have it completed by the end of 2003. At the beginning of the year, however, I had not written one word, and wondered how I would be able to get to grips with it, given my speaking and travelling schedule and other writing projects such as *Every Day with Jesus*. To find the time to write what amounted to 15 editions of *Every Day with Jesus*, seemed an impossible task.

In January I had a medical check-up and discovered I was diabetic. It explained why I had been feeling so unwell after all the sweet things I had eaten at Christmas time. It was diagnosed as Type 2 diabetes and tests showed that it could be controlled by diet. After a visit to Sri Lanka in the company of Phil Greenslade,

Jeannette Barwick and Colin Nelson in February to conduct a Sri Lankan ministers' conference organised by Hilary Fernando, in co-operation with the Evangelical Alliance. On my return I had to see my oncologist once again due to a pain that had developed in my knee. He arranged for me to have an MRI (Magnetic Resonance Imaging) scan. This gives a quite detailed picture of the problem and can detect tiny changes of structures within the body. It showed, in my case, that there were now aggressive cancer cells at work in my right knee. A further course of radiotherapy was recommended, but as the waiting list for the radiotherapy machines in some hospitals is so long it was almost eight weeks before I could start my treatment. During that time I survived on painkillers – and of course, the grace of God.

One of the dreams John Muys had had ever since I finished the book *Christ Empowered Living* was to put the course on video. The year of my seventy-fifth birthday it became a reality when a team from LifeWay, the Baptist organisation based in Nashville, came by previous arrangement to Waverley to begin filming the course. The Waverley Room was transformed into a studio for two days and before an invited audience I presented the course. There were eight sessions, each one lasting about half an hour, and for each session I was required to have change of clothing. Betty, the LifeWay film crew member in charge of make-up and wardrobe, insisted that I could not wear white shirts, as 'the camera doesn't like them'.

As I am not a great lover of coloured shirts I did my best to resist this, but when she told me that she had been involved in the make-up and wardrobe of several US presidents and they had never given her any difficulty over her suggestions about what they should wear, I decided it would be best to do as I was told. The result was that I appeared for each session in a different coloured shirt, ranging from a disgusting pink to a nauseating green!

On 27 April 2003 I celebrated my seventy-fifth birthday. I spent the day with the Special Ministries Team from Waverley who work closely with me – Robin, Bridget, Marilyn, Nicky Sue – in the home of Jeannette. They are such a support and strength to me that almost every time I think of their love and concern for me tears come into my eyes. The next day, Monday, I was treated to another birthday celebration, this time by the CWR staff. Several short speeches made by some of the staff moved me deeply. The love and respect I receive from those with whom I work always gives me a conscious taste of how God feels about me. For that I am deeply grateful.

Once that first part of the filming of Christ Empowered Living was over the crew returned to the USA for a few weeks before coming back to film me on location, partly at Waverley and partly in South Wales. A particularly meaningful moment for me was when we visited the little mission hall in Fochriw where I was converted. I did a piece to camera standing close to the spot where I surrendered my life to Christ and talked about that life-changing moment.

My knee was continuing to give me a good deal of pain and in May, I was given a slot in the Royal Surrey Hospital in Guildford for five sessions of radiotherapy. This greatly helps to relieve the pain, but it does take time for things to settle down and for a while actually increases the pain and discomfort. For about five weeks the only way I could get around was on crutches. Then no sooner had that pain diminished than another cancer 'hot spot', as they are called, occurred – this time in my foot – and I had to take to the crutches again. That meant another session of radiotherapy and a further five weeks before I was free of pain and able to get around unaided. Altogether it took five months to deal with the problems in my knee and my foot, during which time I was mainly housebound.

As a result, I was unable to attend a number of meetings during this period, including a trip to Uganda in June to present the Caring seminars to the several hundred cell group leaders in the Kampala Pentecostal Church. Mick and Jeannette, who are very familiar with the material, substituted for me and did a wonderful job. At the end they received a standing ovation – something, I understand, not normally done in this Ugandan church.

I was able to participate in CWR's first Summer School at Waverley Abbey House in August when I presented a new seminar on spiritual direction over three mornings. This is a subject, I believe, that is going to occupy the attention of many in the coming days. Spiritual direction is different from counselling in the sense that it is a prayer process in which one person helps another to develop a deeper relationship with God. It has been practised by a number of Catholic and Anglican churches for centuries, but it is a ministry that has been largely ignored by evangelicals. My purpose was to take this ancient form of ministry and set it within an evangelical framework. I do not consider myself to be a prophet in the sense of foretelling events, but I believe that in the future spiritual direction is a practice that will be taken up by many in our evangelical churches.

My health problems prevented me from travelling to the USA and Canada in September, first to receive an award for my work of 'soul care' from the AACC (American Association of Christian Counsellors), and secondly to speak in the famous People's Church, Toronto, now pastored by an Englishman, Charles Price, who was for some years Principal of Capernwray Bible College. The latter engagement was to have been followed by a Christ Empowered Living seminar over two nights organised by our *Every Day with Jesus* distributors in Canada, C.H. Cook. It was disappointing to have to cancel these two events, but everyone was sympathetic and considerate in the light of my personal difficulties.

I was, however, able to go to Bangor, Northern Ireland that month to spend a day with some of the CWR partners. The venue was the West Presbyterian Church in the city, pastored by a good friend of CWR, the Revd Charles McMullen.

Towards the end of the year I experienced another physical problem that caused me a few days of deep distress and concern. I woke up one morning in early November unable to see properly out of a part of my right eye. I telephoned my doctor, who urged me to get someone to drive me at once to the emergency unit of Frimley Park Hospital in Surrey. Robin, one of the special ministries team, drove me to the hospital where after investigation I was diagnosed as having a detached retina. I was told to get to the Moorfield Eye Hospital right away and the next day I was operated on. The surgeon told me I had come within just a day or two of losing the sight in my right eye.

I find it interesting that the concern I had at the beginning of 2003 about writing my autobiography was taken care of by the fact that I was housebound for five months and had to cancel a number of meetings. Like the apostle Paul writing in prison, although I have been impeded in one direction, I have been released in another. And for that I am once again deeply thankful.

Although the past few years of my life have been filled with many problems, especially the loss of my family and my constant battle with cancer, I have found that out of these struggles has grown an empathy and an understanding that I didn't have before – a deeper compassion for others. The poet Rilke, writing in an age when language was used in a rather different way from today said:

If only we arrange our life according to that principle which counsels us that we must always hold to the difficult, then that which now seems to us most alien will become what we trust most and find most faithful.

Holding to the difficult is not easy. Malcolm Muggeridge said that he learned more from his troubles than his successes. In the end it is the difficulties that have proved 'most faithful' to my soul.

In the last paragraph of a letter to an aspiring young poet, Rilke said:

Do not believe that he who seeks to comfort you lives untroubled among the simple and quiet words that sometimes do you good. His life has much difficulty and sadness and remains far behind yours. Were it otherwise he would not be able to find the words.

Were it otherwise I would never have been able to find the words, either. And for that, too, I am deeply grateful.

EPILOGUE

One of the questions asked by members of each generation from time to time is: what does the future hold? The young ask in a different way from those who are older. For me it is a question that seems to be raised to almost cosmic proportions as I come to this final chapter of my story. As Malcolm Muggeridge said in a television interview as he was heading for his eightieth year: 'It will not be long now before some young, brilliant, white-coated doctor may look me over and put me in the NTBR (Not To Be Resuscitated) bracket.' That is a sentiment I can now fully share with the great man.

My mother is still alive and as I write has just celebrated her ninety-seventh birthday. She has all her faculties and is as feisty as she was when she was 27. Often when I see her I ask myself, 'Will I live to that ripe old age?' When I was diagnosed with prostate cancer in 1995, I was writing an edition of *Every Day with Jesus* on the theme of heaven and wondering whether it might be the last one I would produce. Through the prayers of thousands and expert medical attention, however, I am still here, joyfully pursuing the work God called me to nearly 60 years ago.

Many years ago, high up in the Swiss Alps, on the grave of a young climber who fell to his death on his very first ascent, I saw inscribed the words 'He died climbing'. Ever since my conversion I have always had a thirst to know more of God and His Word and to share that knowledge with others. My prayer is that I will be able to go on doing that until the day I die.

In the last couple of decades the thought of heaven has impinged upon my thinking more and more.

C.S. Lewis wrote, in *The Problem of Pain*:

There have been times, I think, when we do not desire heaven, but more often I find myself wondering whether, in our heart of hearts, we have ever desired anything else.[1]

It was Lewis who also said,

If I find in myself desires which nothing in this world can satisfy, the only logical explanation is that I was made for another world.[2]

We should not be surprised that thoughts of a future life come into our minds from time to time. After all, Scripture says that God has set eternity in our hearts (Eccl. 3:11). Because of that, everyone, deep down in their hearts, whether they realise it or not, has a sense of homesickness, a nostalgia for heaven.

Modern-day Christians don't seem to talk much about heaven. Church history shows that Christians in bygone days made a great deal of heaven and were effective on this earth for doing so. In his book, *The Eclipse of Heaven*, A.J. Conyers said, 'We live in a world no longer under heaven.'[3] I believe that many of our problems as Christians (and all the problems of those who are not yet Christians) stem from this fact.

As Brent Curtis and John Eldridge put it in *The Sacred Romance*:

All the addictions and depressions, the rage that simmers just beneath the surface of our Christian façade and the deadness that characterises so much of our lives has a common root; we think this is as good as it gets. Take away the hope of heaven and our journey is but a death march.[4]

One of my regrets, as I draw near to the end of my journey here on earth, is that I did not tune in earlier to this longing for home that God has built into every one of us. I think it would have made my Christian walk more effective and enhanced my life in so many ways – ways which I am enjoying now but could have enjoyed much sooner. I think I was probably afraid that a preoccupation with heaven would inhibit my usefulness here on earth. I certainly preached about heaven, but I have to confess that it did not have the 'pull' it has had upon me in the past couple of decades. Living in the light of heaven need not make us less keen to help others, but it can be a constant reminder to us that the most permanent dwelling earth provides is only a tent and at any time word may come to pull up the pegs. We are indeed strangers and pilgrims here below.

Some words of Jesus come home to me with particular force nowadays whenever I read them:

In my Father's house are many rooms; if it were not so, I would have told you. I am going there to prepare a place for you. And if I go and prepare a place for you, I will come back and take you to be with me that you also may be where I am (John 14:2–3).

I find the thought that Christ has prepared a place for me tremendously moving. Some time ago I walked into a crowded meeting room and I was wondering whether I would find a seat when someone said, 'Sit here, Selwyn. I have saved a place for you.' It was a wonderful feeling that someone had thought about me enough to keep a place for me. There is a place reserved for me in heaven. I won't have to scramble for it. It is waiting for me and I have no doubt I will be led to it by the Lord Himself.

There was a wonderful moment in recent history when the Apollo 13 spacecraft arrived home. The mission had got into trouble and there was a fight against the odds to bring the men back safely. All the world could do was to watch. Would the heat shield hold? Would the parachutes unfold in time? Would the capsule survive re-entry? Seconds seemed like hours as the astronauts disappeared into the blackout. All eyes were fixed on the blank television screen. Suddenly the capsule appeared, with the parachutes opening beautifully.

'Hello Houston, this is Odyssey. It's good to see you again.'

'Odyssey, this is Houston. Welcome home. We're glad to see you.'

For me, heaven will be like that. A preacher one said that heaven can be missed by 18 inches – the approximate distance between your head and your heart. In the end it is not *what* you know but *who* you know that matters. Make certain Christ is in your *heart*.

I often wonder *when* I will die, *where* I will die, and *how* I will die. But none of those things can be foretold, and what I do know for sure is that after death will begin the most joyous adventure I have ever known.

There was a time nearly ten years ago when I said I was ready to go but eager to stay. Now, however, things are different.

Now I am eager to go but willing to stay.

Notes

1. C.S. Lewis, *The Problem of Pain*, HarperCollins, 2001.
2. Ibid.
3. A.J. Conyers, *The Eclipse of Heaven*, InterVarsity Press, 1992.
4. Brent Curtis and John Eldridge, *The Sacred Romance*, STL, 1998.

National Distributors

UK: (and countries not listed below)
CWR, Waverley Abbey House, Waverley Lane, Farnham, Surrey GU9 8EP.
Tel: (01252) 784700 Outside UK +44 (0)1252 784700

AUSTRALIA: CMC Australasia, PO Box 519, Belmont, Victoria 3216.
Tel: (03) 5241 3288

CANADA: Cook Communications Ministries, PO Box 98, 55 Woodslee Avenue, Paris, Ontario.
Tel: 1800 263 2664

GHANA: Challenge Enterprises of Ghana, PO Box 5723, Accra.
Tel: (021) 222437/223249 Fax: (021) 226227

HONG KONG: Cross Communications Ltd, 1/F, 562A Nathan Road, Kowloon.
Tel: 2780 1188 Fax: 2770 6229

INDIA: Crystal Communications, 10-3-18/4/1, East Marredpalli,
Secunderabad – 500026, Andhra Pradesh.
Tel/Fax: (040) 27737145

KENYA: Keswick Books and Gifts Ltd, PO Box 10242, Nairobi.
Tel: (02) 331692/226047 Fax: (02) 728557

MALAYSIA: Salvation Book Centre (M) Sdn Bhd, 23 Jalan SS 2/64,
47300 Petaling Jaya, Selangor.
Tel: (03) 78766411/78766797 Fax: (03) 78757066/78756360

NEW ZEALAND: CMC Australasia, PO Box 36015, Lower Hutt.
Tel: 0800 449 408 Fax: 0800 449 049

NIGERIA: FBFM, Helen Baugh House, 96 St Finbarr's College Road, Akoka, Lagos.
Tel: (01) 7747429/4700218/825775/827264

PHILIPPINES: OMF Literature Inc, 776 Boni Avenue, Mandaluyong City.
Tel: (02) 531 2183 Fax: (02) 531 1960

REPUBLIC OF IRELAND: Scripture Union, 40 Talbot Street, Dublin 1.
Tel: (01) 8363764

SINGAPORE: Armour Publishing Pte Ltd, Block 203A Henderson Road,
11-06 Henderson Industrial Park, Singapore 159546.
Tel: 6 276 9976 Fax: 6 276 7564

SOUTH AFRICA: Struik Christian Books, 80 MacKenzie Street, PO Box 1144,
Cape Town 8000.
Tel: (021) 462 4360 Fax: (021) 461 3612

SRI LANKA: Christombu Books, 27 Hospital Street, Colombo 1.
Tel: (01) 433142/328909

TANZANIA: CLC Christian Book Centre, PO Box 1384, Mkwepu Street,
Dar es Salaam.
Tel/Fax (022) 2119439

ZIMBABWE: Word of Life Books, Shop 4, Memorial Building,
35 S Machel Avenue, Harare.
Tel: (04) 781305 Fax: (04) 774739

For email addresses, visit the CWR website: www.cwr.org.uk
CWR is a registered charity – number 294387

Day and Residential Courses
Counselling Training
Leadership Development
Biblical Study Courses
Regional Seminars
Ministry to Women
Daily Devotionals
Books and Videos
Conference Centre

Trusted all Over the World

CWR HAS GAINED A WORLDWIDE reputation as a centre of excellence for Bible-based training and resources. From our headquarters at Waverley Abbey House, Farnham, England, we have been serving God's people for 40 years with a vision to help apply God's Word to everyday life and relationships. The daily devotional *Every Day with Jesus* is read by over three-quarters of a million people in more than 150 countries, and our unique courses in biblical studies and pastoral care are respected all over the world. Waverley Abbey House provides a conference centre in a tranquil setting.

For free brochures on our seminars and courses, conference facilities, or a catalogue of CWR resources, please contact us at the following address.
CWR, Waverley Abbey House, Waverley Lane, Farnham, Surrey GU9 8EP, UK

Telephone: **+44 (0)1252 784700**
Email: **mail@cwr.org.uk**
Website: **www.cwr.org.uk**

Every Day with Jesus
Selwyn Hughes

With three-quarters of a million readers worldwide, this bestselling daily Bible reading tool offers practical help with life's challenges and insight into the deeper truths of Scripture. It is designed to challenge, inspire, comfort and encourage readers in their spiritual walk as they study six topics in-depth each year.

ISSN: 0967-1889
£1.99 (plus p&p) per issue

UK Subscription from CWR
£11.50 (6 issues)

Also available in Large Print format
ISSN: 0967-4381
£1.99 (plus p&p) per issue

And by daily email
EDWJEMAIL
£8.00 per year

EDWJ for New Christians
Selwyn Hughes

A powerful and relevant guide for people new to the Christian faith or for people who need the basics presented to them clearly and dynamically. A favourite with churches across denominations.

ISBN: 1-85345-133-9
£1.99

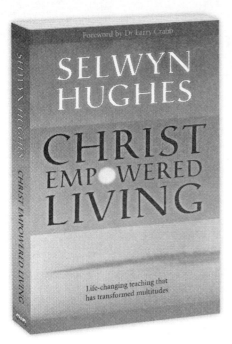

Christ Empowered Living
Selwyn Hughes

Christ Empowered Living is Selwyn Hughes' dynamic core teaching in one easy to digest volume.

It will help transform your life with essential principles of Christian living and develop you to your full spiritual potential. You will dicover biblical insights that will revolutionise your approach to the way you live and help to renew your mind.

This new edition improves readability and gives larger margins for notes.

ISBN: 1-85345-201-7
£7.99

Christ Empowered Living Resources Pack
Selwyn Hughes

This Christ Empowered Living seminar will help you understand more clearly just what Christ meant when He said: 'I have come that they may have life, and have it to the full' (John 10:10). Selwyn Hughes takes us on a journey from the Fall to complete restoration as we learn to depend on God and accept Jesus as the power and source of life as God intended.

This pack includes:

Two DVDs (including eight half-hour sessions)

One workbook (including comprehensive leader's guide)

Code: CELRP
£59.99

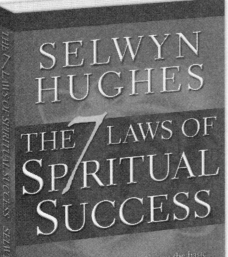

The 7 Laws of Spiritual Success
Selwyn Hughes

Just as there are laws in nature that hold our physical world together, so there are laws for life that make our spiritual walk a success. This book is Selwyn Hughes' legacy to future generations and essential reading for anyone who has been inspired by his teaching and ability to apply God's Word to everyday life and relationships.

ISBN: 1-85345-237-8
£7.99

Applying The 7 Laws of Spiritual Success
Selwyn Hughes

This workbook which accompanies Selwyn Hughes' *The 7 Laws of Spiritual Success*, has much to encourage the reader to read and reread Selwyn's book. The workbook also has probing questions, and action plans to challenge the reader to put into practice Selwyn's teaching and apply it to their daily lives.

ISBN: 1-85345-297-1
£5.99

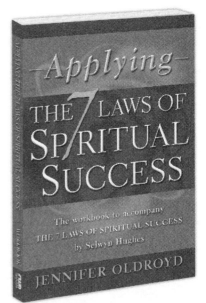